BIG DATA? QUALITATIVE APPROACHES TO DIGITAL RESEARCH

STUDIES IN QUALITATIVE METHODOLOGY

Series Editor: Sam Hillyard

Recent Volumes:

STUDIES IN QUALITATIVE METHODOLOGY VOLUME 13

BIG DATA? QUALITATIVE APPROACHES TO DIGITAL RESEARCH

EDITED BY

MARTIN HAND
Queen's University, Canada

SAM HILLYARD
Durham University, UK

Emerald

United Kingdom – North America – Japan
India – Malaysia – China

Emerald Group Publishing Limited
Howard House, Wagon Lane, Bingley BD16 1WA, UK

First edition 2014

British Library Cataloguing in Publication Data
A catalogue record for this book is available from the British Library

ISBN: 978-1-78441-051-3
ISSN: 1042-3192 (Series)

ISOQAR
REGISTERED
ISOQAR certified Management System, awarded to Emerald for adherence to Environmental standard ISO 14001:2004.
Certificate Number 1985
ISO 14001

INVESTOR IN PEOPLE

CONTENTS

LIST OF CONTRIBUTORS

Angus Bancroft	Sociology, School of Social and Political Sciences, University of Edinburgh, Edinburgh, UK
Andrew Goffey	Department of Culture, Film and Media, University of Nottingham, Nottingham
Lindsay Hamilton	Keele Management School, Keele University, Staffordshire, UK
Martin Hand	Department of Sociology, Queen's University, Kingston, Canada
Mariann Hardey	Institute of Advanced Research in Computing (iARC) Durham University, and Durham University Business School, Durham, UK
Sam Hillyard	School of Applied Social Sciences, Durham University, Durham, UK
Emma Hutchinson	Department of Sociology, University of Warwick, Coventry, UK
Martina Karels	Sociology, School of Social and Political Sciences, University of Edinburgh, Edinburgh, UK
Christine Lohmeier	Department of Communication and Media Research, LMU Munich, Germany
Órla Meadhbh Murray	Sociology, School of Social and Political Sciences, University of Edinburgh, Edinburgh, UK
Lynne Pettinger	Department of Sociology, University of Warwick, Coventry, UK

Robin James Smith	School of Social Sciences, Cardiff University, Cardiff, UK
Ewen Speed	School of Health and Human Sciences, University of Essex, Colchester, UK
Nik Taylor	School of Social and Policy Studies, Flinders University, Adelaide, Australia
Daniel Trottier	Department of Media and Communication, Erasmus University Rotterdam, NL
Jonathan Tummons	School of Education, Durham University, Durham, UK
Jade Zimpfer	Sociology, School of Social and Political Sciences, University of Edinburgh, Edinburgh, UK

DIGITAL SOCIAL RESEARCH: POTENTIAL AND OVERVIEW

We live in societies where, over the last two decades, digital technologies have become woven into almost every sphere of human experience. In daily life, people acquire and live with digital devices and systems that in turn mediate a growing range of digitized services, media forms, cultural objects, social interaction and experiences. Such activities take place across the domains of work, home, transport, education, and leisure, combining and sometimes redefining these domains. Digital technologies have also become the infrastructure of broader dimensions of social, economic, political and cultural life: the ways that people connect, converse and relate to each other, understand and experience culture, negotiate and organize the content and boundaries of work and leisure, public and private life. Many forms of digital mediation are altering established conventions of how time and space are organized and experienced, from notions of being 'always on' in a perpetually connected 24/7 society, to how instant communications appear to constitute new times and places *for* sociality, to the ways in which people's identities seem less anchored to location and more by technologically mediated communication. Public and private institutions of every kind have had to adopt and adapt to digital infrastructures, processes and practices, producing a range of intended and unintended consequences and concerns around ethics, privacy, rights, surveillance, knowledge and power.

The above indicates a changing landscape of sociotechnical relationships, but also potentially novel *ways of knowing* about social change. This collection of papers is orientated around qualitative approaches to what we have called 'digital social research'. This encompasses a wide range of perspectives, disciplines, conceptual and methodological orientations, empirical research, all of which attests to the mainstreaming and diversification of digital technologies and data in social life today.

The term 'big data' in the title of this volume is currently the focus of significant debate among policy makers across government, health, business, education, science and so on. It refers to 'our newfound ability to crunch a vast quantity of information, analyse it instantly, and draw sometimes astonishing conclusions from it' (Mayer-Schonberger & Cukier, 2013). An outcome of the continuing development of ubiquitous computing, new corporate/state informational infrastructures and ordinary practices of data production and circulation in daily life are raising hugely important questions for the social sciences. The question mark applied to big data signals the ambivalence of the term in its technical definitions, the narratives of promise and threat through which it is articulated, the unintended consequences of its production and circulation and so on. We are also ambivalent about the term in this book, in lots of different ways. Nonetheless, we use the term here to recognize its rhetorical power and also the ways in which it has prompted critical reflection on broader issues related to ongoing digitization. Indeed, researchers have begun to map critical questions about data transparency and privacy, freedom and suppression of data, invasive marketing and analytic purchase (Boyd & Crawford, 2012). Some of the current debates about digitization are part of a far broader set of reflections on the jurisdiction of the social sciences in an era of ubiquitous data, and a questioning of the 'tools of the trade'. Many issues around the challenges of the digital landscape to social science itself have been taken up, regarding the tools and concepts of sociology (Orton-Johnson & Prior, 2013), the ontological and epistemological assumptions of social science methods (Ruppert, Law, & Savage, 2013), the potential of 'digital methods' (Rogers, 2013) and the emergence of the 'digital sociologist' (Lupton, 2012). Concerns around 'data' at the current time are the locus of a wider range of issues around the complex relationships between social research and the digital landscape.

There are many emerging and potential directions suggested here. For some, the imperative is to critically examine the ways in which the socio-political use of data within and across institutions is reconfiguring experience, in the city, the workplace, the home, through consumption, and in the constitution of the self. For others, there is the tantalizing promise that social research could operationalize digital byproduct data to better understand patterns of behaviour, squaring the circle of 'what people do' with 'what they say they do'. Needless to say there is much debate and disagreement about the significance and potential trajectories of digital social research both in terms of 'big data' and beyond.

This volume moves forward and pinpoints many different ways of pursuing and developing these critical discussions, bringing together a wide range of explorations that focus on qualitative approaches to digital research. It draws upon an international field of scholars conducting research that encompasses different concepts, elements, tools and practices of digital research. The volume offers critical insight into the questions being asked of new kinds of data, platforms and media, their implications for the future and how best can we actively conduct research in relation to these. This collection is necessary eclectic and multi-faceted. It asks new questions concerning the familiar objects of qualitative research into digital media, a range of new data objects that challenge existing methods, situates digital data within a number of diverse fields and practices and explores digital research in terms of key categories of social scientific inquiry. In so doing, the volume captures the significance of digital data in its many forms for the conduct of qualitative research and, most importantly, recognizes and engages with its *diversity and ambivalence*. The benefits of big data and digital research more broadly are heralded across many disciplines and domains. Aside from predictable dystopian predictions, there is also legitimate uncertainty and a need for specificity in terms of just how transformative digital data and techniques are for the ways that qualitative research is actually conducted, analysed and presented. What are the emerging relationships between established methodological frameworks and novel digital techniques? How do researchers both analyse and utilize digital data in the field? Are there new ways of knowing emerging with digital devices and data? In what ways are digital methods performative? What can people's uses of digital data tell us about society? How do researchers contextualize and situate digital data methodologically?

The volume begins with a critical review of some current trajectories in digital social research by Martin Hand. He traces the shift from research focused on 'cyberspace' to the 'dataverse', picking out different combinations of concepts and methods being used in response to, but also in constituting, the shifting empirical phenomena labelled 'digital'. Hand pinpoints and discusses three profitable debates at the present time that have significant implications for qualitative research: the conceptualization of 'social' in 'social data'; the role of infrastructures of knowledge in the production of 'data'; and the distinction between 'digitized' and 'digital' methods. The chapter argues for the continued significance of interview, observation and ethnographic work in addressing some of the epistemological challenges of constructing 'thick' social media data. The volume is subsequently organized around the following five thematic clusters each articulating quite different conceptualizations of what digital social research, data and methods are and could be.

INSTITUTIONAL MOBILIZATIONS AND APPROPRIATIONS OF DATA

Data is produced, maintained, mobilized and circulated within specific contexts. These may be institutional contexts with long histories and knowledge practices, particular locations with established senses of 'place', or novel spaces of data circulation such as social media platforms and their underlying infrastructures.

In the chapter by Andrew Goffey, Lynne Pettinger and Ewen Speed, the politicization of big data in the National Health Service in the United Kingdom is explored. As part of a longer term restructuring of public institutions around the 'information revolution', new data policies and practices are being promoted and enacted. Arguing for the significance of ethnographic and institutional analyses to 'unpick' taken for granted assumptions about software and systems, particularly their 'neutrality', the operation of data and information are revealed as messy, complex tools for bureaucratic administration. The relative balance between the provision of care and the production of information is being altered, with huge consequences. A range of established qualitative methods can help perform the important work of demystifying the rhetorical power of digitization 'from within', if they attend to the specificities of setting, including its histories. Data is a contested concept but is also mobilized as part of struggles to articulate and shape social realities. As Goffey et al. show, the promises of data are often used to pursue 'inevitable' futures in institutional settings.

The complex political, economic and social character of data infrastructures and practices are often forgotten or hidden. In a chapter about the strategic uses of social media data by individuals and police agencies, Daniel Trottier argues that there are a range of institutional difficulties experienced by law enforcement agencies in attempting to use social media data as 'evidence' and 'intelligence'. Through the construction of case studies and in-depth interviews, Trottier delineates the ways in which the affordances of social media data construed as 'evidence' can lead to what he calls 'social harm from above and below'. But, as in the NHS, he also finds that intended efforts to use such data for surveillance purposes is less straightforward than it appears, due to the regulatory contexts and (lack of) expertise in law enforcement. All of which, Trottier suggests, necessitates detailed empirical research into practices of data production, circulation and appropriation, if we are to understand how the *ambivalence* of big data leads to multiple and often contradictory social 'effects'.

In both chapters we get a real sense of data and information being put to work by political and policy interests. In both cases data legitimates a host of potentially unpopular reforms and procedures. The institutional deployment of new data practices may (will) never live up to its promises of smooth re-organization and efficiency, but they will have social consequences regardless.

FIELDS AND SITES

If digital data is 'everywhere', then what happens to some of the established categories of qualitative research in different disciplines, in terms of research sites outside of institutional settings? This issue has been explored at some length in considerations of 'virtual' or 'online' ethnography (e.g. Hine, 2000, 2008). With the present emphasis on increased data production and circulation across devices and social practices, the question is revisited in two different ways here. Christine Lohmeier provides a critical overview of how 'big data' is being approached in communications scholarship, particularly around analyses of Twitter data. There are emerging differences between quantitative and qualitative approaches to digital data, but there are more fruitful avenues to explore by bringing together a concern for digital data with developments in digital ethnography. She goes on to articulate how big data and ethnographic approaches might be conjoined in order delimit the potentially 'never-ending field' of digital social research. Thinking through issues of materiality and context, alongside the novelties of ubiquitous data, raises difficult challenges around privacy, ethics and access to data that are highlighted here.

The difficulties of defining the field site in 'online ethnography' are taken up in detail in a chapter by Emma Hutchinson, where the ethical dilemmas of privacy in online forums are shown to present ethnographers with several challenges. Hutchinson explores the salience of using online forums as part of broader online ethnographies through a participatory study of an online gaming forum. On the one hand, much like social media data, online forums seem to be 'easy pickings' for social research. On the other hand, they require careful attention to other users' privacy. Through a longitudinal study, Hutchinson navigates issues of researcher 'lurking' and audience perceptions, detailing how forum (participant) observation in concert with interviews reveals articulations of identity in gaming communities that might otherwise remain obscured.

In paying attention to the evolution of online spaces and the methodological tools used to explore them takes account of novel issues around data, but reminds us of the continued importance of diverse online cultures. Advances in techniques and tools, coupled with recognition that field sites may be increasingly spreadable, also demand new reflection on the ethics of digital social research.

DIGITAL, DIGITIZED AND PARTICIPATORY METHODS

The above chapters use, imply or argue for the deployment of mixed qualitative methods in digital social research, whether in combination with big data analyses or in isolation.

Mariann Hardey utilizes digital methods to work with digital data produced through marketing narratives. Her chapter critically evaluates the literature on digital consumer data and the ways in which it can be used in digital social research. The chapter illuminates how researchers have to conceptualize and negotiate digital data, focusing upon ethical and procedural challenges of employing digital methods. Necessarily, her approach draws upon and integrates a broad research literature from sociology, digital media studies, business and marketing. Collectively, these have opened up new directions for research design and method. Whilst new visibilities of consumer data are shaped by related processes of branding and the interactivity of content, this recognition heralds too a new need for an ethical responsibility in the context of the longer-term presence of data records. The chapter is therefore mindful of not only the reach but consequences of interpenetrated data.

Angus Bancroft, Martina Karels, Órla Meadhbh Murray and Jade Zimpfer also touch upon the ethical issues of digital data usage, ownership and participatory research projects. They use crowdsourced data as a way of doing participatory research. They place such an approach in its historical context understanding that dairies are one way in which social scientists have in the past attempted to break down traditional hierarchies of power. Their chapter discusses how the ambition to use digital data is difficult to realize in practice. Using their own empirical work exploring alcohol consumption amongst young people, they deconstruct the multiple layers that constitute qualitative fieldwork, analysis and writing. They conclude crowdsourcing data has the potential, albeit not realized in their own case specific discussion, to open up the research process to a more egalitarian relationship between researchers and researched.

Jonathan Tummons is similarly optimistic regarding the way technology has opened up possibilities for the management of qualitative datasets. He speculates that there may be new avenues for rich archives of qualitative data and that the *speed* of communication makes the management, communication and inter-team organization of datasets more robust. This does not replace the need for reflexive analysis, but rather renders more transparent the logic – and evidential basis – underpinning qualitative analytic procedures. Using his own participation in an international research team, he demonstrates how digitalization has transformed what types of qualitative data can be captured – and collectively analysed – in the research process.

VISIBILITIES, ROUTINES AND PRACTICES

As discussed above, one of the key claims for the significance of digital data for social research is that, on the one hand, it has generated a range of novel practices to be understood, and on the other hand makes previously obscure practices *visible* and thus available for research. Much has been made of this, particularly the notion that 'small data' traces are automatically produced through ordinary conduct mediated by devices. What are the implications of this for qualitative research that has aimed at mapping and accounting for such conduct? The question is addressed in a detailed theoretical chapter by Robin James Smith, in which he critically addresses the relationships between sociological discipline and method, and the ways in which qualitative methods are being 'reduced, re-used and recycled' in digital sociology in the context of the 'crisis' in social science research. By drawing upon two ethnographic cases and recovering some of the key insights of ethnomethodological scholarship, Smith excavates what he sees as the divergences between data and lived experience in digital research, arguing that this 'space' is often 'filled' by ideological interests. Qualitative methods are particularly well suited to intervene in such spaces, and Smith outlines potential contributions, including analyses of the ways that big data is actually constructed, and detailed studies of how people, devices and traces are co-constituted through practice.

This latter point is taken up by Martin Hand in his chapter on the routine uses of cameras, smartphones and social media, and the 'negotiation of traces' enabled through those uses. In the context of digital memory, traces of daily life produced through photography and other visual practices appear to deconstruct prior distinctions between private and public, personal and collective, active and passive memories in modernity. By reflecting upon two qualitative studies – of digital photographic practices and smartphone mediated memory practices – Hand shows how the combination of the increased routine production and visibility of digital data presents novel challenges for both researchers and participants. Hand suggests that qualitative studies of *how* digital data is routinely produced, negotiated, recursively worked upon and circulated – how digital data is *socialized* in daily practice – can provide insight into the continuities and discontinuities of digitization as a corrective to the dominant assumption of novelty. He stresses the need to take individual's reflexive engagements seriously while also paying attention to the handling, use and agency of mundane digital devices.

INVISIBILITIES, GAPS AND WAYS OF KNOWING

The scale, scope and pervasiveness of digital data should not imply that this increases representativeness of that people, things and populations are not routine excluded from the new data landscape. On the one hand, there are issues of bias and selectivity in the production and visibility of digital data, especially in social media metrics. On the other hand, there are other modes of invisibility that require considered reflection. Firstly, we might ask, even in the affluent global north are there places and practices largely ignored by the big data practitioners and academic research on digitization? One example explored here is that of 'the rural'. Digital social research has almost exclusively focused upon the urban, and while there are good reasons for this, explorations of the experience of digitization in rural settings can provide new insight. Digital rural research might explore both the lived experience of digitization unexplored settings, and potential new ways of knowing the rural through digitization. Sam Hillyard articulates these important issues in the context of theoretical innovation in 'rural sociology', in a chapter that explores two very different appearances of digital data in the rural context. Birdwatching and the management of datasets evaluating firearm licence holders suitability are discussed and analysed. Whilst rural spaces are shaped by how people consume them, the chapter also moves to recognize that datasets can also have unanticipated consequences. How rural digital datasets are constructed and accessed therefore may well shape the activities that are ultimately performed there. The digital, in this case, therefore has the potential to shape what rural spaces then become.

Many of the most hyperbolic claims for big data and new knowledge concern 'big science'. Do new ways of collating and sharing data in the natural sciences provide new ways of knowing nature? How and why might the social sciences incorporate such data? The final chapter by Nik Taylor and Lindsay Hamilton examines new theoretical frontiers relating to nature, animals and social practices. They argue that animals have typically been excluded from social science research and see the potential for datasets *around* animals to be used to break down some of the traditional distinctions about human–animal relations. This entails grappling with some of the troubling, often vexatious methodological issues involved in human–animal research. That is, by realizing that a datafication of everyday life has already occurred, then the field of post-humanism similarly opens up areas for social investigation that would not have been possible before. Their chapter is critical, in that it considers research methodology and potential barriers to multi-disciplinary research in the field of human–animal relationships. Using a brief example to illustrate this, they define an emerging method of Multi Species Ethnography (or MSE) as an exciting new debate offering a number of suggestions for further analysis and speculation. Digitalization as part of a qualitative research toolkit may also offer up theoretical opportunities for future MSE.

The emphases in the chapters as a whole are on capturing the dynamics of qualitative approaches to digital research at the conceptual level and through grounded empirical accounts. They are therefore in keeping with – and extend – the exploratory spirit of past volumes in the series. The breadth of focus outlined above seeks to explore digital research from many angles, illuminating the subtle tensions and ambivalences of pervasive digital data in social life, offering an ambitious road map for how this can be researched and critically understood.

Martin Hand
Sam Hillyard
Editors

REFERENCES

Boyd, D., & Crawford, K. (2012). Critical questions for big data. *Information, Communication and Society*, *15*(5), 662–679.

Hine, C. (2000). *Virtual ethnography*. London: Sage.

Hine, C. (2008). Virtual ethnography: Modes, varieties, affordances. In N. Fileding, R. M. Lee, & G. Blank (Eds.), *The Sage handbook of online research methods*. London: Sage.

Lupton, D. (2012). *Digital sociology: An introduction*. Sydney: University of Sydney.

Mayer-Schonberger, V., & Cukier, K. (2013). *Big data: A revolution that will change how we live, work and think*. London: John Murray.

Orton-Johnson, K., & Prior, N. (Eds.). (2013). *Digital sociology: Critical perspectives*. Basingstoke, UK: Palgrave.

Rogers, R. (2013). *Digital methods*. Cambridge, MA: MIT Press.

Ruppert, E., Law, J., & Savage, M. (2013). Reassembling social science methods: The challenge of digital devices. *Theory, Culture & Society*, *30*(4), 22–46.

FROM CYBERSPACE TO THE DATAVERSE: TRAJECTORIES IN DIGITAL SOCIAL RESEARCH

Martin Hand

ABSTRACT

Purpose – *To outline the current trajectories in digital social research and to highlight the roles of qualitative research in those trajectories.*

Design/methodology/approach – *A secondary analysis of the primary literature.*

Findings – *Qualitative research has shifted over time in relation to rapidly changing digital phenomena, but arguably finds itself in 'crisis' when faced with algorithms and ubiquitous digital data. However, there are many highly significant qualitative approaches that are being pursued and have the potential to contextualize, situate and critique narratives and practices of data.*

Originality/value – *To situate current debates around methods within longer trajectories of digital social research, recognizing their conceptual, disciplinary and empirical commitments.*

Keywords: Dataverse; cyberspace; digital social research; digital methods; big data; social data

Big Data? Qualitative Approaches to Digital Research
Studies in Qualitative Methodology, Volume 13, 1–27

ISSN: 1042-3192/doi:10.1108/S1042-319220140000013002

INTRODUCTION

Over the last 25 years, social science research into digital media and technologies has expanded dramatically and changed its character considerably. To put it relatively crudely, the emphases in digital social research have shifted from interpreting 'life online' to researching a far broader range of 'mediated life'. The title of this chapter suggests a general shift from a largely external phenomenon to be researched in terms of its distinctive differences, to the sense that *life in general* has been interpenetrated by digital data. That social life is being reconfigured through the *routine* production, circulation and performativity of vast amounts of data appears incontestable. This includes the proliferation of infrastructures, networks and screens, plus social media and networking, compound devices and algorithms, and all the institutions and practices that have formed around these. This mutual embedding of digital media technologies and institutional and personal life has led to new questions, concerning the roles of infrastructures and expertise, the shaping of personal relationships, the public visibility of private life, and the continuous surveillance of people, things and transactions.

However, rather than simply being a 'from-to' story, it is more accurate to say that there has been a multiplication and diversification of the objects, subjects and methods of digital social research over this period. Digital media technologies, like those before them, have become routine and normalized but there is much debate about the substantive, theoretical and methodological implications of this. Emergent infrastructures and practices of digitization are challenging the ways that research in the social sciences and humanities are conducted and legitimated. In research *about* digital transformations to research *with* the digital, there is an acute sense of a turning point in our relations with data and devices. Digitization is opening up the potential for change in both the methods and the objects of analysis in social science research.

As a starting point, we can observe that digital social media are now integrated into social life to such an extent that they multiply mediate social life. That is, they enable novel ways of organizing the social while at the same time rendering the social amenable to established and emerging modes of analysis, most clearly in terms of the *visibility* of social media interactions. Digital data is both a taken for granted aspect of daily life and a source of hyperbolic claims for novel regimes of truth. The term *big data* has become the dominant metaphor for the vast data production, storage, circulation and calculation occurring in the world today. Much commentary about big data is really discussing a far broader and diverse range of data, but the *idea* of big data is both rhetorically persuasive and materially pervasive in shaping institutional, commercial and personal life. Present concerns with (big) data need to be understood as part of the more *general methodological problems of digitization:* changes in the objects and means of qualitative research, from how research is conceptualized, conducted, disseminated and of course valued.

With this in mind, this chapter provides a review of current trajectories in what can broadly be termed 'digital social research'. Much of this is concerned with new forms of data and their relationship to method, but a key aim here is to contextualize the current fascination with big, small, open and linked data within longer trajectories in analyses of digitally mediated society and culture. The full range of social research about the Internet, Web 2.0, social networking and social media and so on, is outside the scope of this chapter. As such, this chapter limits itself to tracking how the emphases in theory and method have shifted from conceptions of digitally mediated space to the datafication of everyday life. A second aim is to illuminate some of the key similarities and differences emerging under the umbrella of digital social research across disciplines and locations. At present there are several related trajectories dominating the field, from those working in sociology and media in the United Kingdom, to communications in North America, and digital media in northern Europe, among others.

This chapter discusses current debates about method in the context of digitization in the following ways. Firstly, the objects and subjects of digital social research have changed markedly over the last 25 years as digital devices and data have increasingly penetrated institutional and personal life. Secondly, a series of new claims for knowledge associated with the 'dataverse' have become dominant, to which many social researchers are responding. Many of those responses are specifically focused on questions of methodological expertise and disciplinary boundaries. This chapter then reviews three current debates in digital social research. The question of the social in so-called 'social data' is discussed, followed by the role of infrastructures and devices in framing the possibilities of analytics. Then the differences between digitized methods and digital methods are discussed in relation to the above. Finally, the chapter reiterates the need for digital social research to be flexible about the specificity of particular methods for approaching digital phenomena.

DATA, DATA EVERYWARE

> [W]e have conceived ourselves and the natural entities in terms of data and information. We have flattened both the social and the natural into a single world so that there are no human actors and natural entities but only agents (speaking computationally) or actants (speaking semiotically) that share precisely the same features. It makes no sense in the dataverse to speak of the raw and natural or the cooked and the social: to get into it you already need to be defined as a particular kind of monad. (Bowker, 2013, p. 169)

There have been several transformations in the range and nature of digital media technologies and the methods employed to understand their social significance over the last 25 years. This has involved a multiplication and diversification of the objects, subjects and methods of digital social research. This also intimates dramatic shifts in the information and data *imaginary*, in tandem with the increased embedding of digital technologies within social life and the popularity of social networking and social media.

Briefly, during the late 1980s and early 1990s the metaphor of *cyberspace* was dominant, imagining information as an autonomous cultural environment 'out there'. This 'space' was conceptualized as a non-physical environment (Bolter & Grusin, 1999, p. 181) with the promise of transcending 'the bloody mess of organic matter' (Wertheim, 2000, p. 19) and the limitations implied by containment within the ethnic, gendered, embodied 'meat' of human flesh (Flichy, 2007, p. 130). The emphasis in early accounts was on the radical possibilities for self-transformation and community formation. For the new communitarians, it was not a matter of 'where' individuals might be physically, but whether the interactions between them were sufficient to form 'webs of personal relationships' (Rheingold, 1993, p. 5). While mostly about discussion forums using the Internet, this idea also shaped research into 'virtual reality', role-playing games such as the 'virtual worlds' of MMORPGs and MUDs, all of which largely involved people who rarely met off screen and were, in this view, unrelated to place. Initial critiques tended to reproduce this notion of cyberspace in more dystopian terms. Jones (1997) and Sardar (1996) argued that community is not simply a matter of communication; the fact that they are formed through bonds of transient mutual interest rather than mutual obligation or proximity makes them *simulations of community*. In terms of the self, cybercultural research into 'virtual identity' tracked anonymous identity choices being made as users were 'authors', not *enacting* but *re-writing* given identities in a 'post-social' world (Hayles, 1999). In postmodern theorizing, the sheer contingency of cyberspatial interaction precipitated a democratization of communication where 'The magic of the Internet is that it is a technology which puts cultural acts, symbolizations in all forms, in the hands of its participants' (Poster, 2001, p. 184). Research in computer-mediated communication and social psychology (Turkle, 1997) argued that MUDs offered the opportunity for players not only to create the text (or graphics) of the game but also to construct '… new selves though social interaction' (1997, p. 12), encouraging performances of multiple selves, further enhanced through the possibility of non-linear identities and a 'distributed presence' (1997, pp. 12–13).

A series of empirical interventions shifted the field from the late 1990s, including the political economy of communication, ethnographic explorations of user's practices, and the integration of the Web in social network analyses, all of which had the effect of *disaggregating* cyberspace and *destabilizing* the offline and online distinction as the appropriate ground for digital social research. With the advent of the World-Wide Web in 1991, commercial browsers in 1995, and rapid institutional and personal adoption of networked technologies, research into the political economy of cyberspace traced the penetration of advertising, marketing and e-commercial applications. The material and mythical *production* of cyberspace as proliferating new markets and the accompanying efforts to regulate and monitor Internet traffic, to enforce laws of private property, represented a 'perfect alignment' between technology, capital and culture (Taylor & Harris, 2005). Critical attention was directed towards the longer military and commercial history of information processing and how the apparent immaterialism of cyberspace and the related notion of cultural empowerment were revealed as necessary mythologies of informational capitalism (Mosco, 2004).

A second empirical trajectory has dismantled cyberspace from the ground up. Digital ethnographic research has followed two main directions: detailed immersion studies of 'life online' (Hine, 2000, 2005; Kozinets, 2010; Markham, 1999) and ethnographies of how the practices of everyday life incorporate and integrate (or not) elements of Internet technology into the rhythms of place and practice (boyd, 2014; Miller & Slater, 2000; also Horst & Miller, 2006; Miller, 2011). In this latter development, 'the Internet' or 'social media' has been dissolved into their multifarious components that may or may not be assembled into 'online spaces' by people in daily life. A significant element to Miller and Slater's (2000) groundbreaking ethnographic work was its location in Trinidad, revealing the ways in which Euro-American assumptions about individualized computer use, alienation and postmodern identity politics had structured previous models of cyberspace. Instead of conceptualizing the Internet or cyberspace as a vehicle for identity performance or of disembedded and dematerialized community building, it was convincingly shown that people incorporate elements of media into existing material-symbolic arrangements and, in this case, counter-intuitively used the Internet to 'make concrete' rather than virtualize *national* identities. Similarly, the relationships between new media-orientated practices and childhood (Livingstone, 2011), activism (Lievrouw, 2011) and migration (Madianou & Miller, 2012) provided counter-intuitive findings.

Attempts to 'contextualize cyberspace' through detailed ethnographic exploration has been a complex arena for debate (Hine, 2000) because of the shifting ground of where access to cyberspace takes place (home, library, cybercafé, mobiles) and the proliferating range of possible uses related to ever-evolving technologies and techniques (chat, games, education, shopping, dating). As more connected technologies have become simply a part of ordinary experience the relations between those technologies and the contexts in which they are used has become more complex. Like those doing ethnography, those drawing upon social network analysis have also argued that in reality the so-called 'on-line world' is an extension and often an enhancement of pre-existing social relations which themselves have become increasingly orientated through 'networks' rather than predominantly physical spaces or places (Baym, 2010; Rainie & Wellman, 2012; Wellman & Haythornwaite, 2002). This also entailed the recasting of 'community' itself as a network formation, preferring the concept of 'networked individualism' to describe how people find themselves spatially dislocated and seek to maintain social ties with dislocated others in ways that are both individually orientated yet densely connected (Barney, 2004). Recent work in this area, predominantly employing case studies, has focused upon the intended and unintended creation of 'networked publics', as social media enable people to form ad hoc publics around key issues or events (Bruns & Burgess, 2012; and see Papacharissi, 2009).

In tandem with this phase of (often very different) empirical accounts of the Internet, there have been other theoretical and substantive developments signalling the 'end of cyberspace' as the primary object of digital social research. For example, the growing influence of concepts drawn from empirical work in science and technology studies (STS) has further dismantled technology/user and active/passive dichotomies, considering *how* technical objects actively 'define a framework of action together with the actors and the space in which they are supposed to act' (Akrich, 1992). Instead of either only shaping or being shaped by social actions and interests, technologies co-evolve with the dynamics of systems of which they are part, technical characteristics can be said to evolve in tandem with shifting conventions and practices of use (Oudshoorn & Pinch, 2002), and the dynamics of *uses* will reconfigure future trajectories of innovation.

Conceiving of technologies as active elements within a broader framework of action has been augmented by the proliferation of technologies designed to 'act together' materially and facilitate continual data flows between them. From laptops, tablets and smartphones, to iPods, smart watches, fabrics and glasses, a proliferating materialization *and* informationalization of social life has occurred through the mobility of bodies. Accounts of an 'Internet of things' and of 'knowing capitalism' (Thrift, 2005), suggest that these things are also increasingly constitutive of everyday life in the form of interoperable mobile environments that become all but routinized. In other words, what was once cyberspace – a cultural space to be accessed and entered through the PC – is now, in Thrift's terms, a material 'screeness' that is portable and independent of any particular container. It is everyware. Institutionally, politically, socially and culturally.

Over the last 10 years, this has been raising important conceptual and methodological issues for digital social research. Firstly, the technical objects of research have altered dramatically. Without wishing to simply focus on gadgets, changes in the quantity, range and character of technological devices has enabled different practices to emerge. While people still spend time in 'virtual worlds' it is the ways in which these technologies now facilitate continual 'interfacing', connected presence and enable the 'mediation of everything' (Livingstone, 2009) that facilitates a rethinking of what we think of as 'the social' in terms of data flows.

Secondly, the characteristics of social media and applications enable the reconfiguring of cultural forms. They enable vast amounts of user-generated content to be shared and circulated, often in the form of private information (thought, images, tastes) placed in the public domain, encouraging a reversal of the relation between 'public' and 'private' life that characterized the modern archive (Gane & Beer, 2008). By contrast to many early uses of the Internet, social media is resolutely non-anonymous; others speak of how social media and relational databases seem to necessitate the ever more detailed codification of habitus (Burrows & Gane, 2006) and the circulation of personal data *as* popular culture (Beer, 2013). In cultural terms, the graphics, moving images, sounds, shapes, spaces and texts mashed together and re-formed through metadata 'tagging' in social media and microblogging have indeed 'become computable; that is, they comprise simply another set of computer data' (Manovich, 2001, p. 20). These new cultural objects are liquid in form. Unlike the objects of Benjamin's mechanical reproduction they can produce infinite *variations* not copies.

Thirdly, and this is perhaps the most palpable sense of us 'living among data', is the reversal of the idea of access. Algorithmically produced data now accesses us, intervening and mediating nearly all aspects of everyday life whether we know it (like it) or not. On an individual level, we are informed of what we like, what our interests are (or should be), how we compare with others and so on as the result of algorithmic assessment of our previously mediated actions. The materials of cyberspace are now infrastructural and anticipatory, 'knowing' where to find us (Thrift, 2005), often constructing aggregate representations of an 'us' or 'we'. Instead of existing as an externality (cyberspace) or set of extensions (networks), data now re-structures actual geographic territories (city, neighbourhood) through automated classification systems such as neighbourhood profiling, Google maps, GPS systems, loyalty cards, Wi-Fi and so on (Kitchin, 2013; Kitchin & Dodge, 2011). What we see here are often invisible processes of structuring and re-structuring due to the proliferation of software – as it becomes materialized in more devices and institutional settings – and the increasing significance of classification and metricization as the data produced does not 'represent' but performs *judgement* in Latour's sense (2005).

All of the above has shifted the agenda towards thinking about the digital in terms of continual mediation and of the increasing production, circulation and multifarious uses of data. Networked and mobile digital technologies now routinely mediate daily life in ways that produce vast amounts of data about interactions between people and things. Such data is produced in multiple ways and takes diverse forms. Data is produced both intentionally and unintentionally, it is both extracted from users and volunteered, it is often automated and more purposively directed, it is attached to people, objects and processes or transactions, it is gathered by states, corporations, individuals and groups, much of it is open and public but most of it is closed and inaccessible.

RHETORICS OF THE DATAVERSE

So how does *big* data figure here? The term is generally being used to describe (largely unstructured) data sets that are too vast for conventional servers. While there is no standard definition of big data (what counts as 'big' will change), there are several common attributes within the technical literature that provide a sense of the key features: *Volume* (terabytes or petabytes of data), *Variety* (visual, textual, structured and unstructured), *Velocity* (real-time produced), *Scope* (vast or entire populations), *Relational* (multiple data sets combined), *Flexible* (new fields and scales), *Fine Grained* (high resolution and detail), among others (see, e.g. Laney, 2012). It is the ways in which such datasets can be searched, cross-referenced and aggregated that is the focus of attention (boyd & Crawford, 2012). These features are routinely drawn upon to underpin significant ontological and epistemological claims and related implications. With some similarity to earlier rhetorics of cyberspace, and more empirical accounts of the 'network society' (Castells, 1997) or the 'new social operating system' (Rainie & Wellman, 2012), enthusiasts for big data often conjure a 'dataverse' where the world is now *made of data*. This is sometimes construed as nothing less than a new social ontology:

> We will no longer regard our world as a string of happenings that we explain as a natural or social phenomenon, but as a universe comprised essentially of information. (Mayer-Schonberger & Cukier, 2013, p. 96)

For some, this social ontology of ubiquitous data problematizes existing methods for analysing it (e.g. Burrows & Beer, 2013, p. 75). In the most radical view, it is not simply a question of adjusting our methods accordingly, but of rethinking our epistemological commitments *tout court*:

> This is a world where massive amounts of data and applied mathematics replace every other tool that might be brought to bear. Out with every theory of human behavior, from linguistics to sociology. Forget taxonomy, ontology, and psychology. Who knows why people do what they do? The point is they do it, and we can track and measure it with unprecedented fidelity. With enough data, the numbers speak for themselves. (Anderson, 2008)

Of course, the idea that data simply displaces theory-driven knowledge has been well critiqued from inside and outside of social science. But the lingering corollary – that the need for *interpretation* is displaced by the need for *description* in the face of data deluges pervades much of the commentary at the present time. On the one hand, the call for description has been employed as a cautionary note to avoid simply repeating the hyperbole of earlier enchantments with digitization (Beer & Burrows, 2007). On the other hand, models of automatically produced, linked and relational data that simply has to be visualized is cast as 'pre-analytic' or 'pre-conscious' and we need to 'let the data speak' (Mayer-Schonberger & Cukier, 2013, p. 14). In other words, it is thought that as digital data appears produced automatically *through* social action it provides us with a ready-made analytics *of* the social.

Such a conception has profound implications for how qualitative methodologies are valued and legitimated as devices for intervening, interpreting and explaining the social. The dataverse promises a new descriptive-predictive analytics of pattern and correlation, prioritized over meaning and causation. In what might be called a pristine empiricism, the scale, pattern and complexity of vast relational datasets enables a model of analysis in which 'Correlation is enough' (Anderson, 2008). Not only that, the questions one might ask of data are likely to be immanent to the dataverse itself:

> Ayasdi has managed to totally remove the human element that goes into data mining and, as such, all the human bias that goes with it. Instead of waiting to be asked a question or be directed to specific existing data links, the system will -undirected – deliver patterns a human controller might not have thought to look for. (Clark, 2013)

This prioritization of pattern has led Crawford (2013) and others to critique what she sees as an emerging 'data fundamentalism', a rhetoric in which '...[C]orrelation always indicates causation, and that massive data sets and predictive analytics always reflect objective truth'. Such a reification of data shifts due attention from methodological questions concerning data construction, sampling, interpretation and analysis, and the ways in which data 'trends' have themselves been shaped by commercial interests and contingent sociotechnical processes (Gillespie, 2013; van Dijck, 2013). What we think of as 'social' – especially interaction, practice and symbolic communication – is being structured and codified by digital infrastructures of one kind or another and made available for analytics regardless. For example, some of the data generated through social media communication can be accessed through the 'application programming interfaces' (APIs) of platforms such as Facebook and Twitter. This kind of potentially big data is thought to provide researchers with 'live' data about public life in the present (Bruns, 2013). Similarly, 'real-time research' that utilizes digital technologies to reorder the relation between data capturing, analysis and dissemination promises more collaborative methods and increased accessibility (but see Bancroft, Karels, Murray, & Zimpfer, 2014).

Many of these ideas rest on the notion that social research, broadly conceived as discourse about the social, appears to be occurring 'everywhere' in social media. There has been a generalization of 'sharing' personal narratives in social media that appear to replicate some qualitative forms of inquiry (such as the interview). But this is arguably a superficial reading of social media practices and a defensive reaction to what looks like the outsourcing of a sociology of everyday life through new modes of popular cultural circulation (Beer, 2013). At its worst, 'commercial sociology' might simply provide us with 'trends', implicitly endorsing the myth of such publicly available data as the 'roar of the crowd' (see van Dijck, 2013) and naively valuing aesthetic visualizations. Nonetheless, the prevalence of ubiquitous data generated through social media practices raises significant questions about how this data deconstructs established and unquestioned sociological models of society. For example, it has been argued that there are instances involving digital data where the relation between that data and external realities is perhaps mute, as the updating of 'whole population data' in real time raises the question as to whether this data needs to be 'grounded' in an external (see Adkins & Lury, 2012).

On the one hand, the majority of researchers in the social sciences and humanities will not be utilizing big data per se, but in conducting digital social research are concerned about how to position themselves in relation to such data and the knowledge claims that are accompanying it. On the other hand, given the diversity and flexibility of qualitative methods, there are forms of 'smaller' digital data that seem to offer novel possibilities for methodological innovation. Both of these trajectories have recently lent themselves to a sense methodological crisis.

METHODOLOGICAL CRISIS AND RENEWAL IN THE SOCIAL SCIENCES

The promises and threats associated with ubiquitous data have prompted a great deal of critical self-reflection within the social sciences and humanities regarding the perceived need (and opportunity) for methodological innovation, in light of the potential 'emptying out' of methodological and technical expertise. Recent articulations of 'digital sociology' (Orton-Johnson & Prior, 2013), 'digital anthropology' (Horst & Miller, 2012) and 'digital humanities' (Berry, 2012) have attempted to chart the ways in which disciplines might rethink themselves for the digital age, especially in terms of methodological commitments and research practices. Much has been made in the last few years of the 'crisis in the empirical social sciences' (Savage & Burrows, 2007; Ruppert, 2013). The broader context for this concern is the increased visibility and *measuring* of academic practice in a market-based system of higher education, arguably leading to a curious mixture of conventionality and potential irrelevance (Burrows, 2012). But at the core of this crisis is thought to be the shrinking role of social science methods such as the survey and in-depth interview, as new forms of 'social data' and the expertise to collect and analyse it shifts to the domain of corporate and governmental institutions. In some respects, core sociological methods have been outsourced to a mixture of corporations, technology/media companies, and individual social actors.

A matter of both limited access to, and a lack of expertise with, huge volumes of transactional and other data, social science researchers arguably find themselves somewhat disconnected from the new digital data analytics. The task, as Ruppert (2013, p. 270) puts it, is to 'innovatively, critically and reflexively' engage with emerging forms of data. This requires, at the very least, a turn to interdisciplinary and collaborative ways of approaching data, drawing upon expertise in computation and data analytics alongside social-scientific insights. This jurisdiction problem is happening across many fields of professional life, where expertise previously embedded within the domains of journalism, science, education and law is arguably undergoing a partial redistribution through publicly available data and associated calls for public participation in the constitution of expert knowledge (e.g. 'citizen science').

What role for qualitative methods in digital social research here? For those explicitly concerned with big data, the distinction between quantitative and qualitative methods is one of the key obstacles to developing data-literate analyses of the emerging landscape. A broader view of digital data, one that situates new forms of data within the specificities of digital social transformations, recognizes the continuing salience of qualitative methods in interpreting and analysing the production and implications of digital data. In one influential account, Marres (2012) argues that we should recognize that society is different as a result of digitization and that sociological methods should remain flexible and dynamic in order to negotiate data, technique, context and medium in digital societies. Marres thus advocates 'inventive empiricism' that pulls together and reconfigures multiple and mixed methods, data, and analysis. One of the key questions for those advocating a digitization of disciplines is whether digital social research that operationalizes social media platforms as analytic 'devices' helps us to understand the dynamics of Twitter rather than the dynamics of Twitter-in-social-life (Marres, 2012; see also Couldry, 2012; van Dijck, 2013). It is precisely this difficulty in analytically demarcating between 'the social' and 'data' that contributes to such an intensive reflection on method, expertise and disciplinary domains.

The problem of methodological expertise in the face of digital data has been taken up Ruppert (2013), recognizing that much of the available data is produced as a byproduct of ordinary practice rather than through the intervention of 'experts' – data produced by device enabled transactions rather than as constituted in, say, a survey. Rather than think of this as the 'corporatization of methods', both Marres and Ruppert suggest that a 'redistribution of expertise' across disciplines and the division of labour is occurring (Ruppert, 2013; cf. Marres, 2012). Drawing upon an STS perspective, methods are always 'in process', performative and thus implicated in the ongoing constitution of 'the social'. If 'social science methods' are, in part, being codified *within* digital technologies (the analytics of the 'real-time Web') then perhaps digital social research can employ these material devices to gain insight into both social and media dynamics and their co-constitution. Indeed, Ruppert (2013) has argued that big data represent methodological opportunities rather than crises, if handled in the right way. She argues that it is an opportunity to think beyond method as 'external' to or 'detached' from the social, but as a source of internal or immanent critique developed through collaborative networks of actors. The precise issues around such 'digital methods' will be explored in the section below.

Other questions around methodological expertise have centred upon simply gaining access to this data, the limited 'public' forms it takes, the ethical problems of 'scraping' and 'harvesting' (boyd & Crawford, 2012; Crawford, 2013), the limited data infrastructures of academic institutions and the barriers to building expertise in data analytics and visualization techniques among citizens and community organizations (Bassett, 2014). The 'private enclosure' of big data and the lack of access to 'relevant forms of expertise' present social researchers with a different set of methodological issues – how to conduct robust research into data processes that both constitute 'publics' (often through data visualizations) *and* remain black-boxed and obscured from public scrutiny (Kennedy & Moss, 2014). Key concerns over big data privacy, the surveillance of social media interactions and the impact of new modes of measurement *in* social life, also contribute to the sense of urgency within the social sciences and humanities to successfully negotiate digital methods *and* critically interrogate the digitization of social life.

DEBATES ABOUT DATA, SOCIETY AND METHOD

There is some general agreement that we need to critically engage with emerging forms of data and the contexts in which they emerge, rather than simply dismissing 'data' or 'big data' as solely a corporate or economic vehicle for restructuring. Across sociology, communications, anthropology, STS, information science and so on, alternative ways of proceeding are emerging, many of which are interdisciplinary. For some scholars, the promises of big data can be taken up in the social sciences and humanities by developing robust *quantitative* methodologies for discovering large-scale patterns of communication and interaction on social media platforms (see Bruns & Burgess, 2012). For others, the use of a range of *qualitative* methods such as in-depth interviewing, discourse and content analysis, has proved particularly useful in contextualizing a range of social media data (see boyd & Crawford, 2012). This is sometimes referred to as 'small data research' – a combination of quantitative metrics and qualitative techniques such as observation in a particular field site and/or interviewing with diverse producers and users of social media. It is not that new modes of quantitative research enabled through big and small data replace qualitative data and analysis, but they might complement one another or be recombined in interesting and productive ways that problematize previous divides between 'surface' (quantitative) and 'deep' (qualitative) data on large and small populations respectively (see Manovich, 2011). New patterns might be spotted at one 'scale' than lead to novel questions at another, for example.

What's Social about 'Social Data'?

An expanding range of social and technical practices leave digital traces that can, in principle, become data of one sort or another. There are many difficulties in assessing what such data can tell us about society. Perhaps the most promise has been attached to claims for the *visibility* of social life through digital traces, many of which are the outcome of transactional processes between 'things' rather than the specific activities of people (Ruppert, Law, & Savage, 2013). Coupled with institutional practices of data visualization, visible data raises crucial methodological questions about how visualizations get made, how are they 'seen' and interpreted, and whether they fundamentally alter existing concepts of 'society'. The prefix 'social' is routinely used for much of this data. But what does it really mean to say that data is *social* and what are the methodological implications of this?

As discussed above, one of the key claims about digital data is that much of it is automatically collected 'social data' and as such can provide unproblematic (even 'authentic') descriptions of social activity ('we can now see what people do') and relationships between things hitherto unavailable ('we can see the missing masses of the social'). Of course, few researchers make such unqualified claims, acknowledging that visible metrics are themselves the products of a politics of measurement shaped by commercial interests and also problematized by the simple question of 'where, what and how do you count' in a landscape of fragmented media and audiences (Baym, 2013, p. 4). As Baym argues:

> That social media platforms usually show visible metrics of a page or user's popularity is no accident …[A]ll this commodification of affect through likes, follows and so on accrues to the platforms themselves, making platform designers powerful actors behind the kinds of data available online and the kinds of practices that motivate the creation of those data in the first place. (2013, p. 8)

In this sense, the 'social' in social data is a *construct* that problematizes any simple measurement of *what* people are doing, before we even consider *why* they are doing it or what it *means* to them or indeed us. Even the automated processes that result in data should not be taken to be neutral or disinterested (see Vis, 2013). Baym observes that the social media metrics are designed to enable 'positive affect' (i.e. 'likes') and that this alone skews what we can know as 'the Like economy is all about approval (2013, p. 9). Social media metrics are also non-representative, in terms of the counts, the invisible populations and social groups and the sentiments that are 'mined'. We have no real sense from such data what the motivations behind engagement and disengagement might be or how socioeconomic and other structural factors might be shaping patterns of activity. Most importantly, there is a basic question of meaning to be applied to so-called 'big social data'. Baym (2013) and others argue that social media metrics are 'inherently ambiguous' in their meaning. Any form of data mined is necessarily extracted from its context, from the 'flow of action in order to become data' (Baym, 2013, p. 10). This, it seems to me, is the fundamental issue at stake for qualitative research in the face of algorithmic processing. The contexts of meaning, understanding and practice cannot be 'read' from data metrics, the visibility of apparently 'obvious' sentiment in social media text, or what we can see on screens (Hand, 2012, 2014). Baym (2013, p. 14) persuasively argues that:

> In a time when data appear to be so self-evident and big data seem to hold such promise of truth, it has never been more essential to remind ourselves what data are not seen, and what cannot be measured …[A]s metrics, especially visible metrics, rise as vectors for assessing worth, we need to remain keenly aware of the inherent multiplicity of

> meanings they collapse, the contexts in which they are embedded, and, perhaps most importantly, the depth of what they do not reveal.

Indeed, one of the key difficulties of social media research focusing on Twitter is defining an object of study that does not simply construct an abstraction that is completely at odds with the notion of capturing automated 'live data'. As Bruns (2013, p. 3) has observed:

> Researchers focus on Hashtag datasets in order to simplify data gathering and analysis processes, but in so doing they create and describe a new reality which does not necessarily represent the lived experience of any one user.

On might of course level the same charge at the heavily quoted interview, but the 'opportunistic' use of social media data – capturing data organized by hashtags for example – has serious drawbacks of simply not being able to contextualize much of that data within more complex realities, motivations and unpredictable or accidental turns that communicative events might take. Notions of 'live methods' might also lead to accusations of *presentism* in much digital research (Uprichard, 2012). As Bruns (2013) also observes, the ability to acquire a more comprehensive and nuanced data set that would avoid this requires a data storage and analysis infrastructure outside the remit of scholarly researchers, precisely the point being made by those sensing a crisis of expertise.

Can We Socialize Digital Data?

> Data need to be imagined as data to exist and function as such, and the imagination of data entails an interpretive base. (Gitelman & Jackson, 2013, p. 3)

A key claim of big data enthusiasts is that it exists prior to interpretation, and is thus able to provide transparent patterns and connections that tell us about the social. The great insights of Bowker and Star (1999) and Bowker (2005) in their analyses of infrastructures-as-processes are how the conditions for the possibility of information gradually become invisible and eventually 'naturalized' and 'inevitable' until they break down. Digital data is often seen as floating externally, as disembodied or immaterial (see Hayles, 1999 on this problem), rather than the outcome of complex value-laden 'standards', protocols and technologies that make up the infrastructures of heterogeneous data sets. If we reduce phenomena to data, they are divided and classified, often obscuring the ambiguity, ambivalence, conflict and contradiction involved (Bowker & Star, 1999; Gitelman, 2013). The forgetting of this gives credence to the notion that routinely and automatically produced digital data produces a 'distanced objectivity' and thus a specific claim to truth. In recent accounts of the social and cultural history of data, it is argued that, on the contrary, data of any kind is always-already an interpretation. For example, with regard to the terms 'raw' and 'cooked' applied to big data, Boellstorff (2013, p. 9) argues:

> [T]hese categories are incredibly important with regard to big data. One reason is the implication that the "bigness" of data means it must be collected prior to interpretation – 'raw'. This is revealed by metaphors like data 'scraping' that suggest scraping flesh from bone, removing something taken as a self-evidently surface phenomenon. Another implication is that in a brave new world of big data, the interpretation of that data, its 'cooking', will increasingly be performed by computers themselves.

The turn towards social media data in sociology, media and communication studies is usefully complimented, then, by the 'material turn' related to scholarship in science and technology studies (see Goffey, Pettinger & Speed, 2014; Hand, 2014; Lohmeier, 2014). Data does not exist outside of its material substrate, and is shaped by ethico-political constraints and agendas, engrained practices and technical knowledge, regulations and protocols, orientations towards valued outcomes and so on. This includes the ways in which specific disciplines imagine and construct data as part of 'the operations of knowledge production more broadly' (Gitelman & Jackson, 2013, p. 3). In this sense, it has been argued that data is 'co-produced' through application programming interfaces (APIs) and researchers themselves, who make and select data, and also by the tools used to delimit and make that data visible and amenable for analysis (Vis, 2013, p. 2).

The notion that the social sciences and humanities should simply take 'the computational turn' (Berry, 2012) is thus highly contested, raising complex issues about what forms of 'the social' are being constructed and enacted through *designed* computational processes *and* the disciplinary methods employed to analyse and interpret them. Thinking carefully about the powerful effects of data in shaping social life, while at the same time being able to critically engage with its sociotechnical ambivalences and affordances, would seem to require a range of approaches and modes of expertise. New media scholars have drawn upon work in STS and histories of media to situate data in relation to the material and semiotic conditions of its production *as data*, and the processes through which it becomes black-boxed, stabilized and mobilized in a variety of contexts.

A second way of socializing digital data turns its attention to the socio-technical processes at work in structuring the flows of data in the first instance, asking how algorithms and other devices become stabilized, and most importantly, asking how does this form of data become and remain a legitimate and persuasive form of knowledge? Bruns (2013, p. 4) argues that:

> There is a substantial danger that social media analytics services and tools are treated by researchers as unproblematic black boxes which convert data into information at the click of a button, and that subsequent scholarly interpretation and discussion build on the results of the black box process without questioning its inner workings.

Drawing on insights from STS and software studies, the black boxing of algorithms is taken up in detail by Gillespie (2013) who argues that, on the one hand, researchers must strive to deconstruct the workings of algorithmic processes, but on the other hand recognize the obdurate affordances of these processes that are designed to remain invisible:

> Computational research techniques are not barometers of the social. They produce hieroglyphs: shaped by the tool by which they are carved, requiring of priestly interpretation, they tell powerful but often mythological stories – usually in the service of the gods (Gillespie, 2013, pp. 191, 193)

As a critique of the naïve interpretation of algorithmically produced data, Gillespie (2013) observes that algorithmic procedures are not well known, they are selective and likely to be ridden with error, manipulation, failure, commercial and political interests and so on. In a not particularly optimistic vein he argues that:

> A sociological inquiry into algorithms should aspire to reveal the complex workings of this knowledge machine, both the process by which it chooses information for users and the social process by which it is made into a legitimate system. But there may be something, in the end, impenetrable about algorithms. They are designed to work without human intervention, they are deliberately obfuscated, and they work with information on a scale that is hard to comprehend (at least without other algorithmic tools) … [S]o in many ways, algorithms remain outside our grasp, and they are designed to be. (Gillespie, 2013, p.)

A third trajectory is to socialize data by examining the recursive conditions of its production and consumption. Taking up the question of 'the social' directly, Couldry (2012) has advocated a practice-orientated approach to digital media in general, and more recently has called for a 'hermeneutics of big data' that involves 'doing digital phenomenology in the face of algorithmic power' (2014). By way of contrast with Google analytics, digital analytics and the kind of cultural analytics proposed by Manovich (2012), Couldry and Fotopoulou (2014) describe *social* analytics as 'the sociological study of social actors' (more or less reflexive) uses of analytics to further their own social ends'. Analytics here means both the multiple ways in which practices are being algorithmically measured, evaluated and tracked, but also reflected and acted upon by social actors. As a form of critique that utilizes digital data but also qualitatively explores its affective and contested dimensions in social life, the emphasis here is precisely on understanding how people are *making sense* of the data they produce and is produced about them (being watched, counted and categorized). Couldry, like van Dijck (2013) is concerned with developing an informed critique of the 'platformed sociality' being co-constituted through social media and its users (e.g. 'sharing' and 'liking'), treated as a transparent mechanism for generating social knowledge. There are distinctly ethical considerations here, seeking to understand the constitution and recursivity of data in order to think about alternative ways of imaging the social:

> If data are so central to our lives and our planet, then we need to understand just what they are and what they are doing. We are managing the planet and each other using data – and just getting more data on the problem is not necessarily going to help. What we need is a strongly humanistic approach to analyzing the forms that data take; a hermeneutic approach which enables us to envision new possible futures even as we risk being swamped in the data deluge. (Bowker, 2013, p. 171)

Identifying 'the social' in digital social research is relatively problematic in that, while the quantity and visibility of data produced through ordinary activity appears limitless, there is much debate about the relative agency of computational technologies in designing and shaping the possibilities of sociality in the first instance. Recognizing the 'cooked' character of digital data does not mean that it is not performative in intended and unintended ways. Indeed, digital data often appears to have 'a life of its own', as it morphs into different contexts (such as other databases, borders, financial records) and is constitutive of life chances in uneven ways (Lyon, 2003). Digital data is involved in constituting 'data-subjects', in reducing phenomena to particular modes of measurement and calculation, in manufacturing and modelling contemporary risks, in framing the possibilities of research questions and in providing the rhetorical basis for argument (Gitelman, 2013). All of these processes are opportunities for qualitatively orientated interpretation and critique.

Is the Medium the Method?

In what ways might social research employ digital media technologies to do research? On the one hand, new devices for filming, recording, imaging and interfacing with the objects and subjects of research promise collaborative and participatory ways of capturing and rapidly disseminating the dynamics social life. On the other hand, a second concern is how social research of various kinds might still utilize the prevalence of social media platforms in social life while recognizing that the data available is not pre-analytic but *already mediated.* Responses range from the development of a detailed 'social literacy' about big data (Ruppert, 2012) and ethically orientated 'social analytics' (Couldry & Fotopoulou, 2014) to the development of specifically 'digital methods' (Rogers, 2009, 2013). All agree at some level that the pervasiveness of digital assemblages and data in the world requires serious engagement and does, in several ways, unsettle the role of the qualitative researcher.

At the risk of oversimplification, a core question concerns the extent to which traditional qualitative methods should be augmented with digital analytics or develop novel specifically digital methods. In the latter case, debates focus on whether we can *use* the digital *as* a method and technique for studying the social, on what epistemological grounds, and whether such a method requires any empirical external 'grounding' through quantitative or qualitative means (Rogers, 2013). One way this is being approached is through *repurposing*. The amount of digital data generated and made available online has prompted some to appropriate automated techniques such as 'scraping' for 'collecting, analyzing and visualizing social data' (Marres & Weltevrede, 2013, p. 313). As a technique of social research, scraping occupies a set of devices for gathering data about what is occurring in 'real time'. As Marres and Weltevrede (2013) argue, such techniques produce data that is already an interpretation (it is 'formatted'), but this in itself can provide potential insights for social research. Indeed, scraping tools are now routinely used in archival institutions as they also grapple with capturing and preserving new spatiotemporal orderings of social life conducted *through* the web (see Hand, 2008, pp. 131–156). Marres and Weltevrede (2013) argue that 'scraping' has 'an epistemology built in', formatting processes of data collection and analysis along specific lines that constitute particular forms of knowledge making (i.e. as 'extraction' and 'distillation' of overwhelming amounts of data). The methods of the medium enable the automatic capturing and repurposing of 'fresh data' in ways that have some affinities with social science methods that seek to 'follow the actors' (Latour, 2005). As Rogers puts it 'By continually thinking along with the devices and the objects they handle, digital methods, as a research practice, strive to follow the evolving methods of the medium' (2013, p. 1).

The broader point here is that by understanding, following and appropriating how online data is organized and structured researchers can use digital objects to study how sociality is being organized. For example, Rogers (2013, p. 153) discusses what he calls 'postdemographics', where researchers study the data in social networking platforms to look at how profiling is and can be performed (see Hardey, 2014). This data is that which is beyond traditional classifications employed by social scientists – for example, using software to plot connections between the cultural tastes of different social networking profiles that support particular political candidates. Such 'metaprofiling' (2013, p. 153) uses multiple sources of such data and tries to 'mash' the data and get a sense of how profilers recommend information on the basis of these data. In other words, the digital method builds upon and repurposes the tools being used in social networking platforms to understand how the social is an ongoing accomplishment. For example, Rogers (2013) shows how *Wikipedia* can be approached as a cultural reference in its own right, as revealing interesting cultural differences and similarities in the ways that pages are developed and maintained. In this way the web can be *source* of big and small data (Rogers, 2013, p. 203) that does not necessarily require grounding in the offline, through studies of users. Data gathered through the web is not necessarily 'dirty' or messy': indeed, the *ways in which* online data deteriorates, is incomplete, is ordered and altered are themselves potential avenues for researching the temporality of contemporary social processes (Marres & Weltevrede, 2013).

Such digital methods are aimed at simulating innovation in audience research for media and communications, rather than, say, reconfiguring ethnographic or interview-based methods. But the emphasis on rethinking the relationship between technique, method and object in digital social research has a wider significance. The sense of altering methods such that they capture the present – or the 'happening of the social' (Lury & Wakeford, 2012) – also follows this line of thought. It forces us to think about whether methods that are immanent to the phenomena should be developed and utilized to better understand digitally mediated social life.

The opportunities to use existing web tools to pull together and triangulate web data of many kinds – for example, Twitter feeds with geolocational and temporal data – might in many cases be more fruitful than 'offline data', if one is trying to understand the mediation of social activities. This is especially significant for digital social research that seeks to re-appropriate the forms of automated expertise at play in constituting 'publics' (visualized, mapped, represented through data) that are then subjects to be acted upon (e.g. by the state). In other words, questions of data analytic expertise are being explored by researchers trying to utilize them and also qualitatively by researchers asking critical questions about the *politics* of this 'redistribution of expertise' (Bassett, 2014; Kennedy & Moss, 2014). Big data is an intensification of the automation of expertise (Bassett, 2014), where expertise is being redistributed between humans and machines in ways that are not always progressive let alone democratic. For example, how are analytics framing the ways in which 'publics' are constituted and understood, and to what extent do people outside of big data companies have a say in what become powerful inscriptions and representations? How might publics be enabled by analytics? Could analytics be used to form more 'knowing publics'? How might analytics be drawn upon to *form* public opinion (as a process), rather than *represent* it (as captured)?

There are also limits to this approach if one is trying to understand the conditions through which this data has been *produced as data*. Here, I would suggest, is the continuing value of ethnographic approaches that situate digital technologies within the fabric of people's lives (i.e. boyd, 2014; Miller, 2011) and try to understand the complex forms of negotiation that are taking place that both constitute much of the data in the first place and are the contexts within which people reflexively engage with that data. Any account of the recursive processes of data circulation must surely benefit from detailed explorations of this kind. In this regard, Crawford (2013) makes an explicit call for developing robust combinations of big and small data studies, computational social science with 'traditional qualitative methods'. She argues that:

> … by combining methods such as ethnography with analytics, or conducting semi-structured interviews paired with information retrieval techniques, we can add depth to the data we collect. We get a much richer sense of the world when we ask people the why and the how not just the 'how many'. This goes beyond merely conducting focus groups to confirm what you already want to see in a big data set. It means complementing data sources with rigorous qualitative research. Social science methodologies may make the challenge of understanding big data more complex, but they also bring context-awareness to our research to address serious signal problems. Then we can move from the focus on merely 'big' data towards something more three-dimensional: data with depth.

CONCLUSION: TOWARDS THICK SOCIAL DATA?

In this essay I have aimed to do several things. I have sought to provide a partial but hopefully useful reading of how digital social research has shifted much of its emphasis from studies of mediated spaces, to networks, to mediated life in a *dataverse*. Bowker (2013) employs this term while acknowledging its hyperbole to force us to think about how data is coming to define us and our actions, as well as what we claim to know about the world and each other. This is what many researchers in the social sciences and humanities are responding to: the sense of a world being remade through data and the need to critically engage with these processes and their implications, in terms of both the conduct of social research and the lives of the researched. In briefly discussing three key debates at the present time I have simply sought to identify what I think are profitable trajectories. By resolutely returning to the ongoing problems of *contextualizing* and *localizing* digital data, qualitative research can, I think, make major contributions to our understanding of digital data-in-society.

One important central contribution is the ability to develop empirically informed critiques of the grandest claims of digital data and also the concrete effects such claims might be having 'on the ground'. In the traditions of STS and institutional ethnographies, we need detailed accounts of how data is being produced and analysed by practitioners and the tools and techniques they develop and employ. Developing grounded analyses of the institutions and practices of data production and analysis can also serve to avoid two forms of data reductionism: the uncritical acceptance or dismissal of data. Moreover, engaging with data practitioners in these ways also facilitates the development of critical interventions in how 'publics' are constituted and acted upon through data (Bassett, 2014; Kennedy & Moss, 2014).

Secondly, as alluded to throughout, there is a dearth of qualitative empirical attention being paid to the ways in which people *make sense* of their own and others data in the course of everyday life. We know quite a lot about the kinds of data that appear in social media, and how these are structured and classified by software and so on. Developments in those research fields need to be complimented and enhanced by varieties of 'small data' that focus on the permanent production of data by ourselves, such as ethnographic analyses of the conditions in and though which people routinely produce and consume data. Digital data is indeed routinely produced and circulated, but it is also reflected upon, negotiated, deleted and analysed by those producing it in presumably diverse ways not immediately accessible to the data scraper. In trying to situate data analytics (and, e.g. the 'quantified self') in this way, digital social research might provide much needed detail about emerging alternative projects of self-knowledge, and the ways in which people are or might use analytics 'against the grain'.

REFERENCES

Adkins, L., & Lury, C. (Eds.). (2012). *Measure and value*. Oxford: Wiley-Blackwell.

Akrich, M. (1992). The de-scription of technical objects. In W. Bijker & J. Law (Eds.), *Shaping technology/building society: Studies in sociotechnical change* (pp. 205–224). Cambridge, MA: MIT.

Anderson, C. (2008). *The end of theory: The data deluge makes the scientific method obsolete*. Wired. Retrieved from http://www.wired.com/science/discoveries/magazine/16-07/pb_theory. Accessed on May 29, 2014.

Bancroft, A., Karels, M., Murray, O. M., & Zimpfer, J. (2014). Not being there: Research at a distance with video, text and speech. In M. Hand & S. Hillyard (Eds.), *Big data? Qualitative approaches to digital research* (Vol. 13, pp. 137–153). Studies in Qualitative Methodology. Bingley, UK: Emerald Group Publishing Limited.

Barney, D. (2004). *The network society*. Cambridge: Polity.

Bassett, C. (2014). Plenty as a response to austerity: Expanding big data expertise in cultures and communities. Paper presented at the International Communication Association Annual Conference, May 2014, Seattle, WA.

Baym, N. (2010). *Personal connections in the digital age*. Cambridge: Polity.

Baym, N. K. (2013). *Data not seen: The uses and shortcomings of social media metrics*. First Monday, 18(10). Retrieved from http://firstmonday.org/ojs/index.php/fm/article/view/4873/3752. Accessed on May 29, 2014.

Beer, D. (2013). *Popular culture and new media: The politics of circulation*. Basingstoke: Palgrave.

Beer, D., & Burrows, R. (2007). *Sociology and, of and in web 2.0: Some initial considerations*. Sociological Research Online, 12(5). Retrieved from http://www.socresonline.org.uk/12/5/17.html

Berry, D. (Ed.). (2012). *Understanding digital humanities*. Basingstoke: Palgrave.

Boellstorff, T. (2013). *Making big data, in theory*. First Monday, 18(10). Retrieved from http://firstmonday.org/ojs/index.php/fm/article/view/4869/3750. Accessed on May 29, 2014.

Bolter, J. D., & Grusin, R. (1999). *Remediation: Understanding new media*. Cambridge, MA & London: MIT Press.

Bowker, G. (2005). *Memory practices in the sciences*. Cambridge, MA: MIT Press.

Bowker, G. (2013). Data flakes: An afterword to raw data is an oxymoron. In L. Gitelman (Ed.), *Raw data is an oxymoron* (pp. 167–171). Cambridge, MA: MIT Press.

Bowker, G., & Star, L. (1999). *Sorting things out: Classification and its consequences*. Cambridge, MA: MIT Press.

boyd, D. (2014). *It's complicated: The social lives of networked teens*. New Haven, CT: Yale University Press.

boyd, D., & Crawford, K. (2012). Critical questions for big data. *Information, Communication and Society*, *15*(5), 662–679.

Bruns, A. (2013). *Faster than the speed of print: reconciling "big data" social media analysis and academic scholarship*. First Monday, 18(10). Retrieved from http://firstmonday.org/ojs/index.php/fm/article/view/4879/3756. Accessed on May 29, 2014.

Bruns, A., & Burgess, J. (2012). Researching news discussion on Twitter: New methodologies. *Journalism Studies*, *13*(5–6), 801–814.

Burrows, R. (2012). Living with the H index? Metric assemblages in the contemporary academy. *The Sociological Review*, *60*(2), 355–372.

Burrows, R., & Beer, D. (2013). Rethinking space: Urban informatics and the sociological imagination. In Orton-Johnson & Prior (Eds.), *Digital sociology: Critical perspectives*. Basingstoke: Palgrave.

Burrows, R., & Gane, N. (2006). Geodemographics, software and class. *Sociology*, *40*(5), 793–812.

Castells, M. (1997). *Rise of the network society*. Oxford: Blackwell.

Clark, L. (2013). *No questions asked: Big data firm maps solutions without human input*. Wired, 16 January. Retrieved from http://www.wired.co.uk/news/archive/2013-01/16/ayasdi-big-data-launch. Accessed on May 29, 2014.

Couldry, N. (2012). *Media, society, world*. Cambridge: Polity.

Couldry, N., & Fotopoulou, A. (2014). Social analytics: Doing digital phenomenology in the face of algorithmic power. Paper presented at the international communication association annual conference, May 2014, Seattle, WA.

Crawford, K. (2013). *The hidden biases of big data*. Harvard Business Review Blog, 1 April. Retrieved from http://blogs.hbr.org/2013/04/the-hidden-biases-in-big-data/. Accessed on May 29, 2014.

Flichy, P. (2007). *The internet imaginaire*. Cambridge, MA: MIT.

Gane, N. (2006). Speed-up or slow down? Social theory in the information age. *Information, Communication and Society*, *9*, (1), 20–38.

Gane, N., & Beer, D. (2008). *New media: The key concepts*. Oxford: Berg.

Gillespie, T. (2013). The relevance of algorithms. In T. Gillespie, P. Boczkowski, & K. Foot (Eds.), *Media technologies: Essays on communication, materiality, and society*. Cambridge, MA: MIT Press.

Gitelman, L. (2013). *Raw data is an oxymoron*. Cambridge, MA: MIT Press.

Gitelman, L., & Jackson, V. (2013). Introduction. In L. Gitelman (Ed.), *'Raw data' is an oxymoron* (pp. 1–14). Cambridge, MA: MIT Press.

Goffey, A., Pettinger, L., & Speed, E. (2014). Politics, policy and privatisation in the everyday experience of big data in the NHS. In M. Hand & S. Hillyard (Eds.), *Big data? Qualitative approaches to digital research* (Vol. 13, pp. 31–50). Studies in Qualitative Methodology. Bingley, UK: Emerald Group Publishing Limited.

Hand, M. (2008). *Making digital cultures: Access, interactivity, and authenticity*. Aldershot: Ashgate.

Hand, M. (2012). *Ubiquitous photography*. Cambridge: Polity.

Hand, M. (2014). Persistent traces, potential memories: Smartphones and the negotiation of visual, locative and textual data in personal life. *Convergence* August 2014. Online First.

Hand, M. (2014). Digitization and memory: Researching practices of adaption to visual and textual data in everyday life. In M. Hand & S. Hillyard (Eds.), *Big data? Qualitative approaches to digital research* (Vol. 13, pp. 205–229). Studies in Qualitative Methodology. Bingley, UK: Emerald Group Publishing Limited.

Hardey, M. (2014). Marketing narratives: Researching digital data, design and the in/visible consumer. In M. Hand & S. Hillyard (Eds.), *Big data? Qualitative approaches to digital research* (Vol. 13, pp. 115–135). Studies in Qualitative Methodology. Bingley, UK: Emerald Group Publishing Limited.

Hayles, N. K. (1999). *How we became posthuman*. Chicago, IL: CUP.

Hine, C. (2000). *Virtual ethnography*. London: Sage.

Hine, C. (Ed.). (2005). *Virtual methods*. Oxford: Berg.

Horst, H., & Miller, D. (2006). *The cell phone: An anthropology of communication*. Oxford: Berg.

Horst, H., & Miller, D. (Eds.). (2012). *Digital anthropology*. Oxford: Bloomsbury.

Jones, S. (Ed.). (1997). *Virtual culture*. London: Sage.

Kennedy, H., & Moss, G. (2014). Making analytics public: Really useful analytics and public engagement. Paper presented at the International Communication Association Annual Conference, May 2014, Seattle, WA.

Kitchin, R. (2013). Big data and human geography: Opportunities, challenges and risks. *Dialogues in human geography*, *3*(3), 262–267.

Kitchin, R., & Dodge, M. (2011). *Code/space: Software and everyday life*. Cambridge, MA: MIT Press.

Kozinets, R. V. (2010). *Netnography: Doing ethnographic research online*. London: Sage.

Laney, D. (2012). *Deja VVVu: Others claiming Gartner's construct for big data*. Retrieved from http://blogs.gartner.com/doug-laney/deja-vvvue-others-claiming-gartners-volume-velocity-variety-construct-for-big-data/last. Accessed on May 29, 2014.

Latour, B. (2005). *Reassembling the social: An introduction to actor-network theory*. Oxford: Oxford University Press.

Lievrouw, L. (2011). *Alternative and activist media*. Cambridge: Polity.

Livingstone, S. (2009). 'On the mediation of everything'. ICA presidential address 2008. *Journal of Communication*, *59*(1), 1–18.

Livingstone, S. (2011). *Children and the internet*. Cambridge: Polity.

Lohmeier, C. (2014). The researcher and the never-ending field: Reconsidering big data and digital ethnography. In M. Hand & S. Hillyard (Eds.), *Big data? Qualitative approaches to digital research* (Vol. 13, pp. 75–89). Studies in Qualitative Methodology. Bingley, UK: Emerald Group Publishing Limited.

Lury, C., & Wakeford, N. (Eds.). (2012). *Inventive methods: The happening of the social*. New York, NY: Routledge.

Lyon, D. (2003). *Surveillance as social sorting*. London: Routledge.

Madianou, M., & Miller, D. (2012). *Migration and new media*. London: Routledge.

Manovich, L. (2001). *The language of new media*. Cambridge, MA: MIT Press.

Manovich, L. (2011). *Trending: The promises and the challenges of big social data*. Retrieved from http://www.manovich.net/DOCS/Manovich_trending_paper.pdf. Accessed May 29, 2014.

Markham, A. (1999). *Life online*. Lanham, MD: Rowman and Littlefield.

Marres, N. (2012). The redistribution of methods: On intervention in digital social research, broadly conceived. *The Sociological Review*, *60*, 139–165.

Marres, N., & Weltevrede, E. (2013). Scraping the social? *Journal of Cultural Economy*, *6*(3), 331–335.

Mayer-Schonberger, V., & Cukier, K. (2013). *Big data: A revolution that will change how we live, work and think*. London: John Murray.

Miller, D. (2011). *Tales from facebook*. Cambridge: Polity.

Miller, D., & Slater, D. (2000). *The internet: An ethnographic approach*. Oxford: Berg.

Mosco, V. (2004). *The digital sublime: Myth, power, and cyberspace*. Cambridge, MA: MIT.

Orton-Johnson, K., & Prior, N. (Eds.). (2013). *Digital sociology: Critical perspectives*. Basingstoke: Palgrave.

Oudshoorn, N., & Pinch, T. (Eds.). (2002). *How users matter*. Cambridge, MA: MIT.

Papacharissi, Z. (2009). *A private sphere*. Cambridge: Polity.

Poster, M. (2001). *What's the matter with the internet?* Minneapolis, MN: University of Minnesota Press.
Rainie, L., & Wellman, B. (2012). *Networked*. Cambridge, MA: MIT Press.
Rheingold, H. (1993). The virtual community. Reading, MA: Addison-Wesley.
Rogers, R. (2013). *Digital methods*. Cambridge, MA: MIT Press.
Ruppert, E. (2012). The governmental topologies of database devices. *Theory, Culture Society, 29*: 116–136.
Ruppert, E. (2013). Rethinking empirical social sciences. *Dialogues in Human Geography, 3*(3), 268–273.
Ruppert, E., Law, J., & Savage, M. (2013). Reassembling social science methods: The challenge of digital devices. *Theory, Culture & Society, 30*(4), 22–46.
Sardar, Z. (1996). Cyberspace as the darker side of the west. In Z. Sardar & J. Ravetz (Eds.), *Cyberfutures*. London: Pluto Press.
Savage, M., & Burrows, R. (2007). The coming crisis of empirical sociology. *Sociology, 41*(5), 885–889.
Taylor, P., & Harris, J. (2005). *Digital matters: The theory and culture of the matrix*. London: Routledge.
Thrift, N. (2005). *Knowing capitalism*. London: Sage.
Turkle, S. (1997). *Life on the screen: Identity in the age of the internet*. New York, NY: Simon and Schuster.
Uprichard, E. (2012). Being stuck in (live) time: The sticky sociological imagination. *The sociological Review, 60*(1), 124–138.
van Dijck, J. (2013). *The culture of connectivity: A critical history of social media*. Oxford: OUP.
Vis, F. (2013). A critical reflection on big data: APIs, researchers and tools as data makers. *First Monday, 18*(10).
Wellman, B., & Haythornwaite, C. (Eds.). (2002). *The internet in everyday life*. Oxford: Blackwell.
Wertheim, M. (2000). *The pearly gates of cyberspace*. New York, NY: W. W. Norton.

PART I
INSTITUTIONAL MOBILIZATIONS AND APPROPRIATIONS OF DATA

POLITICS, POLICY AND PRIVATISATION IN THE EVERYDAY EXPERIENCE OF BIG DATA IN THE NHS

Andrew Goffey, Lynne Pettinger and Ewen Speed

ABSTRACT

Purpose – *This chapter explains how fundamental organisational change in the UK National Health Service (NHS) is being effected by new practices of digitised information gathering and use. It analyses the taken-for-granted IT infrastructures that lie behind digitisation and considers the relationship between digitisation and big data.*

Design/methodology/approach – *Qualitative research methods including discourse analysis, ethnography of software and key informant interviews were used. Actor-network theories, as developed by Science and technology Studies (STS) researchers were used to inform the research questions, data gathering and analysis. The chapter focuses on the aftermath of legislation to change the organisation of the NHS.*

Findings – *The chapter shows the benefits of qualitative research into specific manifestations information technology. It explains how*

Big Data? Qualitative Approaches to Digital Research
Studies in Qualitative Methodology, Volume 13, 31–50

ISSN: 1042-3192/doi:10.1108/S1042-319220140000013003

apparently 'objective' and 'neutral' quantitative data gathering and analysis is mediated by complex software practices. It considers the political power of claims that data is neutral.

Originality/value – *The chapter provides insight into a specific case of healthcare data and. It makes explicit the role of politics and the State in digitisation and shows how STS approaches can be used to understand political and technological practice.*

Keywords: Digital data; big data; information; infrastructure; STS; healthcare

INTRODUCTION

In this chapter, we explore digitisation and big data in the context of the 'information revolution' (Department of Health [DH], 2010) of the UK National Health Service (NHS) since the reforms of the 2012 Health and Social Care Act. We discuss an ongoing qualitative research project that locates current NHS data practices within the context of long-established political, institutional and technological structures. We explore the in-between stages of a multimethod qualitative project to consider what such methodologies can usefully contribute to understanding the social and political contexts within which specific kinds and uses of big data are discussed and operationalised, both in the ongoing policy context and in the lived experience of producing big data. In order to see how qualitative research has (and could) be used to study digitisation and big data, we suggest it is important to see precise details of the case being studied. Therefore, this chapter presents the technical and political empirical details of how information is used as a regulatory device in the NHS.

There is considerable discussion amongst sociologists about digital data in general, and big data in particular, which questions how such data seems to challenge the legitimacy of the social scientist, and established – quantitative and qualitative – social science approaches. Big data by definition (in its focus on correlations not causation, inclusion of all cases not a sample, and its acceptance of messy, not clean, data) challenges the scientism of traditional social science quantitative methodologies. The divination of new methods (e.g. data scraping, twitter sentiment analysis) is one possible response, but, we suggest, this hides the politics of big data. Our contribution to these discussions is to argue for the importance of understanding of the specificities of the digital in institutional contexts. (Qualitative) sociologists have good reason to be wary of the hyperbolic claims that are made on behalf of (or in critique of) big data – something easily and naturally produced 'out there', that is eminently desirable, or a cause for envy. We suggest that qualitative researchers, trained in being suspicious of what is taken for granted, are able to unpack the promises made on behalf of digitisation and to unpick the technological processes through which digitisation is put into practice. Qualitative methods are themselves diverse and multiple, and evolve in relationship to the research questions to which they are applied. In the chapter that follows, we talk through this simple methodological principle in relationship to an ongoing research project that looks at information in the post-reform NHS, and contextualises big data within the broader contexts of: digitisation of information practices, streams of information flows; long-established institutional and technological structures that make big data possible; and the relationship of big data to information and other modes of knowledge. We ask: what research questions are raised by recent changes to the organisation of the NHS and to digital data? How are the promises of digitised information harnessed to the agenda for change?

In order to understand the status and presence of information, digitisation and big data in Britain's NHS, and to understand what a qualitative project can and cannot get to grips with, we begin by presenting a very short history of information in the NHS and a slightly longer account of how state actors – a coalition government composed of a dominant right-wing Conservative party and a subordinate centrist Liberal Democrat party – discussed information in public documents generated in the build up to a major reorganisation of the NHS via the Health and Social Care Act of 2012. This is intended to set out the first of the points we want to make in relation to the overall theme of the edited collection: that for qualitative research to ask questions about how big data practices are enacted, it must pay attention to how policies around information, data and infrastructures are formed and implemented (including by policy makers with a strong, if ill-informed, beliefs in the power of information). In the second section of the chapter, we look specifically at selected dimensions of how a new information infrastructure is being introduced in the NHS and explore the powerful mediating role of specific software practices. This contributes to the second point we want to make: that a prerequisite for doing this kind of qualitative research is knowledge of the political context and the technical infrastructures of which they speak. This second section also reveals just how intense and contingent are the mediations that produce 'data'. We draw on science and technology studies in this section, paying particular attention to the significance of policy and discourse within these assemblages.

INFORMATION AND THE NHS

We suggest that understanding big data and information technology more generally must involve recognition of the singularity of the practices with which we are dealing (something that qualitative researchers may feel at home with). In the first instance, this means seeing the singularity of the NHS context. In the second instance, it means avoiding the temptation to tell a predictable story (e.g. that big data has contributed to an existing and well-established linear movement from an NHS that supports 'cradle to grave' welfare to a broken and fragmented service where clinical expertise has ceded power to 'evidence' of all kinds via a simple dynamic of marketisation), that is, to over-interpret. Instead, getting to grips with singularity means understanding the trajectories, translations and transformations that specific practices undergo as they move out of, say, computing science departments into the labs of IT corporations, into the corporate and political world, and, here, then into healthcare. And it means, in turn, that we should also avoid conferring on 'big data' the status of a unitary, finished, 'thing'. Like the NHS context that we are examining, big data itself is made up of a set of practices themselves in movement. Together, each of these – and other – moments, encounters and translations sees software differently and frames 'big data' differently. How then can we think about information in the NHS? And what affect do specific manifestations of digitisation and big data have for the always fraught questions of NHS organisation?

The current status of data in the NHS may be usefully understood against the broader backdrop of what Agar (2003) refers to as the 'hollowed-out state'. Since the 1960s and Wilson's era of white hot technology the 'Organizations and Methods' (O&M) movement within the civil service has pushed for more and more automated bureaucratic processes. However, civil service reform in the 1970s and 1980s meant that some of the necessary expertises that groups such as O&M possessed, and which were required to see through information technology developments, were lost. The net effect was that whilst government departments increased their dependency on IT, the control of those technologies to a large extent passed into the hands of private companies. It looks also as though government information technology projects themselves act as agents of privatisation by virtue of the forms of expertise that are needed to get such projects off the ground. Private sector technology appears then as a chisel for hollowing out the state. SERCO starts providing administrative 'back office' support, then moves to the front office and from there into health-care provision itself (Deith, 2013). The growing involvement of private companies in the government use of information technology requires us to acknowledge not just the presence of transnational corporations and the commercial imperatives that drive them, but the significant extra layers of mediation that they introduce into the processes that determine who or what gets counted, and how. Understanding this mediation gives us another dimension of insight into the wedge driven into the political concordat around health and social care, between the state, the professions and the public, as well as more tools with which to understand the apparently magical position of information as an evidence base beyond influence.

We can interpret the failure of large government IT projects, including considerable elements of the National Programme for Information Technology (NPfIT) in the light of this fairly developed historical trend. NPfIT was the previous (Labour) government's attempt at an integrated patient data system. Reasons for the failures of NPfIT are many, but not least was the enormity of the project and the complex problems of 'interoperability', of getting many unique information systems, including paper records, to speak to each other, coordinating between the private sector IT firms that were commissioned to do the work, and developing IT systems that would work across the NHS as a whole. That considerable (but not all[1]) elements of this reorganisation of IT infrastructures failed within recent memory has not given the current coalition government pause for thought: the seductive promises of what software *could* do are hard to resist, it seems, coupled to a naïve belief that *better* software will circumvent the structural problems that beset NPfIT. And indeed, for those outside IT, the difficulties might seem daft. Remember though, that changing how, say, millions of patient's records are kept is different to designing a new system that can keep those records: the NHS was not 'born digital' and the legacy of decades of paper-based records is not something that can simply be ignored, especially not for a properly contextualised approach to big data practices.

The Health and Social Care Act (Health and Social Care Act [HASCA], 2012) marked a radical shift in how the NHS is organised. Information is at the heart of this change: new information processes have emerged across clinical and administrative contexts. Clinical outcomes data measures and patient outcomes data measures are now explicitly used in the commissioning of local healthcare provision; all of the 'any qualified providers' (AQP) now providing healthcare must collate and share clinical and administrative data about their commissioned services; and new forms of quality assurance data are generated as AQPs and Clinical Commissioning Groups (CCGs) must routinely feed data about what they do into the Care Quality Commission (CQC, the quality regulator) and Monitor (the sector regulator) to ensure they are operating to centrally set national standards. Under the legislation, all healthcare providers, across the NHS and the private sector, effectively become 'any qualified providers', all tendering against each other to provide commissioned services. These unprecedented demands for the acquisition and analysis of different kinds of information are intended to enable better local and national provision/commissioning, and increased population metric levels of health observation and surveillance. The complexities and details of knowledge practices – such as recording information – are rather too easily simplified, and much of what is laboriously and contingently constructed comes to assume a weight of inevitability that belies this complexity. To put it another way, it is too easy to ignore the practices that make data, and so the politics of big data are hidden behind a rhetoric of transparent, readily available information that can all too easily preclude any consideration of the infrastructural shifts that make this possible. Elsewhere, one of us has argued that the shift to new information metrics facilitates a new metric for rationing healthcare that, at a stroke, revokes the state's traditional reliance on the medical professions to perform this function (Speed & Gabe, 2013). The 'data' takes the role of the professions in determining what treatments are and are not available, and the apparent neutrality and naturalness of data appears to provide evidence free of interference. We will now look at how 'data', 'big data' and information have been framed in recent political discourses, and at how these framings have informed the changes to the organisation of the NHS. Finding an effective politicisation of big data requires us not to amalgamate things too quickly, to slow down, not to launch precipitously into asking the kinds of questions that we can and do ask when we are dealing with a set of processes and practices that are assumed to have become 'one', stabilised and self-evident 'thing'. The political context is a significant part of this.

Former Health Secretary Andrew Lansley, in the white paper that preceded the HASCA, characterised an NHS 'information revolution' (DH, 2010) whereby care should be commissioned following assessment of current international best evidence and clinical practice, clinical outcome data, patient outcome data and patient experience data. The power of information, we are told, will lead to more integrated services (through increased sharing of information across providers), better quality of care (through the requirement for more routine analysis of administrative and clinical data), safer care (through routine comparisons of what works across different healthcare settings and providers) and more efficient and effective care (through comparisons of clinical and patient data on what worked and what did not). Similarly, it is claimed that the shift to new models of commissioning, predicated on clinical and patient outcome measures, as well as patient experience data, will lead to a leaner, more localised and responsive mode of healthcare delivery. Those providers that perform well will be invited to tender for more commissions, and those that perform poorly will not. An apparently objective, evidence-based medicine model is given primacy. The foundational premise is that it is the data that determines provision, rather than any human actor. To those trained in critiques of the 'scientific method' and claims to 'objectivity', such claims seem wilfully naïve. Outcome measures, and the data that constitutes them, are flawed products, vulnerable to manipulation, and are mediated by the IT that constitutes them.

The care.data debacle is an apposite example here. This issue came to a head in early 2014 when the much-vaunted government roll out of patient data sharing was suspended amidst concerns about the disclosure of pseudo-anonymised individual level hospital episode statistics (HES) and related concerns about the options for patient opt-out from the data-sharing scheme. This measure was very much a piece of the HASCA, but it somewhat divided critics. Pollock, perhaps one of the most vocal critics of NHS reforms (Pollock & Price, 2012a, 2013), came out in favour of data sharing (see Pollock & Price, 2012b), from the context of the massive potential public health gains that such a process could facilitate. She was however opposed to the way in which the data-sharing programme was set up, and was deeply sceptical of the privileging of private interest that the proposed model provided. Other critics were deeply sceptical of shared data ever being able to exist in a solely public health domain; such is the value of health related big data, and as such rejected the very principle of data sharing (see Taylor, 2014). There is clearly money to be made out of this sort of data.

It is in this type of context that we can begin to see the political utility of an 'information revolution'. Decisions about who and more importantly who does not, get treatment can be legitimised through an apparently objective evidence base, based on routinely occurring data. Healthcare takes on the appearance of a matter of best practice and never one of economics or ideology. For example, consider the second Caldicott review (2013) into information governance in the NHS, which, whilst framed as being concerned with patient confidentiality, contains a notable principle (number 7) that states 'The duty to share information can be as important as the duty to protect patient confidentiality'. The implication is that information, neutral and undifferentiated, can only improve services, it brings no problems of its own, it is a public good worth giving out. In the post-reform NHS context, where the 'AQP' formula means NHS and private providers are competing with each other, sharing patient information prevents established providers getting any insider advantage, and limits the ability of all to think in the long term. Reynolds and McKee's (2012) suggestion that the reforms are intended to break the NHS treatment monopoly seems plausible.

The ubiquity of this rhetoric of the positive beneficent power of information in the post-reform NHS and associated calls for disruptive technological 'innovation' sit uncomfortably alongside a clear political and organisational failure to elaborate how these processes are actually going to work (something that has caused many headaches for our research participants). A 2011 Department of Health document, with the bluntly biopolitical title 'Innovation, Health and Wealth: Accelerating Adoption and Diffusion in the NHS' rather blandly links together, and confuses, the use of medical technologies for clinical use with administrative technologies for purposes of rationalisation. It calls for 'innovation' to become the 'core business' of the NHS. In this, it draws on ideas about 'disruptive technology' developed in a widely different institutional setting to argue that disruption causes positive change, a claim that must sound hollow to anyone who has observed the last 20 years of organisational change in the NHS, and that reflects the common misreading of technology as generic and transferable across contexts.

It seems to us, then, that the government expects the most significant changes to NHS care to come from the use of technology, in particular from technologies that will generate reliable data and yield information that can be meaningfully assessed in an international context, transform an engrained institutional culture and 'level' the playing field for healthcare provision. It is difficult to argue the case 'against' more information, given the rhetoric of the benign beneficence of data and information. But this makes it all the more important to understand where information comes from, how it is managed, and how it is mediated, particularly when infrastructures for data capture, processing and circulating seem to constitute an evidence base that is somehow miraculously beyond the realm of professional or political influence. There are qualitative research questions to be asked about science, information and politics here and issues of digitisation and big data have a part to play in these broader questions.

Whilst big data is typically framed in terms of a dramatic, epochal shift (using the language of 'paradigm shifts', 'game changers', 'turns', 'revolutions' and so on), several early research papers that profile the computational innovations that mark out big data (Cafarella, Downey, Soderland, & Etzioni, 2005; Franklin, Halevy, & Maier, 2005) address more prosaic and specific technical issues, to wit those associated with working on data extracted from the internet. The framing of these issues as marking an epoch-making shift is strikingly absent at this early point. Subsequent broader attempts at getting others interested, however, present big data practices as a rational way of responding to the vast quantities, the 'deluge' of data generated through clickstreams, social media content, business transactions and so on. A special issue of the *Harvard Business Review*, for example, dealing with the so-called management revolution accomplished as a result of big data presents the shift to data-driven decision making as a response to an apparently spontaneous 'explosion' in digital data. These framings of big data force us to consider not just 'what' constitutes the 'data' (a function of an uninterrogated growth of a disparate and sometimes messy set of web-based epistemic, technical, social, cultural and economic activities – see 'The politics of interoperability' below), but also that big data analytic practices have largely emerged as a side-effect of the proliferation of processes of digitisation, the extension of information infrastructures and the shifts in corporate practices into 'the net'. Yet big data frequently appears as a solution to undefined issues of corporate metrics, it is self-evidently there and ready to use; generated 'in the wild'; not unlike the kind of 'naturally occurring' data that one might expect to gather in a field science.

A crucial issue for us to consider, then, and one that gets forgotten rather easily when data, especially big data, is treated as a raw given and a reality sui generis (the technical counterpart of the idealisation of the revolutionary virtues of information) is to address some of the ways in which data gets captured, to consider the infrastructural machinery through which data gets constituted, and the complex processes and practices through which that technology is generated. Big data is inseparable from the massive infrastructural shift towards networked computing and the dynamics of this shift has implications for the kinds of contextual issues qualitative researchers must address.

INVERTING INFRASTRUCTURES

Despite the apparent naturalism of current discourse about big data, early accounts that defined it in apparently negative terms as data that are 'too large' to be located in traditional relational database systems usefully draw our attention to a shift in the nature of knowledge infrastructures on which new data processing practices depend. The 'traditional' database has arguably been something of a key marker for the informational infrastructure as it developed throughout the 19th and 20th centuries (see Bowker, Baker, Millerand, & Ribes, 2010). Talking about big data in such terms flags up a connection between big data and the information infrastructures of knowledge practices per se and points towards a set of issues that qualitative research is in principle at least well attuned to. Infrastructural shifts in knowledge practices don't attract all that much attention in the frothy commentary about big data – other than in terms of what Mosco (2004) has referred to (in a different context) as the 'digital sublime'. In the NHS context, however, they are crucially relevant because headline grabbing stories about the predictive capacities of big data, on the one hand, and policy rhetoric on the other, have as their flipside a less well understood set of processes of the redefinition of healthcare practices through their 'socio-technical' rearticulation of healthcare practices. Following Bowker and Star (1999), themselves following Becker (1982) and Clarke and Fujimura (1992), we think that teasing apart the different threads of what big data is or might be doing in the NHS requires the methodological practice of 'infrastructural inversion'. They define this (p. 34) as 'a struggle against the tendency of infrastructure to disappear (except when breaking down). It means learning to look closely at technologies and arrangements that, by design and by habit, tend to fade into the woodwork'. In this context, it means in the first instance understanding that how data (big and standard) are defined and captured must be considered to be heavily dependent on the historical development of the processes and activities that have been and can be translated into the algorithms and data structures of software. This means understanding, in turn, that data – and, by extension, information – is less a scientifically defined given that technology then merely extracts, than something that is produced in a series of historically specific social and technical processes. Linking big data back to these processes and insisting on its connections with infrastructure offers a way of situating and contextualising its claims to our attention and, perhaps, of cutting through some of the hype with which it is associated.

For example, GP surgeries now use IT more extensively than other sectors of UK healthcare. Computerisation here was helped in no small measure by the brevity of the earlier reporting structures (i.e. the very cursory format of the 'Lloyd George' form for general practice medical records – see Benson, 2002a, 2002b). In addition, the relatively low-levels of organisational complexity of GP surgeries and the generalist quality of the service provided explain the comparable success of IT here. But contrast this to the complexity of secondary healthcare provision, for which the Department of Health (DH) recognises 60 different kinds of clinical (surgical and medical) specialty, along with a range of others (HSCIC Data Dictionary), many of which have their own organisational bodies, intensely complex organisational practices within hospitals, different temporalities of data capture, and so on. Translating the work of these specialties, themselves with geographical variations, into the kind of data that might sit comfortably in a national database, let alone producing the kind of software that could generate big data that might be clinically meaningful, means capturing complexity, including natural language diagnoses, with all the nuances they may involve. Doing this is a rather different kind of task to developing a technology to capture more readily uniform GP data collection practices, and the failure of the National Programme for IT (NPfIT) (House of Commons Committee of Public Accounts, 2013), often attributed to an attempt to develop a 'one size fits all' solution for the NHS as a whole, reminds us of how hard standardisation is. Yet it is standardisation that is at the heart of justifying the benefits of evidence-based decision making, and in the NHS context it is standardisation that is the tacit condition for the large-scale processes of aggregation characteristic of what we currently understand by big data.

The Politics of Interoperability

Prior to the development of networked computing from the early 1990s, the existence of a very large number of different information systems in relative isolation was not questioned. The patient here might carry their own notes (as is common in maternity care), or the GP might hold a brief record of treatment. Now that broadly interoperable networks of digital technologies are common in many settings and facilitate flows of information (and much of the awareness of the possibilities of using big data that has caused such fuss in the social sciences derives from the growth of similar flows of traffic in globalised information infrastructures of massively networked communication technologies). To put it simply, big data is predicated on interoperability. But the achievement of interoperability in a setting as complex as the NHS, where IT infrastructures are dated, poorly resourced and designed to stand alone is hardly a straightforward process, as the NPfIT found. Evidence-based thinking requires that for meaningful comparisons to be made, the same kinds of data items must be being collected. The interoperability toolkit in the NHS sets out protocols to enable different technologies to talk to each other by setting out the basic structures of the vast number of messages that are or will be exchanged between systems. Such protocols and other kinds of technical standards are not unproblematic. And interoperability as such envelops a broader, global dynamic that it is worth unpacking a little. Consider briefly the tacit 'standard' embodied within Microsoft software. Sharp corporate practices have, for example, enabled Microsoft to get the Open XML format (which was developed by the ECMA, a commercially orientated industry-run standards body) accepted as a standard by the ISO, despite the earlier approval of the Open Document Format, which was developed out of an open source software initiative. Adoption of one or other standard matters in a day to day format – small differences in the 'implementation' of a standard in a piece of software can make all the difference between a document that opens and formats correctly and one that someone has to spend many hours tidying up to achieve appropriate formatting quality. This is the case with something like Microsoft Office 2010 which implements only certain versions of agreed standards (on all this see Lai, 2007 and the commentary by Bhatnagar, 2012). Given that Microsoft had a virtual monopoly on desktop software in the NHS until 2010 and had a central role in the NHS in the development of what is known as the 'Common User Interface' in the NHS and also the standards against which software is procured, issues of backwards compatibility that emerge within interoperable systems are not insignificant, and can mitigate against the adoption of say open source software, and leave information officers with the financial and logistical nightmare of playing perpetual catch up with corporate software development practices. One commentator has argued more broadly that standardisation issues globally are actually a form of 'neocolonialism' (Upgrove cited in DeNardis, 2010, p. 214), and whilst this may not be an apt descriptor for the NHS it does at least point towards the complex power issues raised by reliance on less than entirely open standards.

But the kind of standardisation aimed at by interoperability of the kind sought in the NHS also operates in other ways. Here we would point to the use of medical coding systems. Such systems are used widely because of the way in which they allow for the more reliable generation of what is colloquially referred to as 'good, clean data'. Historically, ICD10 codes offer a good example of an alpha-numerical system designed to standardise the recording of medical diagnoses. Yet such a coding system has had considerable significance beyond what it facilitates in the easy recording of data. Bowker and Star (1999) relate the development of standardised codes at the core of information infrastructures to the development of the State. As they put it 'Building the ICD involved building the State as much as developing medical knowledge' (p. 123), in the sense that ICD codes facilitated the work of the State as central point for the gathering of information. So it is perfectly licit to want to question and explore the broader impact of the many kinds of systems of standardisation and structuring of data that we observe in the NHS today. Some of these – SNOMED and HL7, for example, not unlike the better known DSM codes, are intrinsically bound into the private healthcare insurance industry in the States and it is noteworthy that the 'information revolution' in the NHS coincides with unprecedented structural reform that many commentators have described as lurch towards US style health insurance model of provision (Leys & Arnold, 2011). We might argue then that like ICD10 in its development, but in a different direction, the new standards and shift towards interoperability perhaps testify as much to a process of redefining the position of the UK state in relation to medical knowledge, as information is parsed and passed on to private providers. Information in this context is used (disingenuously) to allow the state to abrogate its responsibility for providing healthcare, under a rhetoric of 'what does it matter who acts on the information, the most important thing is we have the information to act upon'. In this context, information works to enable the state to 'promote' a system of universal healthcare (which, is all it is required to do under the health and social care act, see Pollock & Price, 2012a, 2012b).

Furthermore, discussions of big data are frequently predicated on the idea that it renders old-fashioned expertise in knowledge production redundant. Yet such claims can all too easily make us forget that 'data', 'information' and 'knowledge' are not the same thing at all: computing, and the ability to understand what is happening with the data deluge with which big data has mistakenly become synonymous, entails some complex dynamics. Computing scientists and software developers will routinely distinguish between data, as the kind of thing that acts as an input to generate an output from some bit of software, and information as a possible semantically meaningful 'interpretation' of data, and will generally treat knowledge as something to be modelled ('engineered' is the expression of choice) in terms of algorithms and data structures. But in any case, the distinction between data and information is complex and relative. Castells (2000, p. 17) suggests that information is composed of data where and when data have been organised and communicated, for example, a characterisation that is perhaps most consonant with the way in which information *qua* the information revolution might be imagined to work. But we might risk missing some of the importantly political qualities of such a revolution if we fail to factor in the relationship between information and knowledge, a point made most forcefully by various A2K (Access to Knowledge) movements. In a review of the historical development of the latter, Kapczynski has suggested that 'knowledge … is a capacity more than it is an object or a possession – a power immanent to intellectual, social, cultural, and technological relations between humans. Information, in turn, is the externalised object of this capacity, the part of knowledge that can be systematised and communicated or transmitted to others' (2010, p. 46). The crucial point, however, is that the technologies that are designed to capture data from practices within healthcare, and to transform that data (of whatever size) into information, have an impact on the way in which those practices can organise and develop in turn. We have explored some this in the earlier discussion of interoperability where we mentioned, for example, the role of medical coding in the generation of standardised data. We can extend this issue into a discussion of the kinds of transformations of practices that can occur through digital mediation.

AUTOMATING CARE?

Interoperability within the NHS correlates with the insistence within the HASC Act on the use of international information standards. Using international standards, it is suggested 'allows information to flow across borders and reduces the amount of tailoring required when buying international IT systems' (Information Standards Board for Health and Social Care, n.d.). In this regard, we might consider the impact of SNOMED, a medical coding system designed to facilitate the generation of 'good clean data' on healthcare practices. Whilst not widely in use yet, it is considered to be what is described as a 'full fundamental standard for clinical terminology' (BCS, n.d.) and its use is predicated – albeit in a rather different way to big data practices per se – on precisely the same 'data deluge' generated by the increasingly extensive and intensive digitisation of practices that apologists for the latter suggested would render 'the scientific method obsolete' (Anderson, 1998). Like ICD10 codes, SNOMED is a system designed to facilitate better recording of data. However, it also generates a 'semantics' to otherwise meaningless data that, crucially, can be understood by machines (cf. discussions regarding the 'Semantic Web'). This makes it possible for IT systems more easily to extract meaningful patterns of information from the data they gather. But more pointedly – and this is quite explicit in discussions of 'formal ontology' (of which SNOMED is a variant) – SNOMED offers the possibility of machines acquiring expertise from the work that clinicians do. In this instance, the data that is being provided is the hard-won expertise of medical staff. What this suggests is that within the so-called data deluge, the simple act of recording data belies a more complex set of relations. It is not simply, as the breezy rhetoric suggests, simply about information flows, it is about a continuation of the classic strategy of automation that has been a feature of information technology since the computer's inception, but this time at the level of linguistic communication itself (see Vetere, 2009). Nowadays, this is understood as 'knowledge engineering' (see Studer, Benjamins, & Fensel, 1998). Given our comments about on the 'neo-colonial' quality of standardisation in IP, the very limited translation of SNOMED into languages other than English (it is restricted primarily to European languages) might give pause for thought.

Care.data

Our final example here concerns the so-called 'care.data' initiative, which hit the headlines in the United Kingdom in early to mid-2014. Care.data is a centralised record of individual patient data, which patients are required to opt out of (rather than in to) in order to prevent their de-identified (although in some cases identifiable) medical records being shared on a national database. The intended benefits are indeed significant: care providers can see patient histories and current treatments at a glance and tailor their care accordingly, based on an apparently objective and unmediated aggregation of what treatments are efficient and effective from the perspective, not just of the financial bottom-line, but in terms of current best international evidence, clinical outcome measures, patient outcome measures and patient experience measures. The ethical and practical problems associated with trying to share this data were discussed above. Also of note, though, is how the care.data initiative transforms patients and citizens into consumers and commodities. This extends into a broader 'epistemic' problem that we can associate with big data. The routine assumption that statistically generated evidence automatically equals objectivity belies the way in which, in scientific practices, objects of investigation are put in the position of being able to *resist* the way in which they are represented – in the laboratory, a laboriously constructed artefact that cannot resist such testing remains just that, and not a fact. Referred to in STS literature in terms of 'recalcitrance', this quality of being put in a position where they are given 'a chance to redefine, on their own terms, what it is to be interrogated by science' (Stengers, 1997, p. xv) seems to be something that is missing almost completely with the care.data initiative. Not only do patients and citizens not have control of their data, they do not have the power to contest the terms on which that data was collected or the assumptions about who or what they are that underlie the information systems through which data about them is collected. In respect of this fundamental asymmetry, then, we might argue that the technical infrastructures and associated practices that generate data of the kind envisaged for inclusion in care.data form part of a power relation associated with the redefined governance of the NHS.

CONCLUSION

In this chapter, we have discussed the recent changes to the NHS that suggest to us that 'information', 'digitisation' and 'big data' manifest in complementary and contradictory ways. The new information recording and reporting requirements placed on service providers are intended to generate 'good clean data' that can usefully be applied to make decisions about future service provision and these rely on the development of new IT infrastructures. Digitisation processes are a necessary condition for these uses of information, as it is through digitisation that the information is able to make a claim to being neutral, and therefore a valid basis for decisions about healthcare. The information revolution is also intended to smooth the passage of patients between services, through electronic record keeping. This should generate joined-up care, with benefits to patients. The digitisation of care records makes it possible for this digital data to become 'big data', that is to contribute to global evidence-based medicine. This is one of the key aims of the care.data programme. Consider how in policy discussions and justifications for the organisational change, 'information' is used as a catch-all term. The form that this 'information' takes, however, is digitised, and in some instances it counts as 'big data'. The political promises of information, then, are bound up with broad discourses on the benefits of 'science', the objectivity of data, and the promises of new solutions that are caught up with the 'epoch of big data'.

Our research, however, suggests that the easy slippages (from data to information, from evidence to decision, and from 'administrative' to 'clinical' data) hide very complex and somewhat problematic practices through which data/informational infrastructures can and do operate. That is to say, software, IT companies, working practices in medical wards and managerial understandings of how information should flow are amongst the chains of mediators that influence the transformation of an occurrence into a bit of data and into the kind of information that provides a basis for decision making. Our understanding is that in representing routinely occurring and routinely collated data as providing a real time reflection of what is going on in the system involves ignoring this kind of complexity. In our discussion, we focused specifically on unpicking taken-for-granted software practices and IT systems to indicate the flaws in claims to the neutrality of data. We have suggested that information reporting requirements can be read as an essentially bureaucratic tool of administration. We are only half joking when we say our documentary analysis of information and IT policy leaves the impression that information collection, analysis and exchange replaces patient care as the purpose of the NHS.

In this chapter we have used techniques of discourse analysis, ethnography, and key informant interviewing, informed by STS approaches to understanding assemblages. The process of unpicking and unpacking that we are able to do using these techniques reveals the extraordinary organisational, institutional, political and technological complexity of information in the NHS. As qualitative researchers, we would not want to deny or hypothesise away this kind of complexity, but we also soon hit the limits of what we can feasibly say about such a complex case, given the constraints of academic publishing, our own expertise and the politically charged and ever-changing landscape of digitisation in the NHS. Our contribution, therefore, to discussions of the implications of digitisation on qualitative research is to stress two features. First, that any setting is distinct and requires careful understanding and description of its specificity, including awareness of its history. This means that 'digitisation' here differs from other healthcare settings, even as some of the push to 'big data' is influenced by global healthcare corporations. Second, that digitisation is effectively understood from 'within', that is, expertises – in this case, understanding of the NHS as a complex institution, and of the workings of software – generate qualitative research that comes closer to meeting the criteria for good quality' research: it has credibility and dependability.

We suggest that qualitative researchers in future may helpfully address digitisation by interrogating the institutional and political contexts within which specific kinds of big data are formed and used, that is, qualitative tools can investigate the politics, technology and lived experience of big data, and the kinds of questions qualitative researchers tend to develop are well suited to undoing big data's seductive power. A contextually informed understanding of digitisation and big data might address two key, interconnected criteria: the sets of practices that constitute digitisation and big data, and the implementation of those practices across social, political and institutional contexts, to understand the regulatory, administrative and bureaucratic uses that digital data is put to, and to understand what digitisation does in the social world. Our analysis demonstrates the ways in which digitisation might be used to legitimate otherwise unpopular political decisions. An appeal to the claimed objective, scientific nature of data of various kinds functions to cover-over the very real decisions, made at the level of government about what does and does not count (in very much the same tradition as 'seasonally adjusted' rates of employment). Research that interrogates the institutional and political contexts within which specific kinds of big data are formed and used, that is, the politics, technology and lived experience of big data.

NOTE

1. The so-called 'Spine' of NPfIT was completed successfully, for example.

REFERENCES

Agar, J. (2003). *The government machine: A revolutionary history of the computer*. Cambridge, MA: MIT Press.

Anderson, C. (1998). The end of theory: The data deluge makes the scientific method obsolete. *Wired*, June 23.

Becker, H. (1982). *Art worlds*. Berkeley, CA: University of California Press.

Benson, T. (2002a). Why general practitioners use computers and hospital doctors do not – Part 1: Incentives. *British Medical Journal*, *325*, 1086–1089.

Benson, T. (2002b). Why general practitioners use computers and hospital doctors do not – Part 2: Scalability. *British Medical Journal*, *325*, 1090–1093.

Bhatnagar, A. (2012). *Is DOCX really an open standard.* Retrieved from http://brattahlid.wordpress.com/2012/05/08/is-docx-really-an-open-standard/. Accessed on June 19, 2014.

Bowker, G., Baker, K., Millerand, F., & Ribes, D. (2010). Toward information infrastructure studies: Ways of knowing in a networked environment. In J. Hunsinger, L. Klastrup, & M. Allen (Eds.), *Handbook of internet research* (pp. 97–117). Amsterdam, the Netherlands: Springer.

Bowker, G., & Star, S. L. (1999). *Sorting things out: Classification and its consequences.* Cambridge, MA: MIT Press.

British Computing Society (BCS). (n.d.). *The changing face of medical terminologies.* Retrieved from http://www.bcs.org/content/conWebDoc/43963. Accessed on June 19, 2014.

Cafarella, M. J., Downey, D., Soderland, S., & Etzioni, O. (2005). KnowItNow: Fast, scalable information extraction from the web. In *Proceedings of human language technology conference and conference on empirical methods in natural language processing.* Vancouver, Canada (pp. 563–570).

Caldicott, F. (2013, March). *Information: To share or not to share? The information governance review.* Department of Health. Retrieved from http://webarchive.nationalarchives.gov.uk/20130805112409/https://www.gov.uk/government/uploads/system/uploads/attachment_data/file/192572/2900774_InfoGovernance_accv2.pdf. Accessed on June 20, 2014.

Castells, M. (2000). *The rise of the network society* (2nd ed.). Oxford: Blackwell.

Clarke, A., & Fujimura, J. (1992). *The right tools for the job: At work in twentieth century life sciences.* Princeton, NJ: Princeton University Press.

Deith, J. (2013). A healthy market? Lack of transparency raises doubts about NHS commissioning. *British Medical Journal, 347*, f7115.

DeNardis, L. (2010). The global politics of interoperability. In G. Krikorian & A. Kapcyznski (Eds.), *Access to knowledge in the age of intellectual property.* New York, NY: Zone.

Department of Health. (2011). *Innovation, health and wealth: Accelerating adoption and diffusion in the NHS.* Retrieved from http://webarchive.nationalarchives.gov.uk/20130107105354/http://www.dh.gov.uk/prod_consum_dh/groups/dh_digitalassets/documents/digitalasset/dh_134597.pdf

DH. (2010). *Equity and excellence: Liberating the NHS.*

Franklin, M., Halevy, A., & Maier, D. (2005, December). From databases to dataspaces: A new abstraction for information management. *ACM SIGMOD Record.* Retrieved from http://www.sigmod.org/record/issues/0512/sigmod-record.december2005.pdf#page=28

Health and Social Care Act. (2012). London: Stationery Office.

House of Commons Committee of Public Accounts. (2013). *The dismantled national programme for IT in the NHS. Nineteenth Report of Session 2013–2014* [HC294]. Retrieved from http://www.publications.parliament.uk/pa/cm201314/cmselect/cmpubacc/294/294.pdf. Accessed on June 19, 2014.

Information Standards Board for Health and Social Care. (n.d.). *Health and Social Care Act 2012.* Retrieved from http://www.isb.nhs.uk/setting/hscact2012/index_html. Accessed on June 19, 2014.

Kapczynski, A. (2010). A conceptual genealogy. In G. Krikorian & A. Kapcyznski (Eds.), *Access to knowledge in the age of intellectual property.* New York, NY: Zone.

Lai, E. (2007). Microsoft guns Open XML onto ISO fast track. *Computerworld*, March 12. Retrieved from http://www.computerworld.com/s/article/9012860/Microsoft_guns_Open_XML_onto_ISO_fast_track?intsrc=news_ts_head. Accessed on June 17, 2014.

Leys, C., & Arnold, J. (2011). The NHS: Anatomy of a demolition (Part 1). *New Left Review*. Retrieved from http://www.newleftproject.org/index.php/site/article_comments/the_nhs_anatomy_of_a_demolition

Mosco, V. (2004). *The digital sublime: Myth, power and cyberspace*. London: MIT Press.

Pollock, A. M., & Price, D. (2012a). How the secretary of state for health proposes to abolish the NHS in England. *British Medical Journal*, *342*(2597), 800–803. doi:10.1136/bmj.d1695

Pollock, A. M., & Price, D. (2012b). The break-up of the NHS: Implications for information systems. In P. Watson (Ed.), *Health care reform and globalisation: The US, China and Europe in comparative perspective*. London: Routledge.

Pollock, A. M., & Price, D. (2013). From cradle to grave. In J. Davis & R. Tallis (Eds.), *NHS SOS: How the NHS was betrayed – And how we can save it* (pp. 174–203). London: Oneworld.

Reynolds, L., & McKee, M. (2012). Opening the oyster: The 2010–11 NHS reforms in England. *Clinical Medicine*, *12*(2), 128–132.

Speed, E., & Gabe, J. (2013). The health and social care act for England 2012: The extension of 'new professionalism'. *Critical Social Policy*, *33*(3), 564–574.

Stengers, I. (1997). *Power and invention: Situating science*. Minneapolis, MN: University of Minnesota Press.

Studer, R., Benjamins, V. R., & Fensel, D. (1998). Knowledge engineering: Principles and methods. *Data and Knowledge Engineering*, *25*, 161–197.

Taylor, P. (2014). care.data. *London Review of Books blog*. Retrieved from http://www.lrb.co.uk/blog/2014/01/21/paul-taylor/care-data/. Accessed on June 9, 2014.

Vetere, G. (2009). From data to knowledge, the role of formal ontology. In R. Ferrario & A. Oltramari (Eds.), *Formal ontologies meet industry* (pp. 1–9). Amsterdam, the Netherlands: IOS Press.

BIG DATA AMBIVALENCE: VISIONS AND RISKS IN PRACTICE

Daniel Trottier

ABSTRACT

Purpose – *Social media platforms, along with networked devices and applications, enable their user base to produce, access and circulate large volumes of data. On the one hand, this development contains an empowering potential for users, who can make otherwise obscured aspects of social life visible, and coordinate social action in accordance. Yet the preceding activities in turn render these users visible to governments as well as the multinational companies that operate these services. Between these two visions lie more nuanced accounts of individuals coordinating via social data for reactionary purposes, as well as policing and intelligence agencies struggling with the affordances of big data.*

Design/methodology/approach – *This chapter considers how individual users as well as police agencies respectively actualise the supposedly revolutionary and repressive potentials associated with big data. It briefly considers the broader social context in which 'big data' is situated, which includes the hardware, software, individuals and cultural values that render big data meaningful and useful. Then, in contrast to polarising visions of the social impact of big data, it considers two sets of practices*

Big Data? Qualitative Approaches to Digital Research
Studies in Qualitative Methodology, Volume 13, 51–72

ISSN: 1042-3192/doi:10.1108/S1042-319220140000013004

that speak to a more ambivalent potentiality. First, recent examples suggest a kind of crowd-sourced vigilantism, where individuals rely on ubiquitous data and devices in order to reproduce law and order politics. Second, police agencies in various branches of European governments report a sense of obligation to turn to social data as a source of intelligence and evidence, yet attempts to do so are complicated by both practical and procedural challenges. A combination of case studies and in-depth interviews offers a grounded understanding of big data in practice, in contrast to commonly held visions of these technologies.

Findings – *First, big data is only ever meaningful in use. While they may be contained in databases in remote locations, big data do not exist in a social vacuum. Their impact cannot be fully understood in the context of newly assembled configurations or 'game-changing' discourses. Instead, they are only knowable in the context of existing practices. These practices can initially be the sole remit of public discourse shaped by journalists, tech-evangelists and even academics. Yet embodied individual and institutional practices also emerge, and this may contradict or at least complicate discursive assertions. Secondly, the range of devices and practices that make up big data are engaged in a bilateral relation with these practices. They may be a platform to further reproduce relations of information exchange and power relations. Yet they may also reconfigure these relations.*

Research limitations/implications – *This research is limited to a sample of respondents based in the European Union, and based at a particular stage of big data and social media monitoring uptake. Subsequent research should look at how this uptake is occurring elsewhere, along with the medium to long-term implications of big data monitoring. Finally, subsequent research should consider how citizens and other social actors are coping with these emerging practices.*

Originality/value – *This chapter considers practices associated with big data monitoring and draws from cross-national empirical data. It stands in contrast to overly optimistic as well as well as totalising accounts of the social costs and consequences of big data. For these reasons, this chapter will be of value to scholars in internet studies, as well as privacy advocates and policymakers who are responsive to big data developments.*

Keywords: Big data; social media; surveillance; police; digital vigilantism

INTRODUCTION

Social media platforms, along with networked devices and applications, enable their user base to produce, access and circulate large volumes of data. On the one hand, this development contains an empowering potential for users, who may benefit from technological innovation and make otherwise obscured aspects of social life visible to one another (Anderson, 2008; Mayer-Schönberger & Cukier, 2013). Yet the preceding activities in turn render these users visible to governments as well as the multinational companies that operate these services (Andrejevic, 2013; Morozov, 2013). Between these two visions lie more nuanced accounts of individuals coordinating via social data for reactionary purposes, as well as policing and intelligence agencies struggling with the affordances of 'big data'. A social scientific engagement with big data monitoring must maintain a distinction between the monitoring device, and how the device is utilised. The latter is configured by the developer culture linked to the device, but also the end-user's practices, ambitions and constraints. Institutional cultures as well as individual user cultures matter. These cultures are in turn also reconfigured by the uptake of new technologies. As we will see in the sections below, both police cultures and civic engagement are shaped by the range of information and interfaces linked to big data, as well as the kinds of interventions that these allow. Furthermore, these engagements are not necessarily reflected in public discourses on big data.

This chapter considers how individual users as well as police agencies respectively actualise the supposedly revolutionary and repressive potentials associated with big data. This potential is expressed and substantiated in technological features, but also cultural and institutional practices. This chapter briefly considers how big data is envisioned as a way to make emerging forms of social visibility technically and culturally meaningful. Then, in contrast to polarising visions (Mayer-Schönberger & Cukier, 2013; Morozov, 2013) of the social impact of big data, it considers two sets of practices that speak to a more ambivalent potentiality. First, recent examples suggest a kind of crowd-sourced digital vigilantism, where individuals rely on ubiquitous data and devices in order to persecute other individuals. Second, police agencies in various branches of European governments report a sense of obligation to turn to social data as a source of intelligence and evidence, yet attempts to do so are complicated by both practical and procedural challenges. Taken together, these examples suggest that individuals and police engage with social data and employ methods to interpret it in ways that further existing tendencies and constraints, which are often visibly imprinted on social media platforms. A combination of case studies and in-depth interviews offers a grounded understanding of big data in practice, in contrast to commonly held visions of these technologies. Thus, visions of methods social media visibility are held in contradistinction to this research's methods, which in turn render these techno-cultural practices visible.

WHAT IS BIG (SOCIAL) DATA?

The term big data refers to a current and still-emerging condition of contemporary life. It points to the manner in which interpersonal and institutional activities, through their reliance on information technologies, generate a staggering amount of data. This may be regarded as a by-product (Beer, 2012) of such activities, or as serving an administrative role in the context of these activities. Yet a key feature for big data is that this data – when aggregated – can serve an administrative or interpersonal role in virtually any other context. The major features and conditions of big data are that (i) information technologies that (ii) generate data that (iii) is interoperable and can be repurposed. Therefore, at its core, big data evokes the image of vast databases of personal and transactional information. Indeed, it is often framed as a kind of raw material from which value is extracted (cf. Mayer-Schönberger & Cukier, 2013, p. 16). Similarly, big data is valuable and meaningful in the context of a full array of platforms, devices, infrastructures, practices and users. A fully actualised vision of big data depends not only on any single device or infrastructure, but also fully interoperable relations between infrastructures, which may amount to an assemblage of visibility (Haggerty & Ericson, 2000). Beyond material conditions and social morphologies, big data also amounts to an upset to existing social or institutional functioning. This chapter considers 'data whose size forces us to look beyond the tried-and-true methods that are prevalent at that time' (Jacobs, 2009, p. 44).

From this perspective, big data is closely linked to a broader contemporary media culture. Scholars who wish to study these developments may wonder what are the boundaries: where does the reach of big data end, and the remainder of media culture continue? The fact that both empowering and cautious understandings of big data draw upon so many aspects of contemporary media use, and in turn will shape so many spheres, renders them difficult to delineate. Monitoring on social media is a matter of rendering a targeted social actor visible. Yet in doing so, the watcher is also visible through digital traces. Social scientific research in this area should be methodologically anchored by such traces, but social actors who perform surveillance should also be made visible through methods like semi-structured interviews. This chapter focuses on social actors who in turn use big data to monitor others. This focus highlights the enrolment of social media platforms, users, as well as other social features of contemporary information exchange. As of 2012, Facebook was processing over 500 terabytes of data per day (Constine, 2012). The trans-contextual nature of these platforms means that while this information may have been uploaded for a specific purpose, it will surely be repurposed without the user's awareness or consent. The asynchronous nature of interactions online further facilitates this practice, marking a normalisation of function creep (Trottier, 2012a).

The predictive dimensions of big data visibility and analysis are in turn what render this socio-technical assemblage visible in current public discourse. Its proponents claim that handing previously unmanageable amounts of data will render social life visible in ways that will drastically change social functioning. This rests on the logic that correlation is as meaningful causation; that the numbers can 'speak for themselves' (Anderson, 2008). The idea of handling or transforming big data frames it as a kind of resource, and specifically one that is more or less untapped. Explicitly or implicitly, a lot of public discourse on emerging data practices suggests that we cannot even comprehend the real value and usefulness of big data until it is fully embraced. A first intervention will be to consider the cultural agents narratives that promote these visions. Software and hardware producers (Intel, 2014), technology journalists (Anderson, 2008), futurists (critical (Greenfield, 2006) or otherwise (Jarvis, 2011)) and academics (Andrejevic, 2013) are producing visions of big data visibility, which are then shape public discourse to varying degrees. These accounts simultaneously report on grounded phenomenon based on existing technical possibilities, and extend these possibilities to potentialities by anticipating how these can be taken up as practices of visibility and monitoring. These visions often contradict each other, and there is an element of contentiousness in these formative stages. Several narratives currently surround big data, but two notable strands are considered below.

BIG DATA AND EMPOWERED USERS

One cluster of social actors rendering big data meaningful consider individual empowerment to be an outcome of its proliferation, specifically as everyday tasks become more effective as a result of being data-rich. Advertising Agency Ogilvy published a video depicting a fictional and proto-futuristic 'day in the life' of big data (Ogilvyvids, 2013). This format has also been used in the context of wearable devices (Bhutto, 2012) to demonstrate how an augmented visibility of social information will benefit virtually every aspect of an individual's life. This is accomplished by having large quantities of relevant information collected, processed and rendered meaningful in real time. For example, the video's protagonist rents a bike, and is presented with current data about urban congestion. Other pedestrian activity, like shopping and interacting with friends, is rendered more convenient as a result of the timely and contextual processing of multi-sourced information. Elsewhere, big data can supposedly help anticipate criminal events and the spread of disease (IBM, 2014), and provide a competitive advantage in sports gambling (Giller, 2014; Lee, 2014). Based on the notion that the data in big data is ubiquitous in its origin, it seems reasonable to claim that its benefits are as widespread. This discourse of empowerment appears to fuel appeals for public sector investments in big data (Passingham, 2014). Ostensibly, such investments could lead to a kind of public resource that the head of the Economic and Social Research Council (ESRC) in the United Kingdom describes as 'a significant resource that can be used for the mutual benefit of organisations and academic research' (*ibid.*). It is possible to imagine big data as a kind of public repository, accessible to all as a contemporary incarnation of – or feature of – the public library.

New technologies are often made meaningful by the visions that precede them (Mosco, 2004). These visions present technology in a sublime and transcendental manner, such that they constitute a radical overhaul in terms of how we experience social life, notably in terms of the visibility of social information. These cultural elements and are then followed up with socio-technical conditions and affordances that, while constituting an upset in terms of social configurations, are rendered banal in comparison. These discourses originate from enthusiastic developers (now often called evangelists), and are further promoted by marketers and industry journalists. They present an account of how a specific technology can be used, and reflect the interests of their owners. They hold a considerable influence when speaking about a tangible device like a forthcoming smartphone.

However, big data visionaries like Anderson (2008) are infusing meaning into a broad development that is not tethered to a specific object, which is more ambitious in its scope and projected impact.

Among all of these visions, one recurring theme is being able to make predictions that defy reasonable explanation, for instance, correlations between sales and moon cycles (Gage, 2014). Such examples betray two tendencies in big data visions. First, it is primarily business-driven. Individual users/citizens are typically invoked not as the primary beneficiaries of big data, but as part of the backdrop of a broadly defined business model. Second, these stories call into question the notion of the expert. Although data analysts are touted as an in-demand and even 'sexy' profession (Davenport & Patil, 2012), effectively deployed big data will render them obsolete, or at least drastically lower the threshold of human effort required for the numbers to 'speak for themselves'. This can be framed in the context of a democratisation of expertise (Spillman, Olanoff, & Weissman, 2013; Vos, 2012), yet it is also situated in a context of vast precarity within the information sector. Discussions of an 'end of theory' and valuing correlation at the expense of causation suggests that access to and ownership of information will be more important than conventional expertise. These shifts are also characterised by an enduring trend of invoking selective distrust in the media (Andrejevic, 2013), resulting in a kind of savvy engagement among users that is nevertheless shaped by corporate-owned media.

This partial account evokes a vision that presents big data as broad reaching in scope and vaguely benevolent in its ambition. Its applications are diverse, and it aims to reach and assume itself into virtually any information-dependent sector. It also imposes a particular subjectivity of an empowered individual user, who as a result of the democratisation of expertise and a reconfiguration of the visibility of social life is more informed when they perform everyday tasks. Yet even here, the main tilt favours business applications. An immanent critique of this vision may recognise a broader asymmetry of visibility of social life through big data. In the context of social media, end-users simply cannot access and process the same amount of information as corporate or institutional actors (Kuchler, 2013).

BIG DATA AND SOCIAL HARM FROM ABOVE

As big data concerns information collection and processing on a global and enduring scale, it presents troubling potential for individual well-being.

Some scholars and public figures have placed this potential in the foreground. Privacy and the proper handling of personal details are presented as significant concerns for individual subjects under big data. In the context of centralising patient medical information, the NHS emphasised in a public campaign that any identifiable information would be shielded from unwanted scrutiny. Yet public discourse also featured the possibility that details considered not to be personal could nevertheless point to someone's identity (Aron, 2014). This vision of big data presents privacy and exposure as reversible attributes, based on the cunning of a data scientist. Instead of identification at an individual scale, big data can also be the grounds for categories or typologies of people, sorted out by postal code (Burrows & Gane, 2006), or by medical data yielded from mobile devices (Lupton, 2013). In this scenario, the aggregate and/or anonymised profile may speak on behalf of the individual, regardless of its accuracy. The connection between the big data set and the individual is in negotiation. Claims of enduring anonymity for data subjects are contested. Yet these claims configure the relation between the social self and the social big data set. Between these two, the category, the market segment, and the criminal profile serve as a kind of interface that renders both the data and the individual socially meaningful.

A precautionary framing of big data points to potential for social harm (Andrejevic & Gates, 2014; Bennett, Haggerty, Lyon, & Steeves, 2014), in part through a methodological commitment to making surveillance cultures and practices visible. As indicated above, the relation between a publically meaningful slice of a big database and the individual may result in the profile taking precedence over the individual, and determining their life chances (Andrejevic, 2013; Gandy, 1993). Here, the gravitas of the category trumps accuracy of the data, as even a false category can potentially have life-altering consequences. In the context of the above discussion of an 'end of theory', and correlation becoming sufficient grounds for being socially meaningful, for instance, in public policy, categorisation and identification may take on non-negotiable dimensions. In this sense, the 'big' in big data (not unlike big brother) refers not just to the vast quantity of information, but also the clout with which it shapes meaning.

Other prominent risks include the repurposing of personal information, or what scholars like Lyon have dubbed 'function creep' (2001). Here, information that was authored for one specific function and context becomes meaningful in a separate context. While this was an exceptional possibility prior to big data, the current logic is that 'data is captured not solely for current use, but also to take into account the possibility of any and all future scenarios and possibilities' (Andrejevic, 2013, p. 37). This perceived risk is another way of framing big data's status as a kind of paradigm of knowing, where 'connecting' and 'sharing' are vital to its value. Public awareness of these features and the harm they may trigger is in turn linked to a potential 'chilling effect', whereby speech acts and other public actions are dampened or self-suppressed in recognition of potential harms of exposure through big data (BBC, 2012). Thus, public recognition of the effects of big data in turn shapes public engagement with these technologies.

These potential risks are linked to specific attributes of big data's deployment. First, users are often presented with an enduring and forgettable engagement with big data. Extending from principles of ubiquitous computing (Weiser, 1996), big data is typically framed in terms of an ongoing engagement with an interface, and persistent contribution to a database. Related to this ubiquitous engagement is the perception of big data is permeating contextual boundaries. The user, device and database all seemingly transcend former distinctions (Marwick & boyd, 2011) amplifying the scope and impact of any data processing. Another concern is general uncertainty about the ownership and access of data. Returning to the NHS health records, these were sold to insurance companies (Donnelly, 2014), and this revelation has subsequently shaped public discourse about a big data initiative that may otherwise be framed as type of public good. Not only does this invoke issues of ownership and profit into conversations about big data, but it also points to an asymmetry between individuals with a precarious access to their own records, and state and corporate actors with privileged access.

The materials above present individual users as occupying an uncertain role vis-à-vis big data. One vision sees them as benefitting from a data-infused society, while the other sees them at greater risk of profiling and discrimination. Both visions position individuals as the passive recipients of the technical, cultural and practical features of big data. Both visions position these individuals in relation to a type of 'big other'. This big other may be a vaguely benevolent private or publically owned guide that simplifies daily life. Or it may be an amplification of current forms of malevolence and social harms. In both instances, the extent to which the social side of big data is understood and practised is beyond the remit of the individual user.

In positioning these as competing visions, my intention is neither to claim that they are illusory, nor as contradictory. Both empowering 'business solutions' and social harm are ongoing developments. Yet other instances of big data and social media impacting individuals and institutions warrant scrutiny. What follows are manifestations that depart from the above major visions. These accounts describe how big data affordances, rendered accessible through social media platforms and ubiquitous devices, and rendered meaningful through local cultures and practices, amount to a broader assemblage of big data monitoring and visibility.

DIGITAL VIGILANTISM: USERS DOING BAD THINGS WITH BIG DATA

A more nuanced understanding of user subjectivity in the context of big data depends on an empirical focus of user practices that are either emerging or transforming as a result of contemporary digital media. Individuals are able to coordinate using digital media, and the vast scale of data, but also users and devices, suggests that collective behaviour and social movements are shaped by these conditions. Public and academic discourse may frame citizen-led mobilisation in the Arab Spring, for example, under the banner of user empowerment and benefit, and in opposition to a totalising view of state power described above (Eltantawy & Wiest, 2011; Khondker, 2011). However, the relationship between user activity and state power cannot be reduced to a binary. One reason for this is because user activity that exploits big data may result in the harms typically linked to a malevolent 'big other'.

In the context of moral outrage and law and order politics, users may persecute fellow citizens by rendering them visible in an unwanted frame. These actions not only mark a reconfiguration of peer-to-peer relations through digital media (cf. Andrejevic, 2005), but also relations between citizens and the state. In 2013, Gary Cleary hanged himself in Leicestershire, United Kingdom after being pursued by Letzgo Hunting, an online group that exposes suspected paedophiles. Likewise, in 2011 Nathan Kotylak and his family were forced to flee their Vancouver home after receiving numerous death threats upon being identified on Facebook as a suspected rioter. Both individuals were targeted by a clandestine form of criminal justice: digital vigilantism (DV). DV is a process where citizens are collectively offended by other citizen activity, and respond through coordinated retaliation on digital media, including mobile devices and social media platforms. The offending acts range from mild breaches of social protocol (bad parking; not removing dog faeces) to terrorist acts and participation in riots. The vigilantism includes, but is not limited to a 'naming and shaming' type of visibility. This typically involves sharing the targeted individual's personal details by publishing them on a public site, including highly sensitive details such as the target's home address, employment details as well as financial and medical information, all of which may be retrieved from any number of sources. This is done with the intention of conventional justice through police or other legal channels, as well as unconventional justice such as online harassment. The visibility produced through DV is unwanted (the target is typically not soliciting publicity), intense (content like blog posts, photos and video evidence can circulate to hundreds of thousands or even millions of users within a few days), and enduring (the vigilantism campaign may be the first item to appear when searching the individual's name, and may become a cultural reference in its own right).

Common features of DV include (1) an assembly of digital media users taking offence at a targeted individual. This may include an open discussion or editorialising about the offence; (2) soliciting, collecting and aggregating personal information about the target. The types and sources of this information may vary greatly, and may implicate family members and associates; (3) an enduring visibility of the offence and personal information on a public social media platform. Already we can consider variations in terms of DV, including distinctions between (a) offences and responses that occur in a national or trans-national context (although national boundaries are called into question as a result of digital media affordances, as described below); (b) DV action that occurs exclusively online, or also includes offline and embodied activity; (c) instances where the target is able to comment on the DV, and instances where the target is either unaware or excluded from the campaign.

DV is a by-product of big data, insofar as this is an assemblage of vast databases, but also interpersonal interfaces that allow users to monitor and intervene in the lives of others, coupled with user cultures that treat visibility (self or other) as an effective means of social action. Social platforms like Facebook, Twitter and Reddit allow citizens to discuss a targeted individual, publish their personal details and call for action. In addition, mobile devices such as smart phones enable real-time recording and transmission of an offending act to other citizens. As a product of digital media culture, DV is as much a communicative and mediated act as it is a collective social act (the coordinated mass persecution of a targeted citizen). Current scholarship considers the crowdsourcing of surveillance and criminal justice on digital media (Trottier, 2014), as well as the changing nature of policing and visibility online (Trottier, 2012b). These research streams suggest that bottom-up forms of organisation are facilitated by social platforms and that policing is changing as a result of digital media, which in turn shapes how these technologies are used. While the 'early web' was characterised by a perceived distinction between online and offline, the emergence of social, geo-located and ubiquitous media has led to a dissolution of this barrier, to the extent that digital media activity can have lasting consequences in both local and global contexts. This speaks to the impact that big data may have on grounded practices. Individuals, far from passive recipients of big data innovation, as customers or end-users who are presented with the results of crunched data, take advantage of the features of social data for their own initiatives.

Vigilantism is framed as a kind of 'private violence' (Culberson, 1990) whereby citizens seek to legitimate their own violence as a form of criminal justice. Galtung makes a distinction between direct physical violence, structural violence and cultural violence (1990). DV embodies all three forms of violence, and in particular citizen-led structural violence is a novel and troubling concern. Whereas the state is said to hold a monopoly on violent activity, through vigilantism citizens deny this state monopoly in an attempt to legitimate their own violent acts. In the case of digital media, this legitimation is explicitly posted as text, image and video content. Conventional vigilantism is also related to a single nation, and contained within its borders (*ibid.*). This can be seen through the use of nationalist and xenophobic rhetoric. However, the coupling of digital media and vigilantism complicates the relation to any single nation. While there is evidence that DV retains some nationalist sentiment, it is in no way contained to any single border. The backlash to the 2011 Vancouver riot made a clear distinction between a local 'us' and an outsider 'them' (Schneider & Trottier, 2013). Yet even criminal acts such as uttering death threats and harassment can occur in virtually any jurisdiction in the world. As a result, the relation between vigilantism, citizenship and nationalism needs to be reconsidered in the digital age. It is possible to consider vigilantism as a kind of cultural commentary, where citizen violence is meant to represent a kind of claims-making. It often reflects a kind of us/them identity building that identifies a targeted enemy, along with other statements about contemporary society. This violence appears to be a kind of communication counter-power (Castells, 2007) led by citizens. In particular, groups like Anonymous appear to pose a challenge to conventional state power (Coleman, 2012; Fuchs, 2013). Yet the connection between state power and DV is unclear, and forces a reconsideration of state–citizen relations in the context of big data.

The consequences of big data must be understood in the context of long-standing socio-political practices, including vigilantism. Here, big data assemblages of platforms, devices and users are configured terrains from which individuals may persecute fellow individuals. Slices of individual data are reassembled through dispersed users acting in concert across an assemblage of platforms and devices. These practices resemble a kind of user empowerment, albeit one where individuals are empowered to harm other users. These tendencies are not accounted for in visions that render big data socially meaningful. In distinction to these visions, digital vigilantism indicates that big data's social impact is not simply a radical shift upon users, but also an amplification of existing tendencies and harms.

STATES UNABLE TO DO BAD THINGS WITH BIG DATA

Troubling visions of big data rely a 'big other' with the capacity and resources to watch over social life through unfettered access to social information, with the intention of exerting state and/or corporate power. Big data harms are thus predicated on individuals rendered visible to state and corporate actors. Revelations by Edward Snowden and other whistle-blowers indicate that big data monitoring does occur on a trans-national scale. Yet state-led surveillance of big data is manifest on various scales and budgets. Furthermore, many state agencies encounter material, legal and institutional constraints that shape their engagement. What follows is a consideration of limits to state engagements with big data. This interview data is a necessary intervention in a context when so many actors are making big data visibility socially meaningful. The practices of visibility and monitoring must be considered from actors who are trialling these, but may be otherwise obscured in comparison to social actors presented in the above sections. This draws upon a series of structured in-depth interviews with two groups that were conducted between September 2012 and April 2013. The first group includes 19 officials from regional and national police departments as well as specialized investigative agencies in several European Union member states. The second group consists of 15 representative officials from privacy and data protection government branches from these states, as well as advocacy groups that address such issues. Respondents vary in their institutional affiliation, rank, familiarity with social media and country of operation, and each country has a unique historical and cultural context that situates their use of big data.

Social media monitoring requires hardware, software and staffing. These material requirements are in the context of national budgets, which enable and restrict specific practices. Working with these restrictions, many agencies rely on free and affordable tools. A Bulgarian police respondents notes that the principal software they use 'is an Internet browser, chosen by the personnel who conduct the examination, as well as whatever auxiliary tools he/she estimates'. In this context, auxiliary tools refer to 'additional software, usually freeware'. Respondents in other countries endorse free services, noting that they are especially helpful for agencies with limited budgets. A Romanian police respondent points out that 'from a financial point of view, as compared to necessary time and means of collecting information from classified sources, exploitation of open sources is cheaper. For example, high quality geospatial information can be collected on specialised websites, such as Google Earth, which is a great advantage especially for smaller states, which cannot assign big budgets for the Information Services'. However, they add that processing and analysing this data 'requires a lot of financial resources'. Thus, even if data acquisition is inexpensive, the analysis of this acquired data can be costly. Likewise, a Swedish police respondent notes that scalability and data handling are a financial burden that shapes the feasibility of a big data analysis initiative: 'when it comes to the data acquisition part, it's a little bit trickier because then you're playing around with a lot of data, you have to store it somewhere, and so on'.

When discussing the software used to police big data, a Dutch respondent notes that the licences 'can amount to €750 to €1,250 a month, a person. That is a considerable expenditure, a part-timer's salary'. Staffing costs are clearly a concern that intersects with innovative tools, which do not exist in splendid isolation. Thus, the decision to branch into social media monitoring, on a strained budget, comes at the expense of actual agents. Even within the context of big data policing, two UK-based police respondents note that staff wages and training costs represented that single largest expenditure.

Big data monitoring practices may also transcend legal frameworks, especially if they evade public awareness. Yet many agents are entangled in these frameworks, and their use of social media monitoring is complicated in consequence. Jurisdiction boundaries are unclear, and mapping police practices on digital media it in terms of conventional police work, or more familiar communications technologies is equally troubling. Visibility in practice is marked by a perception of national and European laws as outdated. This lack of legal certainty also suggests that it is currently difficult to establish what actions exceed legal limits. A Bulgarian privacy advocate notes 'in many cases investigators are currently attempting to gain access to information from providers of information society in the fastest possible way and make wide variety of requests for retention of information, and even for tracking future activities of their users from providers. These are requests that often go beyond the permissible by the law and if the actual providers of information society services meet them, then there would be an improper use of the information by the investigating authorities'. As well, national borders and the perception of national jurisdictions when speaking of digital media complicate data sharing and interoperability. A Swedish police respondent remarks that official requests to social media companies located in the United States are problematic, as an investigative agency has to set up a mutual legal assistance, by going from the local office, to the American Department of Justice, to the FBI and who then contacts the company with an American court order. Once the data is obtained, it has to be transported back to the Swedish Police by this same route. This can take anywhere from three to six months, at which point data retention laws might lead to the deletion of potential evidence. In order to offset such risks, the respondent notes that they will first inform the FBI Scandinavian office in Copenhagen, so that they can perform a 'data freeze' by asking the targeted US-based company to save the data in question. Visibility is often fleeting in user-led practice on social media. Big data practices have the potential to retain fleeting content, and thus re-purpose it as part of an enduring archive. While social scientists may consider these methods, they impose ethical considerations, especially as they re-contextualise and amplify the visibility social life. In order to facilitate such interoperability with American companies, they also note that Microsoft has its own law firm that represents them in Sweden. In contrast, Facebook is only represented by a marketing company in Sweden, who is unable to handle any legal inquiries. This respondent also notes that as most major social media companies are American, they are protected by American freedom of speech laws. Thus, interoperability with these companies in an investigation against a neo-Nazi group based in Sweden would be restricted. Indeed, although Facebook has corporate offices in Ireland, and servers in locations that include Northern Sweden, the perception of Facebook as an American company means that Swedish police are bound to American laws. These dynamics underscore how assemblages are neither totalising nor assured in terms of technical capacities, but instead connections may be denied as a result of local laws, or simply the perception of their legal status.

Beyond material and legal constraints, big data and social media monitoring in particular does not amount to a full innovation for agencies. In practice, they raise the risk of harm, and at the outset require specific practices to minimise this harm. The accuracy of information found on social media is not always assured. As a result, investigators are faced with the concern of evaluating whether or not to act on information they retrieved. They run the risk of wasting resources when faced with social media content. The uncertain nature of big data, in contrast to the visibility of social life from a patrol car or even a surveillance camera, leads to ambivalence about acting on this data. A Swedish officer attests that this is a concern, noting that while it is easy to retrieve information, assessing whether it is useful and useable is a necessary step in the investigation. A Bulgarian privacy advocate also remarks that data on social media are 'often not true, or exaggerated, or distorted', which may 'lead to wrong conclusions about the profile of the person under observation'. These are significant concerns for officers, but also for data scientists as well as social scientists that may feel compelled to turn to these assemblages and treat them as landscapes of social life. Beyond any individual inaccuracies, some respondents believe that social media data in general is simply not a good description of a target's social ties. An Austrian privacy advocate believes that there is no 'sensible monitoring measures, because the quality of the communication within social networks is very low. Everybody talks to everybody and there is no structured conversation'. As an example they consider the idea that a Facebook user may have 600 'friends', and questions the accuracy and usefulness of any of these social ties as actionable information. This respondent acknowledges that some criminals may provide evidence on social media that they are committing a crime, but likens this to 'burglars who fall asleep at the place of the burglary. Despite this, the strategy cannot consist in hoping that more burglars will fall asleep'. As well, a Dutch officer notes that by acting on false information found online, fledgling IT-based branches of an agency may develop an internal reputation of being unprofessional.

On the basis of these concerns, a Spanish IT specialist emphasises the need for analysts to review data retrieved from social media. This step in an investigation is not only useful for detecting false positives, but also necessary when making inferences about a target's character on the basis of their online presence: 'from quite a few comments or photos you can extract information about likes and dislikes, attitudes, way of life, but this has to be determined manually by some person'. In the context of detecting child exploitation, this oversight is crucial for handling false positives. The above respondent states that an otherwise innocent user's 'computers are used in file-sharing as a node in a network, and files of which they have no knowledge go via their machines. That requires a deeper investigation, so as to rule all the false positives out of the initial list of suspects provided by the paedophile-monitoring program. It's not so much that the information is incorrect, as that it just requires a later process of manual analysis'. Thus, even seemingly accurate digital evidence, such as the presence of child exploitation material on an individual's computer, requires manual interpretation to determine if the user is a suspected target.

A Dutch officer notes that they not only have to cope with 'deliberate misinformation' online, but also individual differences among the investigators in their team. As a result, their team submits 'all information to the information coordinator for review; he is the police official who checks the information from a legal perspective, a police perspective as well as an editorial perspective. No information is passed on without having been checked first'. Other respondents report that evaluating the accuracy of online data – including data from social media platforms – is an integral step in online investigations. One UK officer notes that they are careful to multi-source data and grade their intelligence. A fellow UK officer specifies that social media data in particular must be both graded and corroborated, as social media sites can be a source of misinformation. In the Swedish context, one officer works with a matrix in order to assess online information. The two axes correspond to the source of the information, and their credibility. This officer notes that by default, information located online would be placed in the lowest category of both axes. Despite the costs and challenges associated with sorting through social media data, a Romanian police respondent notes that the bigger cost to policing would be to exclude the bulk of this data. They note that the despite ease with which users can remain anonymous and dissimulate on platforms like blogs, 'excluding the data flow from the virtual environment would mean excluding the greatest data source available, even if they need to be evaluated and analysed to eliminate judgement errors and misleading information'.

Monitoring big data involves engaging with social media platforms, which invariably results in investigators leaving some degree of a traceable presence. A UK officer notes that investigating officers can sometimes leave behind residual evidence of their investigation. Some suspects are able to recognise these 'digital footprints' that can in turn hamper an investigation. Another UK officer echoes this concern, and notes that this risk is more likely to occur among local police forces, rather than specialised branches or agencies. An Italian officer also notes that 'unqualified personnel' are especially risky in this respect, as they 'could make mistakes in the way in which they acquire evidence'. Such improper handling can endanger an investigation, as a Spanish investigator notes: 'There's a set sequence of actions. The original data can never be changed. A copy or an image is made of it, and it's the copy or image that gets analysed. The original is assigned a digital fingerprint by a mathematical algorithm that yields a number. That allows the data to be associated with a unique number. If the original is altered this number no longer matches, which means the evidence has been manipulated. So, normally an identical copy is made of the original and any work is always done with the copy. This procedure is called a chain of custody'. An Italian police respondent distinguishes between a monitoring tool and the way in which a tool is utilised, attributing the latter to the potential harm to investigative activities. On this note they state that the 'lack of best practices can harm the investigation. There is the risk that the evidence collected be manipulated. Clear guidelines on the phases preceding, accompanying and following the acquisition of evidence are needed. We have to focus on the work practices'.

Not only could improper use of social media monitoring tools render online evidence inadmissible in court, but it could also render their investigation visible to suspects. According to one Swedish officer, police interest in a criminal enterprise's online presence 'tells every member in that group that [the police] know something about us'. While communicating this knowledge may have a strategic value, it may lead targeted suspects to change their communication patterns, such as adopting encryption technologies or moving further into the 'dark web'. It may also be a condition in which that an investigator unknowingly finds themselves. Another Swedish officer notes that online investigators do not always know to which online spaces they will be lead, and that they need to anticipate consequences such as leaving traces on a suspect's website or social media profile.

A related concern is the fact that users may be unknowingly recast as criminal informants. Social media users may speak on one another's behalf through explicit statements as well as implicit implications. Use of this content in investigations means that one user is either knowingly or unknowingly assisting police in pursuing a member of their social network. A Swedish officer notes that during an undercover operation, if they befriend someone as a point of entry into the enterprise, the other suspects may know that they gave police access. A related risk this respondent notes is when constructing a fictitious profile for investigations. If an officer uses a randomly chosen person's face as their profile picture (e.g. by extracting it from an unknown person's profile), they would put that person at risk.

A final cost for police who rely on big data and social media monitoring is career opportunities. Developing social media analysis is not a top-down mandate. Instead, specific officers and investigators take an interest in this field, as a basis of their own personal experiences and professional specialised credentials. These specialists follow unconventional career paths as a consequence. A Swedish officer notes that as a police officer, deciding to be Internet specialist is problematic, as there is only one conventional career path, and that even 'the world's greatest OSINT [open source intelligence] expert' would not get promotion under the current system. They also note that the conventional career path poses obstacles at the entry level. New staff is recruited 'for patrol car work', and even though this respondent predicts that Internet surveillance will continue to grow in importance, current recruiting pre-requisites do not reflect this growth. This marks a tension in terms of the status of experts under big data, as they are simultaneously celebrated (Davenport & Patil, 2012) and obviated (Spillman et al., 2013).

These above findings indicate that while large scale data monitoring is possible, such practices are shaped by situated cultures and material constraints. Fledgling agencies and legal uncertainties are grounds for emerging configurations and unanticipated hazards.

CONCLUSION

This chapter presents a selective account of the social impacts and harms linked with big data, as envisioned in public discourse. After juxtaposing two competing visions, it considers some ongoing developments that complicate these visions. Although a discipline-based or broader understanding of big data may be altered by future revelations or innovations, two points warrant consideration. First, big data is only ever meaningful in use. While they be contained in databases in remote locations, big data do not exist in a social vacuum. Their impact cannot be fully understood in the context of newly assembled configurations or 'game-changing' discourses. Instead, they are only knowable in the context of existing practices. These practices can initially be the sole remit of public discourse shaped by journalists, tech-evangelists and even academics. But, as we see, embodied individual and institutional practices also emerge, and this may contradict or at least complicate discursive assertions.

This leads to the second point: the range of devices and practices that make up big data are engaged in a bilateral relation with these practices. They may be a platform to further reproduce relations of information exchange and power relations. Yet they may also reconfigure these relations. Future research needs to consider the full range of actors involved. This will be challenging when considering the ubiquitous ambition and reach of the technology involved. Quantitative research in particular needs to be attentive to pluralised sources of data, as well as the multiple sources of discursive formation. It is also important to consider the limits to big data's seemingly ubiquitous reach, especially in the context of exclusion and the current state of the digital divide (Crawford, 2013). As a point of departure, future research in this area must anticipate that existing social, political and geographic stratifications will be reproduced and even amplified during the deployment of big data technologies, cultures and policies. The communities that are excluded and remain incomprehensible to big data should not be incomprehensible to those who study these conditions.

REFERENCES

Anderson, C. (2008, June 30). *The end of theory: Will the data deluge makes the scientific method obsolete?* Edge.org. Retrieved from http://edge.org/3rd_culture/anderson08/anderson08_index.html

Andrejevic, M. (2005). The work of watching one another: Lateral surveillance, risk, and governance. *Surveillance & Society*, *2*(4), 479–497.

Andrejevic, M. (2013). *Infoglut: How too much information is changing the way we think and know*. New York, NY: Routledge.

Andrejevic, M., & Gates, K. (2014). Big data surveillance: Introduction. *Surveillance & Society*, *12*(2), 185–196.

Aron, J. (2014). NHS plans leave 'anonymous' medical data vulnerable. *New Scientist*, February 19. Retrieved from http://www.newscientist.com/article/dn25088-nhs-plans-leave-anonymous-medical-data-vulnerable.html

BBC. (2012, October 11). *Social media laws to be discussed in wake of prosecutions*. BBC.co.uk. Retrieved from http://www.bbc.co.uk/news/technology-19910865

Beer, D. (2012). Using social media data aggregators to do social research. *Sociological Research Online*, *17*(3), 10. Retrieved from http://www.socresonline.org.uk/17/3/10.html

Bennett, C. J., Haggerty, K. D., Lyon, D., & Steeves, V. (2014). *Transparent lives: Surveillance in Canada*. Edmonton, Canada: Athabasca University Press.

Bhutto, H. (2012, May 7). *Google Glasses project*. Youtube.com. Retrieved from https://www.youtube.com/watch?v=JSnB06um5r4

Burrows, R., & Gane, N. (2006). Geodemographics, software and class. *Sociology*, *40*(5), 793–812.

Castells, M. (2007). Communication, power and counter-power in the network society. *International Journal of Communication*, *1*, 238–266.

Coleman, G. (2012). Our weirdness is free, the logic of anonymous – Online army, agent of chaos, and seeker of justice. *Triple Canopy*, January. Retrieved from http://gabriellacoleman.org/wp-content/uploads/2012/08/Coleman-Weirdness-Free-May-Magazine.pdf

Constine, J. (2012). How big is Facebook's data? 2.5 billion pieces of content and 500+ terabytes ingested every day. *TechCrunch*, August 22. Retrieved from http://techcrunch.com/2012/08/22/how-big-is-facebooks-data-2-5-billion-pieces-of-content-and-500-terabytes-ingested-every-day/

Crawford, K. (2013). The hidden biases in big data. *Harvard Business Review*, April 1. Retrieved from http://blogs.hbr.org/2013/04/the-hidden-biases-in-big-data/

Culberson, W. (1990). *Vigilantism: Political history of private power in America*. Westport, CT: Greenwood Press.

Davenport, T. H., & Patil, D. J. (2012). Data scientist: The sexist job of the 21st century. *Harvard Business Review*, October. Retrieved from http://hbr.org/2012/10/data-scientist-the-sexiest-job-of-the-21st-century/ar/1

Donnelly, L. (2014). Hospital records of all NHS patients sold to insurers. *The Telegraph*, February 23. Retrieved from http://www.telegraph.co.uk/health/healthnews/10656893/Hospital-records-of-all-NHS-patients-sold-to-insurers.html

Eltantawy, N., & Wiest, J. B. (2011). The Arab Spring: Social media in the Egyptian revolution: Reconsidering resource mobilization theory. *International Journal of Communication*, *5*, 1207–1224.

Fuchs, C. (2013). The anonymous movement in the context of liberalism and socialism. *Interface: A Journal for and about Social Movements*, *5*(2), 345–376.

Gage, D. (2014). Big data uncovers some weird correlations. *The Wall Street Journal*, March 23. Retrieved from http://online.wsj.com/news/articles/SB10001424052702303369904579423132072969654

Galtung, J. (1990). Cultural violence. *Journal of Peace Research*, *27*(3), 291–305.

Gandy, O. (1993). *The panoptic sort: A political economy of personal information*. Boulder, CO: Westview Press.

Giller, G. (2014). The best bracket big data can build. *Scientific American*, March 27. Retrieved from http://blogs.scientificamerican.com/observations/2014/03/27/the-best-bracket-big-data-can-build/

Greenfield, A. (2006). *Everyware: The dawning age of ubiquitous computing*. Berkeley, CA: New Riders.

Haggerty, K. D., & Ericson, R. V. (2000). The surveillant assemblage. *British Journal of Sociology*, *54*(4), 605–622.

IBM. (2014). *Big data in action*. IBM.com. Retrieved from http://www-01.ibm.com/software/data/bigdata/industry.html

Intel. (2014). *Big data analytics beings with Intel*. Intel.com. Retrieved from http://www.intel.co.uk/content/www/uk/en/big-data/big-data-analytics-turning-big-data-into-intelligence.html

Jacobs, A. (2009). The pathologies of big data. *Communications of the ACM*, *52*(8), 36–44.

Jarvis, J. (2011). *Public parts: How sharing in the digital age improves the way we work and live*. New York, NY: Simon & Schuster.

Khondker, H. H. (2011). Role of the new media in the Arab Spring. *Globalizations*, *8*(5), 675–679.

Kuchler, H. (2013, December 4). *Analytics start-ups drink deep from Twitter 'fire hose' of data.* FT.com. Retrieved from http://www.ft.com/cms/s/0/cb3fb18c-5c61-11e3-b4f3-00144feabdc0.html

Lee, D. (2014, March 27). *Big data: Would number geeks make better football managers?* BBC.co.uk. Retrieved from http://www.bbc.co.uk/news/business-26771259

Lupton, D. (2013). Quantifying the body: Monitoring and measuring health in the age of mHealth technologies. *Critical Public Health, 23*(4), 393–403.

Lyon, D. (2001). *Surveillance society: Monitoring everyday life.* Buckingham, UK: Open University Press.

Marwick, A. E., & boyd, d. (2011). I tweet honestly, I tweet passionately: Twitter users, context collapse, and the imagined audience. *New Media & Society, 13*(1), 114–133.

Mayer-Schönberger, V., & Cukier, K. (2013). *Big data: A revolution that will transform how we live, work, and think.* New York, NY: Houghton Mifflin Harcourt.

Morozov, E. (2013). *To save everything, click here: The folly of technological solutionism.* New York, NY: Public Affairs.

Mosco, V. (2004). *The digital sublime: Myth, power and cyberspace.* Cambridge, MA: The MIT Press.

Ogilvyvids. (2013, May 10). *Big data for smarter customer experiences.* Youtube.com. Retrieved from http://www.youtube.com/watch?v=449twsMTrJI

Passingham, M. (2014, February 6). *Public sector big data projects get £73m government investment.* V3.co.uk. Retrieved from http://www.v3.co.uk/v3-uk/news/2327364/public-sector-big-data-projects-get-gbp73m-government-investment

Schneider, C., & Trottier, D. (2013). Social media and the 2011 Vancouver riot. *Studies in Symbolic Interaction, 40,* 335–362.

Spillman, R., Olanoff, D., & Weissman, J. (2013). Behold the end of experts: Why the Goodreads sale really matters. *The Build Network,* April 15. Retrieved from http://thebuildnetwork.com/leadership/end-of-experts/

Trottier, D. (2012a). *Social media as surveillance: Rethinking visibility in a converging world.* Farnham, UK: Ashgate.

Trottier, D. (2012b). Policing social media. *Canadian Review of Sociology, 49*(4), 411–425.

Trottier, D. (2014). Crowdsourcing CCTV surveillance on the internet. *Information, Communication & Society, 17*(5), 609–626.

Vos, D. (2012). Big data spells death-knell for punditry. *The Guardian,* November 7. Retrieved from http://www.theguardian.com/media-network/media-network-blog/2012/nov/07/big-data-us-election-silver

Weiser, M. (1996). *Ubiquitous computing.* Retrieved from http://www.ubiq.com/hypertext/weiser/UbiHome.html

PART II
FIELDS AND SITES

THE RESEARCHER AND THE NEVER-ENDING FIELD: RECONSIDERING BIG DATA AND DIGITAL ETHNOGRAPHY

Christine Lohmeier

ABSTRACT

Purpose – *This chapter considers the challenges and potentials of using so called big data in communication research. It asks what lessons big data research can learn from digital ethnography, another method of gathering digital data.*

Design/methodology/approach – *The chapter first takes on the task of clearly defining big data in the context of communication and media studies. It then moves on to analyse and critique processes associated with the dealings of big data: datafication and dataism. The challenges of data-driven research are juxtaposed with qualitative perspectives on research regarding data gathering and context. These thoughts are further elaborated in the second part of the chapter where the lessons learned in digital ethnography are linked to challenges of big data research.*

Big Data? Qualitative Approaches to Digital Research
Studies in Qualitative Methodology, Volume 13, 75–89

ISSN: 1042-3192/doi:10.1108/S1042-319220140000013005

Findings – *It is proposed that by including the materialities of contexts and transitions between material and mediated realms, we can ask more relevant research questions and gain more insights compared to a purely data-driven approach.*

Practical implications – *This chapter encourages researchers to reflect upon their relations to the object of study and the context in which data was produced through human/human–technical interaction.*

Originality/value – *This chapter contributes to debates about qualitative and quantitative research methods in communication and media studies. Moreover, it proposes that methods which are in the widest sense used in the never-ending digital field benefit from the mutual consideration of both qualitative and quantitative approaches.*

Keywords: Digital ethnography; big data; qualitative research; communication research; material turn

INTRODUCTION

Big data is hyping. The possibilities of big data have received a lot of attention by communication scholars. One of the most recent pieces of evidence for this is the publication of a special issue on big data by the *Journal of Communication*, one of the most prominent and well-respected publications in the field. The magazine *Research Trends* (Halevi & Moed, 2012, p. 5) attests to 'an explosion of publications since 2008'. This chapter considers how big data is used in communication research. Following an assessment of what is meant by 'big data', it outlines the potentials and challenges of (communication) research with big data. In a second step, big data as well as digital ethnography are re-considered from a qualitative research perspective. Over the past two decades, digital ethnography – another research method with a strong focus on the digital world and online activities – has experienced increasing popularity. I propose that approaches to and with big data can benefit from what has been learned in developing and refining digital ethnographies.

BIG DATA IN COMMUNICATION RESEARCH

Big data stands at the intersection of technology and social reality. It is a 'cultural, technological, and scholarly phenomenon' (boyd & Crawford,

2011, p. 663). The term is used to refer to a method and an approach to science and research as well as to large datasets themselves. In the past, big data has caused some over-excitement and even mythologising, meaning a 'widespread belief that large data sets offer a higher form of intelligence and knowledge' with a previously unachieved 'aura of truth, objectivity, and accuracy' (boyd & Crawford, 2011, p. 663). Parks (2014, p. 355) even calls what we are witnessing right now a 'Big Data movement'. As the term suggests, we are talking about 'big' data, but there have always been data sets which – in their time – were considered relatively large, so size 'alone is therefore an insufficient descriptor' (Parks, 2014, p. 355). Even before the term became fashionable, larger datasets than those which are now referred to as big data were already available, such as census data (boyd & Crawford, 2011, p. 663). For communication scholars, the datasets in questions can be 'large social networks (including online networks such as Twitter), automated data aggregation and mining, web and mobile analytics, visualization of large datasets, sentiment analysis/opinion mining, machine learning, natural language processing, and computer-assisted content analysis of very large datasets' (Parks, 2014, p. 355). In communication research, the analysis of big data stemming from Twitter is particularly common at this point in time. This is partly due to the fact that large datasets of tweets are relatively easy to get hold of. Nevertheless, even with regards to Twitter, researchers are somewhat dependent on the benevolence of Twitter Inc. and its regulations; the challenge of data availability will be discussed in more detail below.

CHALLENGES OF DATAFICATION AND DATAISM

Why has big data been given such a prime spot in debates about social sciences over the past few years? The coming together of technological developments, that is computers having the capacity to store and carry out analysis of large datasets, promises new findings – hopefully followed by new insights – that could not be obtained at an earlier stage. At the same time, big data which is of particular interest to communication scholar is continuously being generated by people using and 'feeding' information and communication technologies. This process has been coined as 'datafication' (Mayer-Schönberger & Cukier, 2013). Data is being generated by users and being conceived as something worth looking at by (communication) researchers. These developments are indeed exciting as they allow for new types of research questions.

A second aspect of 'datafication' is linked to the new computational prowess in analysing large datasets. These new capacities allows for the bringing together of multiple 'datasets of different times, from different places, or gathered at different times'. Big data has evoked scholars and commentators to refer to what we are experiencing now as a 'big data revolution' (Mayer-Schönberger & Cukier, 2013). No doubt, the benefits of big data analysis might be ground-breaking in some disciplines and possibly life-saving, for example when it comes to analysing medical data sets. However, big data is also a continuation of how science, including the social sciences, has evolved over the past 100 years (boyd & Crawford, 2012; Parks, 2014). As with other technologies and types of information and data, what was once only accessible to few is now available for more agents, including 'scholars, marketers, governmental agencies, educational institutions, and motivated individuals' (boyd & Crawford, 2011, p. 664). The question of how to go about an analysis of large data sets does not require a trip to the local library: tricks and pitfalls can now be easily found in blog posts (Bar-Joseph, 2013).

The process of datafication, alongside questions on how to deal with the big data sets in question, brings several challenges. Anderson's bold assertion that '[w]ith enough data, the numbers speak for themselves' (2008) has been widely refuted, even in circles of researcher that are strongly associated with quantitative research. Moreover, if we think about the social world from an epistemological perspective, 'data' is ubiquitous; the (digital) ethnographer in the field – just like the big data analyst – is surrounded by data. The challenge then becomes to relate different pieces of data, trace and confirm patterns and make sense of what was found in the larger scheme of things. But often the assumption when it comes to large data sets is that they are (a) intrinsically relevant, (b) holistic and complete in describing phenomena that can be distinguished from other occurrences disconnected to or at least not effected by them and (c) clean – meaning that there are no corrupted data. This type of thinking, the underlying assumption that all answers are to be found by looking at data alone has been coined 'dataism'.

While working towards my PhD, I remember sitting in a doctoral workshop at the University of Glasgow, during which, a senior scholar encouraged us to 'trust our data'. For me, this meant trusting what I have observed during times of ethnographic field work, taking seriously field notes and what research participants had told me in interviews and focus groups. Interpretations, of course, need thinking, re-thinking, questioning. As in other areas of life (Turkle, 2011), there is a latent assumption that technology can do better than humans, that is technically generated or mechanically selected data sets are more reliable than those collected by personally and physically going to a field and gathering data. Dataism is an expression of the tendency to value technically generated or selected data higher, to view it as more objective and therefore more reliable, making theory obsolete. The famous case of correlation between S&P 500 stock index and butter production in Bangladesh (Leinweber, 2007) demonstrates that everything data suggests is neither true nor necessarily significant.

As has been shown for example in the case of large datasets gathered from Twitter, the data received is problematic. First of all, Twitter, like Facebook, offers very limited archiving capacities (boyd & Crawford, 2012). Consequently, there is a bias towards working with fairly recent data or data of the immediate past. Secondly, the data sets obtained are not necessarily complete or selected in a traceable manner. For example, to gather tweets and feed them into a data set, researchers work with an application programme interface (API). The majority of researchers have access to about 10 per cent of public tweets. This is due to terms and conditions set by Twitter Inc. So how are these 10 per cent of all public tweets selected? 'It could be that the API pulls a random sample of tweets or that it pulls the first few thousand tweets per hour or that it only pulls tweets from a particular segment of the network graph. Without knowing, it is difficult for researchers to make claims about the quality of the data they are analysing' (boyd & Crawford, 2012, p. 669). For many data sets relevant to communication research, the quality and therefore the reliability of the data is limited and access often depends on the goodwill of companies: '[O]nly social media companies have access to really large social data – especially transactional data. An anthropologist working for Facebook or a sociologist working for Google will have access to data that the rest of the scholarly community will not' (Manovich, 2011).

Alongside questions of access and data reliability, it is doubtful that research questions can always be answered in the best possible manner purely because of researchers working with a large data set. Java et al. (2007) found that people's motivations for using Twitter were the need to share and seek information as well as to sustain and conserve friendships. These results were based on the analysis of 1.3 million tweets from 76,177 users. But as Marwick (2014) rightly points out, conducting qualitative interviews and participant observation with Twitter users, is likely to bring out a much more refined picture of motivations, human–technology interactions, relationships and other issues at stake. The hype about big data and methods including computational analysis should not mean a turning away from small data sets. They hold very valuable insights too (boyd & Crawford, 2012). More often than not, the true promise of big data research might become apparent in combining big data research with other, perhaps especially, with qualitative research methods.

In the case of big data research on tweets, Axel Bruns and colleagues (Bruns, 2012; Bruns & Burgess, 2012; Bruns, Burgess, Crawford, & Shaw, 2012) have, among others, used big data analyses to map the shape and dynamics of large networks. While this is extremely useful for our understanding of the workings of large networks, such type of analyses tell us little about the meaning of networks, tweets, platforms in people's everyday life. By purposefully taking a small data approach, Stephanson and Couldry (2014) demonstrate that great insights can be gained on Twitter's influence on community and (collective) identity by combining a number of methods and by analysing a relatively small and context-specific number of tweets. The aim here is not to praise the virtue of one kind of research in contrast to the shortcomings of another but to acknowledge that each and every one method and approach comes with advantages as well as shortcomings.

Drawing on the work of Florian Znaniecki on 'the human coefficient', Christians and Carey (1989, p. 360) remind us that 'data always belong to somebody, that they are constructed *in vivo* and must be recovered accordingly'. Capturing data in vivo is of course a challenge in and of itself – and it is certainly not essential for every type of research question. However, Christians and Carey's (1989) point reminds us of two important aspects of data: For one, every insight gained through big data analysis gives information about the past. This is not specific to big data – all forms of content analyses do not provide first-hand information on how data was produced in vivo (e.g. in newsroom, in living rooms, on the go with mobile devices). However, when it comes to big data – because of the sheer amount of users considered – we know little about individual circumstances in which data was produced. Answering the question of whether we can use our understanding of the past to predict the future goes beyond the remits of this contribution. But nevertheless, with only a rudimentary understanding or a good estimate of what goes on 'on the ground' where data originates, the quality of predictions and even of the analyses are likely to decline.

The second point raised by Christians and Carey (1989) relates back to dataism. At times there seems to be an unconscious detachment regarding the origin of data. As social and cultural researchers, we are generally interested in data directly or indirectly generated by humans or through human–technology interaction. Big data research in the field of communication makes use of people's digital footprints or data trails. However, the question of ownership of these data is highly contentious. The recent verdict of the European Court of Justice forced Google Inc. to delete certain information about a Spanish citizen (Travis & Arthur, 2014). In a similar vein, the 'right to be forgotten' – a concept originally coined by Victor Mayer-Schönberger (2009) and taken up by policy makers as well as NGOs and civil liberties groups (Rosen, 2012) – has been discussed widely and, in fact, is a concern to many users. From an ethical perspective, big data then does not happen in a void. Can we imagine a scenario where permissions to use tweets have to be sought from each and every single user in a large data set? For medical records, that is certainly the case. But access to and power over data is not straightforward. Will we allow companies such as Twitter, Facebook and Google to negotiate ethical concerns or even to simply ignore them?

The huge promises of big data are therefore accompanied by a number of serious challenges. The following section will approach challenges big data poses in light of discussions surrounding digital ethnography and the aims of qualitative research more generally.

RECONSIDERING BIG DATA AND DIGITAL ETHNOGRAPHY FROM A QUALITATIVE PERSPECTIVE

From a communication scholar's perspective, digital ethnography and big data are both linked to processes of digitisation and mediatisation. We live with what Couldry (2011) has called a 'media manifold' in which the majority of highly diverse aspects of everyday life are directly or indirectly mediated (Hepp, 2010; Livingstone, 2009). The dynamic configurations of mobile and more or less stationary technical devices form part of everyday life and allow for a 'connected presence':

> We can now, if we wish, be permanently open (and potentially responsive) to content from all directions. Many writers see the practice (or even compulsion) of continuous connectivity as characteristic of the 'digital native' generation. [...] Keeping all channels open means permanently orienting oneself to the world beyond one's private space and the media that are circulated within it. (Couldry, 2012, p. 55)

Communication devices are either at the centre of our actions and attention or on the periphery. Most significantly though, they are ubiquitous

(Hand, 2012) and they intersect, influence, form and arrange aspects of our material world. I will return to this point in greater detail below.

With this in mind, researching media and communication is a highly complex undertaking and several methods have been developed to adhere to research questions and capture the needed data. Along interviews, focus groups, surveys – all methods common to the social sciences more generally, there are some which are more specific to media and communication research, such as different forms of content analysis and media ethnography. Media ethnography is used to gather data on websites or digital media more generally. Of course ethnographies as well as large datasets are possible outside of the digital realm; examples could be large datasets on television viewing habits in a pre-Internet era and ethnographies of newspaper readers. But it cannot be ignored that both of these approaches to research – media ethnography and big data analyses – have gained momentum in the digital era. After introducing digital ethnography in more detail, the chapter will move on to consider in which ways big data research might benefit by considering some of the challenges which digital ethnographic researchers have had to face.

Digital ethnography[1] is based on the anthropological and sociological approach of treating a certain space as a field. In traditional anthropology, this was generally speaking a certain locale which the researcher would travel to and make him or herself 'at home' – as far as that was possible – in order to gather data. An exemplary anthropologist was supposed to 'go native', live just like or at least alongside the 'tribe' she was researching and, once substantial amounts of data were gathered, return home to interpret field notes, recorded conversations and so on. A pivotal characteristic of this type of research is the close, embodied and personal relationship between researcher and researched (see Coffey, 1999). Interestingly, and perhaps in contrast to what one might come to expect, field relations do not end with the researcher leaving the field. A very common experience of ethnographic work is that the field turns out to be 'sticky' as it stays present on the researcher's mind much longer than could be expected. Okely (1994, p. 32) eloquently describes this process:

> [T]he experience of anthropological material is, like fieldwork, a continuing and creative experience. The research has combined action and contemplation. Scrutiny of the notes offers both empirical certainty and intuitive reminders. Insights emerge also from the subconscious and from bodily memories, never penned on paper. [...] The author is not alienated from the experience of participant observation, but draws upon it both precisely and amorphously for the resolution of the completed text.

Following this approach, ethnographic research consists of a mix of methods, including interviews as well as informal chats with people encountered in the field, focus groups and (participant) observation. While the individual methods employed might vary strongly depending on the field and the research questions, the main commonality of ethnographic studies is that the researcher makes a conscious effort of understanding the field and the people he or she researches from *their* perspective. In an ideal scenario, the researcher simultaneously manages to keep a certain level of objectivity and a critical capacity of what he or she encounters which is not easy as field relations quickly become complex and multi-dimensional (Lohmeier, 2014).

Among others, Christine Hine must be acknowledged as one of the pioneers of media or virtual ethnography. Like 'regular' ethnography, media ethnography is a mix of method (see for example Hine, 2000) which has gained ever higher levels popularity in communication research. The opportunity to examine communities and interactions in social information and communication technologies (SICT) has led to a steep increase on studies focusing on communication practices online.

In traditional ethnographies, scholars distinguish between emic and etic approaches to the field. While the former indicates that the researcher is part of the community he or she investigates, the latter implies that the researcher is in fact an intruder who has not been socialised in the context s/he now examines. Both types of field relations have advantages and disadvantages. An emic researcher, for example a person researching the community he or she has been brought up in, might be highly familiar with certain behavioural patterns and structures encouraging or hindering certain actions. In this case, the researcher will need a lot less time of familiarising himself or herself with the field and with what is at stake. Then again, the fact of belonging somewhere and being seen as 'one of us' in the widest sense by research participants, might also have certain disadvantages. If, the field in question is highly polarised, research participants are likely to assign the researcher to a 'side'. Whether this is justified or not, is another matter.

Imagine a research project on the memories of the Troubles in Northern Ireland. Clearly, an etic researcher, who in an ideal scenario even comes from outside of the United Kingdom and Ireland, might have more success of building rapport with informants than someone who is perceived as biased right from the start. On the other hand, there might be complexities and intricacies of the field that the etic researcher might completely miss out on because certain phenomena which are relevant in this particular field are not familiar from her own background. Similarly, there might be prejudices among informants about a researcher coming from a different background. So both ways of doing research, emic and etic, have benefits as well as drawbacks. But whether one or the other, good research ends with insights, understanding and in all likelihood more questions to answer and follow up on. The term 'understanding' is often linked back to qualitative or 'soft' science. However, as Wax (1971, pp. 10–11) points out, understanding is not meant in the sense of empathy:

> Understanding does not refer to a mysterious empathy between human beings. Nor does it refer to an intuitive or rationalistic ascription of motivations. Instead, it is a social phenomenon – a phenomenon of *shared* meanings. Thus a fieldworker who approaches a strange people soon perceives that this people are saying and doing things which they understand but he does not understand. One of the strangers may make a particular gesture, whereupon all the other strangers laugh. They share in the understanding of what the gesture means, but the fieldworker does not. When he does share it, he begins to 'understand'. He possesses a part of the insider's view.

The distinction between emic and etic field relations forms part of practising reflexivity. In ethnographic work, this conscious reflection of field relations and potential blind spots and biases is clearly encouraged. In the case of digital ethnographies, it is not common to make explicit one's relationship to the subject of study.

But what could be gained by doing so, by reflecting on the researcher's relation the subject? What is striking when considering digital ethnography as well as big data, is the prominence of data in our relating to it. But would it not make sense to also consider how we relate to this data at the start and throughout the research process? This is not meant to encourage a normative stance in researchers, labelling something as good or bad. What I'm aiming for here is a subjective perspective of the data analysed. If we stick with an analysis of tweets, short messages published through Twitter as described above, does it make a difference if the researcher uses Twitter himself or herself? Does it matter if he enjoys using it or not? Obviously, for crunching numbers in quantitative analyses, this might not matter so much as the actual calculation seems fairly standardised. But just like in a digital ethnography, the researchers' insights about the way Twitter can be used and put to use for individuals, has an influence on the sort of research questions she might ask.

A bit more than a decade ago, Marc Prensky (2001) coined the concept of 'digital natives' and 'digital immigrants'. In communication research, the distinction of those having grown up with digital technologies and gadgets as opposed to those who have learned how to live with these technologies at a later point in life has been useful. When considering digital data, be it in the form of digital ethnography or big data, the distinction where a researcher stands could be useful too. Drawing on the work of Lash and Lunenfeld, Beneito-Montagut (2011, p. 720) emphasises the following with regard to (digital) ethnography in today's world:

> Ethnography in this dynamic arena eventually necessitates a 'technologized' researcher (Lash, 2002; Lunenfeld, 2000). Moreover, paradoxically, in order to achieve reflexive, critical, precise descriptions of internet phenomena we need both to 'speed-up' to follow our fast-moving objects of analysis and to 'slow down' to understand them properly. [...][Some studies] are more concerned with the features of the technology than with the forms and meaning of social interaction online.

The danger is indeed that a focus on technologies and data becomes an end in itself. As researchers we are at times so enthralled with the wealth of digital data and what could possibly be done with it, that there is a danger is to forget what the most pressing research questions are. Moreover, being critical and reflective of a researcher's relation to technology can be highly useful. Returning to the case of Twitter as an example, boyd and Crawford (2012, p. 669) remind us that, for one, Twitter does not 'represent "all people"' and it is wrong to assume that '"people" and "Twitter users" are synonymous' as some users might have multiple accounts – and some accounts have multiple users. In addition, some accounts are so-called 'bots' which 'produce automated content without directly involving a person'. Some 'users' might never establish a Twitter account but 'listen in' via the web (Crawford, 2009). What do definitions of 'user', 'participation' and 'active' mean in this context? Understanding the technical side of Twitter and its affordances, that is how this technology is and can be used, is absolutely essential when considering the results that come out of big data analyses. This background information is not only highly useful but also essential in making sense of the results.

A second challenge digital research has to face is a re-focusing on contexts. In what has become known as the material turn, researchers are encouraged to pay attention to how objects and the physicality as well as different spaces of life interact with what was originally called the virtual life. What we are experiencing are two simultaneous but highly related developments; for one, there is the increasing mediatisation of everyday life; it seems that for some individuals, all areas of life are mediated and life without media seems unthinkable. Secondly, the material turn in the humanities reminds us that – despite digitisation and the mediatisation of everyday life, objects and the physicality of what surrounds us is still highly significant and should not be neglected in our conceptualisations. The challenge of course lies in creating research methods, which capture online *and* offline life and their intersections.

Studies relying solely or to a great extent on big data or digital ethnography alone, run the risk of being disconnected from social reality. In other words, according to proponents of the material turn, these kinds of studies tell us only about a very limited interaction which research subjects engage with in their everyday life. What it takes, is a multi-sited and user-focused way of research, that does not hold data and thereby datafication in a more esteemed sense than social reality. In the case of digital ethnography, Beneito-Montagut and others (2011, p. 730; see also Christine Hine on the University of Surrey Youtube Channel, 2013) argue for what Beneito-Montagut calls an extended or 'expanded ethnography' which goes beyond looking at single-media use and even viewing the digital world as a field in itself:

> [A]n extended ethnography is multi-situated, user centred, flexible and multimedia. It requires highlighting again that the strength of expanded ethnography lies in its capacity to analyse in-depth complex interactions, avoiding artificial divisions of linked social phenomena and problems for their analysis. Meanwhile, it needs to be considered that such a user-centered approach requires a clear ethic guideline.

Following this criticism and the re-focusing of communication research in digital times, we need theories and research methods which place people and their social practices at the heart of research activities. In times of digital/big data, online and offline spaces overlap to such a great extent and they are so vastly interdependent, that the next big challenge is for research to develop methodologies which allow us to capture these realities:

> Social practices change as digital spaces become embedded in a culture. People may feel anxious if a smart phone is lost or an internet connection gets disrupted, and making a New Year's resolution or celebrating Lent may involve forgoing access to electronic devices. (Hallett & Barber, 2014, p. 310)

The challenge for digital ethnography has been to move away from the one-dimensionality of data. For convenience sake, online activity has often been viewed as an isolated action. Online ethnographies of one particular site are still a legitimate way of gathering data and – depending on the research question – they can indeed bring new insights. However, there is also a strong calling to not view certain media practices as isolated events but see them in the context of a wider media ecology (Hoskins & O'Loughlin, 2010) in which individuals use, read, consume, produce, contribute, collect, share, comment, like, link, create and so on, and in which collectives come together, grow, decline and disintegrate over the space of time. Even with the promises of big data analyses, the challenges will be similar to the ones that digital ethnographers have to address and are still in the process of solving.

CONCLUSION

After an overview of big data use in communication research, this chapter addressed some of the myths and thinking surrounding big data. The criticism of processes coined 'dataism' and 'datafication' is a reminder to refocus and to not get carried away by the sheer availability of relatively large data sets. The never-ending field to be found by the (digital) researcher does not make all data and the results they yield relevant or every sample desirable for analysis. The challenge remains to find methodologies that capture, record and analyse the complexities of media practice as opposed to reducing them.

NOTE

1. Depending on the time and context of writing, the term used might also be 'virtual' or 'media' ethnography.

REFERENCES

Anderson, C. (2008). *The end of theory: Will the data deluge makes the scientific method obsolete?* Retrieved from http://edge.org/3rd_culture/anderson08/anderson08_index.html

Bar-Joseph, U. (2013). *Big data = big trouble: How to avoid 5 data analysis pitfalls.* Retrieved from http://searchenginewatch.com/article/2289574/Big-Data-Big-Trouble-How-to-Avoid-5-Data-Analysis-Pitfalls. Accessed on April 30, 2014.

Beneito-Montagut, R. (2011). Ethnography goes online: Towards a user-centred methodology to research interpersonal communication on the internet. *Qualitative Research*, *11*(6), 716–735. doi:10.1177/1468794111413368

boyd, d., & Crawford, K. (2011). Six Provocations for Big Data. A Decade in Internet Time: Symposium on the Dynamics of the Internet and Society. Retrieved from http://ssrn.com/abstract=1926431. Accessed in September 2011.

boyd, d., & Crawford, K. (2012). Critical questions for big data. *Information, Communication & Society*, *15*(5), 662–679. doi:10.1080/1369118X.2012.678878

Bruns, A. (2012). How long is a tweet? Mapping dynamic conversation networks on Twitter using Gawk and Gephi. *Information, Communication and Society*, *15*(9), 1323–1351. doi:10.1080/1369118X.2011.635214

Bruns, A., & Burgess, J. E. (2012). Researching news discussion on Twitter: New methodologies. *Journalism Studies*, *13*(56), 801–814. doi:10.1080/1461670X.2012.664428

Bruns, A., Burgess, J. E., Crawford, K., & Shaw, F. (2012). *#qldfloods and @QPSMedia: Crisis communication on Twitter in the 2011 South East Queensland floods*. Research report (pp. 1–58). Retrieved from http://eprints.qut.edu.au/48241/. Accessed on June 16, 2014.

Christians, G., & Carey, J. W. (1989). The logics and aims of qualitative research. In G. H. I. Stempel & B. H. Westley (Eds.), *Research methods in mass communication* (pp. 354–374). Englewood Cliffs, NJ: Prentice Hall.

Coffey, A. (1999). *The ethnographic self: Fieldwork and the representation of identity*. London: Sage.

Couldry, N. (2011). The necessary future of the audience … and how to research it. In V. Nightingale (Ed.), *The handbook of media audiences* (pp. 213–229). Oxford: Wiley-Blackwell. doi:10.1002/9781444340525.ch10

Couldry, N. (2012). *Media, society, world: Social theory and digital media practice*. Boston, MA: Polity Press.

Crawford, K. (2009). Following you: Disciplines of listening in social media. *Continuum: Journal of Media & Cultural Studies*, *23*(4), 525–535.

Halevi, G., & Moed, H. (2012). The evolution of big data as research and scientific topic: Overview of the literature. *Research Trends. Special Issue on Big Data*. (30), 3–6. Retrieved from http://www.researchtrends.com/wp-content/uploads/2012/09/Research_Trends_Issue30.pdf. Accessed on April 30, 2014.

Hallett, R., & Barber, K. (2014). Ethnographic research in a cyber era. *Journal of Contemporary Ethnography*, *43*(3), 306–330.

Hand, M. (2012). *Ubiquitous photography*. Cambridge: Polity.

Hepp, A. (2010). Researching 'mediatised worlds': Non-mediacentric media and communication research as a challenge. In N. Carpentier, I. Tomanic Trivundza, P. Pruulmann-Vengerfeldt, E. Sundin, T. Olsson, R. Kilborn, H. Nieminen, & B. Cammaerts, (Eds.), *Media and communication studies interventions and intersections* (pp. 37–48). Tartu, Estonia: Tartu University Press.

Hine, C. (2000). *Virtual ethnography*. London: Sage.

Hoskins, A., & O'Loughlin, B. (2010). *War and media. The emergence of diffused war*. Cambridge: Polity.

Lash, S. (2002). *Critique of information*. London: Sage.

Leinweber, D. (2007). Stupid data miner tricks: Overfitting the S&P 500. *The Journal of Investing*, *16*(1), 721–723.

Livingstone, S. (2009). On the mediation of everything: ICA presidential address 2008. *Journal of Communication*, *59*(1), 1–18.

Lohmeier, C. (2014). *Cuban Americans and the Miami media*. Jefferson, NC: McFarland.

Lunenfeld, P. (2000). *Snap to grid: A user's guide to digital arts, media and cultures*. Cambridge, MA: MIT Press.

Manovich, L. (2011). Trending: the promises and the challenges of big social data. In M. K. Gold (Eds.), *Debates in the digital humanities*. Minneapolis, MN: The University of Minneapolis Press. Retrieved from http://www.manovich.net/DOCS/Manovich_trending_paper.pdf. Accessed on April 30, 2014.

Marwick, A. E. (2014). Ethnographic and qualitative research on twitter. In K. Weller, A. Bruns, J. Burgess, M. Mahrt, & C. Puschmann (Eds.), *Twitter and society*. New York, NY: Peter Lang.

Mayer-Schönberger, V. (2009). *Delete: The virtue of forgetting in the digital age*. Princeton, NJ: Princeton University Press.

Mayer-Schönberger, V., & Cukier, K. (2013). *Big data: A revolution that will transform how we live, work, and think*. Boston, MA: Houghton Mifflin Harcourt.

Okely, J. (1994). Thinking through fieldwork. In A. Bryman, & R. G. Burgess (Eds.), *Analyzing qualitative data* (pp. 1–34). London: Routledge.

Parks, M. R. (2014). Big data in communication research: Its contents and discontents. *Journal of Communication, 64*, 355–360. doi:10.1111/jcom12090

Prensky, M. (2001). *Digital native, digital immigrant*. Retrieved from http://www.marcprensky.com/writing/Prensky%20-%20Digital%20Natives,%20Digital%20Immigrants%20-%20Part1.pdf. Accessed on May 1, 2014.

Rosen, J. (2012, February 13). *The right to be forgotten*. 64 STAN. L.REV.ONLINE 88. Retrieved from http://www.stanfordlawreview.org/sites/default/files/online/topics/64-SLRO-88.pdf. Accessed on June 9, 2014.

Stephanson, H., & Couldry, N. (2014). Understanding micro-processes of community building and mutual learning on twitter: A 'small data' approach. *Information, Communication & Society*. doi:10.1080/1369118X.2014.902984

Travis, A., & Arthur, C. (2014). EU court back 'right to be forgotten': Google must amend results on request. *The Guardian,* May 13. Retrieved from http://www.theguardian.com/technology/2014/may/13/right-to-be-forgotten-eu-court-google-search-results. Accessed on June 9.

Turkle, S. (2011). *Alone together: Why we expect more from technology and less from each other*. New York, NY: Basic Books.

University of Surrey Youtube Channel. (2013). *Christine Hine on online research methods*. Retrieved from http://www.youtube.com/watch?v=No8RZOebhX8. Accessed on May 1, 2014.

Wax, R. (1971). *Doing fieldwork: Warnings and advice*. Chicago, IL: University of Chicago Press.

RESEARCHING FORUMS IN ONLINE ETHNOGRAPHY: PRACTICE AND ETHICS

Emma Hutchinson

ABSTRACT

Purpose – *To examine the potential for including forums in an online ethnography that draws on data from multiple online sites.*

Methodology/approach – *Taking a broadly post-structuralist approach to identity and embodiment online, the research drew on three sources of data: asynchronous email interviews, in-game participant observation and six months of forum observation.*

Findings – *The community in question was socially located around multiple field sites online and forums remain an integral part of the social lives of online gamers. The practice and ethics for examining forums from a qualitative perspective are outlined and how this can fit into an ethnographic account. Some of the data is then presented from this strand of the research to illustrate how researching a forum as a 'lurker' can complement theoretical trajectories and analyses from other parts of the dataset.*

Big Data? Qualitative Approaches to Digital Research
Studies in Qualitative Methodology, Volume 13, 91–112

ISSN: 1042-3192/doi:10.1108/S1042-319220140000013007

Originality – *This research details a novel way of examining forums qualitatively as part of a larger dataset. Furthermore, the chapter posits how relatively unobtrusive methods of observation can bring to the fore the ways in which prejudice still structures online social interaction.*

Keywords: Forums; online gaming; online ethics; heteronormativity

INTRODUCTION

Forums have long been an important part of the internet, with the earliest forerunners, bulletin boards, having been in existence since the early 1980s (Rheingold, 1994). Despite the growth of social media, forums on a variety of topics still play an important role in online social interaction (Bryson, 2004; Hine, 2008; Jones, 1998; Kaigo & Watanabe, 2007; Kivits, 2004; Williams, 2006). In my study of the enactment of identity and the social norms in an online game, forums still featured heavily in the social lives of players who were looking to connect with others to talk about the game. As part of an ethnographic study of the Massively Multiplayer Online Role Playing Game (MMORPG) Final Fantasy XIV, I spent nearly six months conducting a qualitative observation of the game's official forum, which was set up by the development company Square Enix. An examination of players talking about the game was highly revealing of their social attitudes and the framing of how they can enact identity in the game and its related spaces. This chapter initially examines some of the benefits and pitfalls of studying forums, for example the potential for qualitative studies of forums and how they can be established. It is also important to examine the ethics of studying forums since they can seem to be easy pickings for the novice social researcher looking to quickly grab data for a project, but also locate the study of forums in an ethical framework that respects users. The next section examines how to conduct a qualitative study of a forum, with examples of my own practices in the study, such as the approach to sampling and the use of NVivo to code forum data with other data from the study. Finally, the chapter concludes with some examples of forum discussions that were used in relation to the players' attitudes towards gender and sexual norms.

THE BENEFITS AND DISADVANTAGES OF STUDYING A FORUM

Forums are attractive to social science researchers for a number of reasons. It is possible to easily view forums with little prior experience of using the internet or specialist equipment (Hine, 2008). In many cases, it is possible to view a forum without signing up to become a member as they are often publicly viewable. Forums will also have membership options to sign up in different ways, often by selecting a username and password and entering minimal personal details. Typically, only forum users can write messages on threads, which are lists of different users' responses to each other. On some forums, there are also sections that are only visible to registered users. Threads are normally moderated according to a code of conduct set out in the forum's rules by a group of users called either administrators or moderators. This code often revolves around maintaining polite and respectful language when interacting with other users and the avoidance of causing offence through 'flaming' or deliberately making abusive or inflammatory remarks.

In most cases, forums are thus relatively straightforward to access even for those with little experience of the internet. Hine (2008) also points out that this ease also poses a risk to users, where it can seem easy for researchers to systematically harvest data from a forum in one fell swoop without users knowing. Rather, Hine (2008) posits that much more can be learned from a forum by spending time participating as a user, or even as 'lurkers', who are users or casual visitors who only read a forum rather than interact. Orgad (2009) defines the career of a forum user in an interesting fashion. She puts forward how many users initially act as 'lurkers' on a website and may spend time reading a forum before starting to join in. At this stage, they may not even fully sign up as a user but browse any publicly available material to see if it is interesting, or if the community is convivial. After some time, they may start to engage with the forum by writing messages on threads and finding their feet. This user trajectory is helpful for understanding the ways in which internet users utilise forums and how social researchers can also navigate them. 'Lurkers' are often deemed difficult to capture in forum-based research since they remain silent and do not leave any traces (Williams, 2007). This does not necessarily mean that they are not participating, and may even feel they are part of the community even by frequently reading threads. Similarly, Hine (2008) suggests that an online ethnography of a forum necessitates regular visits to the forum to experience how discussions unfold, and where appropriate, participate by writing posts. Social researchers can thus involve themselves in a forum in various ways other than just taking data, with degrees of participation that can be developed over time.

One problem with researching forums that follows is the perception of privacy versus the actual level of privacy afforded by the site set-up. This issue will be returned to in fuller detail in the ethics section, however for now it is important to note that forums and blogs are often viewed as a space intended for a particular audience (Moinian, 2006). Unlike many forums, the official Final Fantasy XIV forum can be read in its entirety without a login, hence the moderators kept reminding users that their posts could be read. Above, I noted the different ways that presence can be interpreted on a forum. Hine (2008) holds that studies of forums need the researcher to experience the forum as a full participant, rather than simply taking data. By necessity, I had to be a 'lurker' observer, but engaged with the forum by visiting it over the course of the day, on an almost daily basis, for nearly six months and looking over the most popular threads and ongoing conversations. These issues will be addressed more fully in the later ethics section.

It is also important to discern the different voices on a forum, where certain users become more vocal and tend to dominate conversation, or how the tone of a community can change over time or in response to particular events. A study of the large Japanese forum Channel 2 ('ni-channeru') suggested that the tone of a forum can change (Kaigo & Watanabe, 2007). Channel 2 is known for its disruptive, aggressive nature, which is often associated with the anonymous nature of interaction since users are not obliged to set up a username to take part and there are no moderators. Nevertheless, certain users became prominent voices on the forum regardless. In response to the circulation of graphic videos of the execution of a Japanese man taken hostage in Iraq in 2004, the tone of the forum changed and moderated itself by removing the offending images and videos from the forum. Certain users also took charge of this process and actively deleted the offending posts and videos. This study was successful since the authors had spent time on the forum and noted the change in interaction, which may not have been so pronounced to someone who had merely taken forum threads for analysis. Additionally, a simple 'harvest' of threads may have even missed such a thread altogether. Spending time on a forum also enables a researcher to effectively map the forum as part of a study, for example the potential to view it as part of an ethnographic project. The remainder of this section sets out how a study of a forum can form an interesting and vivid part of an online ethnography that takes in multiple sites.

Online ethnography still needs to clearly define the field site, which may be less straightforward. Traditionally, ethnography requires time spent in a particular bounded location while undertaking the study (Hine, 2000). In offline ethnography, one must still decide on the field site, which tends to be driven more by a particular location, such as a school, or an interesting group (Hammersley & Atkinson, 2007). Further negotiation may be needed after starting fieldwork to further refine the field site, such as access to a particular class (Delamont, 2002). With online ethnography, the field site is less bounded by a geographical location, though certain examples exist, such as Silver's (2000) study of internet use in Blacksburg, Virginia, where Virginia Tech and the local authorities both contributed to infrastructure improvements to bring the city online at a much faster rate than elsewhere. Another approach can be identified, through the recognition of the researcher's involvement in co-constructing the field site through engagement with respondents and the community being studied.

Boellstorff (2009) makes the claim that online ethnography involves creating a field site by reflexively engaging with respondents within a community and through participant observation. Markham (2005) also points to the need for online research to actively map a field site, which does not exist prior to (or outside of) the research process. This entails the researcher paying attention to her own actions, such as the search terms and search engines used to find the site, as well as examining how respondents construct boundaries in field sites (Markham, 2005). As a result, online ethnography involves an active participation in bounding the field site. Most ethnographic accounts of online games and worlds concern multiple, linked spaces. Taylor (2006) refers to EverQuest and related websites for guilds, databases, and forums for example, noting the 'distributed social sphere' (p. 51) around gaming, as players extend the social space of the game. Pearce and Artemesia (2009) followed the Uru group around different online worlds, such as There.com and Second Life, as well as other websites used by the group.

As part of my study into Final Fantasy XIV, I not only spent time in the game itself and interviewing other players, but also mapped the other types of websites they visited, including YouTube to watch videos of others playing, wiki pages to learn about the game, and multiple modes of interacting with other players. These included social media, blogs, as well as forums for the game. In a broad sense, the field of Final Fantasy XIV and its English-speaking players was thus large. Given the size, I tended to focus on the more popular means for players to interact with each other, and forums remain a key part of the online gaming experience (Williams, 2007). For my study, it was therefore important to incorporate them in some way. The following section considers my approach to the forum in practical terms, as well as how I coded the data.

RESEARCH METHOD AND PLANNING

The research on the forum was intended to be complementary to the rest of the dataset. Initially, I started with three months of participant observation in the game Final Fantasy XIV and mapped the different sites visited by the community, such as forums, blogs, wiki pages, YouTube videos and so on. The next phase included 36 asynchronous online interviews, mostly conducted either over email or private messaging through two popular forums. Some of these were also image elicitation whereby I asked players for images of their avatar to discuss in the course of interviews. In the final phase, I decided to study the official forum for the game, which is run by the development company behind the game, Square Enix.

In March 2011, my original plan had been to spend some time with a group known as a Linkshell. These are informal groups of friends and acquaintances who spend time together in the game. On 8 March 2011, an official forum was finally launched by the developer Square Enix. The above-mentioned forums are independent of the company that develops the game, but there had been nothing officially run by the developers. The forum was launched to enable greater levels of communication between the development team and the fans, following its poor reception in the gaming media, with the game's producer Naoki Yoshida regularly reading both the Japanese and English language forums, though he only posted messages on the Japanese section. The forum proved popular with players very quickly, especially since they believed their thoughts on the game would influence the developers. Following the Tohoku Earthquake on 11 March 2011, the company decided within a day to take the game offline due to the power problems that were affecting Japan. As a result, there were practical considerations in deciding to examine the forum.

During the time when the servers were offline, the new forum became very popular, partly as a way for players to express their condolences about the disaster in Japan, and for players to talk about the future direction of the game. Initially I looked at the forum perhaps as a way of gaining more interviews as I had gained interview respondents via messages posted on other forums. I had originally messaged the moderators on two forums to find out if I could post my message on their forums to look for interviewees and the users stated that they were pleased that I had approached the administrators in this fashion. However, it became apparent that this would not be possible on the new official forum for the game. The forum has a strict policy preventing users from revealing their 'true' identities. Users were constantly reminded that the forum is a public space, since it can be viewed without logging in. If a player mentioned where they were from, or went into too much detail about their life, a moderator would often interject and delete such material from their post. Moderators would also often post messages in threads reminding users to not reveal personal details. This meant that I was unable to reveal myself as a researcher, nor contact moderators separately in the way that I had done before as there was no email address for them. I suspected that without permission from a moderator, my request may be viewed with some suspicion by the other forum users, following my experience with the other forums where players approved of my contact with the administrators, but also that the moderators would probably remove my request as it would be revealing too much about myself.

In order to get a feel for the forum, I read the majority of the threads posted in the first two weeks to see what players were discussing. After a while, it became apparent that so many threads were being posted that it was not possible to either keep up with them, nor would it have been practical to analyse all of them. I decided it would be best to focus on the longer threads, as well as regularly skimming others which would be the most useful for my study. The idea was to flesh out some of the meanings attributed to avatars and parts of their creation, such as online race and gender, following the themes of the interviews. Moreover, the data offered greater insight into the opinions and values held by the players. Official forums for such games are often slightly different compared to those run by fans. Fan-run forums tend to be stricter about politeness and etiquette, but fairly relaxed about users revealing a degree of personal information about themselves. The official forum took a different line where only swearing was an outright problem and arguments were allowed to continue for a longer period of time than on a fan forum. Users were actively prevented from talking about their personal lives as moderators would interject and remove anything deemed too personal from posts. These differences led to variations in the tone of interactions as well as the content especially in regard to homophobia and gender norms. It quickly became apparent that an undercurrent of homophobia pervaded certain types of posts, which gave insight into the values of the players.

I focused on a section called 'General Discussion'. The forum has 50 separate sections for each language area (Japanese, English, French and German), mostly concerned with specific elements of the game. General Discussion was the most-viewed section during this time, and comprised a wide range of topics relating to the game. I visited this section on a daily basis during the observation period and saved the most relevant threads. These were selected partly on the basis of popularity, in terms of page views and number of replies, which were listed next to the title of the thread, and how close the subject matter was to the research questions. Hundreds were saved locally on my computer, but only the most relevant 33 forum threads were included in the dataset.

Coding began during the first phase of interviews, and became a continual process during fieldwork. All of the interviews were saved into Word files then imported into NVivo for coding. Later, forum threads were imported in the same fashion, after being saved locally on my computer then formatted in Word. The speed with which coding can start is one of the benefits of conducting online research in this manner, as the interviews essentially transcribe themselves when conducted via email. Online research thus lends itself readily to using Computer Assisted Qualitative Data Analysis Software (CAQDAS) for coding purposes. CAQDAS is often associated with grounded theory methods of coding, where the researcher examines the data, building concepts until theoretical saturation is reached (Strauss & Corbin, 1998). However, Coffey, Rendd, Dicks, Soyinka, and Mason (2006) suggest that such software can be used to expose how analysis is not a linear process, but can demonstrate hypertextual links within data for example. Though research is expected to be written up into a narrative, the messy nature of much research, and the continuous nature of analysis needs to be recognised (Baym & Markham, 2009). This messiness can be revealed through the use of CAQDAS with larger datasets that encourage the use of technology in coding, especially where different types of data, such as written and visual, can be juxtaposed and linked together in interesting ways.

ETHICS ONLINE

Ethics codes of professional bodies, such as those of the British Sociological Association (BSA) and Economic and Social Research

Council (ESRC), tend to overly problematise online research. Both suggest that online research warrants close exploration of ethics, due to its relatively recent development. Orton-Johnson (2010) holds that online research is overly scrutinised in these ethics codes, with neither differentiating between the internet as a culture, or a methodological tool. By declaring that all research involving an online component warrants a full review of ethics also equates such research with research 'involving more than minimal risk' (ESRC, 2010, §1.2.3). This list includes research with vulnerable groups, covert research, or research which could endanger the researcher and/or respondents, as well as '[r]esearch involving respondents through the internet, in particular where visual images are used, and where sensitive issues are discussed' (ESRC, 2010, §1.2.3).

Orton-Johnson (2010) prefers the Association of Internet Researchers' (AoIR) code of ethics, which takes a more nuanced view of internet research. It encourages the researcher to consider different aspects of online cultures and how ethical frameworks vary between countries, which is important where online cultures can be international (AoIR, 2002). For example, the American perspective tends to consider the utilitarian approach of risk versus cost and liability for the institution, whereas European countries are concerned with the welfare of respondents. This ethical framework also considers how respondents are subjects of the research (thus under the remit of human subjects research), and/or authors of texts that are being researched (e.g. bloggers, journalists, forum users). As a result, the debate over public and private spaces online can become complicated. In a recent update to its ethics statement, the AoIR has established a section of their website where case studies can be published for researchers to refer to, as a way of creating a practice-based approach to ethics as new methods and types of website are created (AoIR, 2012). My research concerns both an online culture, and using the internet as a research tool.

Research into online forums, as well as other textual material drawn from the internet, has been considered problematic. Eynon, Fry, and Schroeder (2008) hold that the main issue is how the internet offers 'privacy in public' (p. 27). The AoIR (2002) also suggests that researchers need to consider how their respondents view their online contributions – do they perceive their forum posts or blogs as for private audiences only? Svenningsson Elm (2009) clarifies the problem further, by positing notions of public and private online as a continuum. She borrows from Gold's notion of the different types of participant observation (from full observer to full participant, and variations along the way), and characterises different levels of public and private: public; semi-public (accessible to anyone but requires registration); semi-private (requires membership dictated by formal requirements); and private. This list is by no means exhaustive, but provides a useful starting point. Svenningsson Elm (2009) also puts forward the idea of 'fuzzy boundaries', which leave users in a potentially precarious position, where they may not realise how public their communication is (p. 77). These ideas also complicate researchers' attempts to garner informed consent. With forums, the questions revolve around the fuzzy boundary, and the audience that the user believes she is writing for.

So, how can forums be approached ethically as a research site? Anyone can view the official Final Fantasy XIV forum, however only players with active accounts could post messages. Moderators constantly reminded users not to reveal personal information about themselves for this reason. Yet, this did not seem to prevent users posting personal material. Moinian (2006) suggests that bloggers believe their audience will be sympathetic towards their posts, and the same could be said of forums. Even where a forum is publicly available, users may assume that only people who are sympathetic will read the forum, especially if it caters towards a particular interest. The perception of privacy (and anonymity) leads to a degree of disinhibition on forums too. Consequently, the material from the forum also needs to be handled sensitively, and usernames are removed. The next section gives some examples of discussions from the forum around the theme of heteronormativity. Part of the study's aims included examining the role of heteronormativity, or the assumption of heterosexuality and gender norms in gaming communities, and the rules of the forum permitted discussion of topics that are often deemed potentially inflammatory elsewhere.

HETERONORMATIVITY AND THE OFFICIAL FORUM

The study pursued a series of questions relating to the intersections of the avatar's identity and embodiment. At the outset of such games, players are expected to create an avatar from a series of options including gender, which is often presented in a binary fashion. In the course of interviews, it had become apparent that many players still relied on heteronormativity to make sense of gender online, whereby biological sex and gender were perceived to match, even between player and avatar. For the most part, players assumed that the gender of the avatar and the sex of the player were congruent, with a few exceptions where self-defined male players switched gender with the avatar. This was sometimes defined in terms of a female avatar as being 'nicer' to look at, which is a long-held stereotype among online gamers (Huh & Williams, 2010). This particular point will be returned to in the next section. When I started to study the official forum, I wanted to continue with this theme by searching for threads that concerned gender and sexuality. One of the noticeable qualities of the official forum is that moderators do not necessarily prevent particular types of discussion taking place. Many forums for online gaming actively prevent players talking about sexuality. Following a series of arguments around erotic roleplay (ERP) and Lesbian, Gay, Bisexual and Transgender (LGBT) guilds in World of Warcraft (Sundén, 2009), many online game forums banned certain search terms, such as 'gay', 'ERP' and others, which are covered by their filters (Kaolian, 2010). The official forum for Final Fantasy XIV does not include such measures, which represented an important opportunity for research into this area.

The heteronormative approach to gender emphasises its relationship to sexuality (Butler, 1990), with the heterosexual ideal structuring how gender continues in a binary fashion such as men needing to be masculine and women feminine. Valkyrie (2011) holds that heteronormativity emphasises authenticity and honesty in intimate relationships online, and in turn leads to scrutiny of the player's 'true' gender to avoid homosexual encounters. This formed part of his research into cybersexual encounters in MMORPGs, where players enact sexual behaviour through the avatar. On the Final Fantasy XIV forum, one post offered the following example, which illustrates how heteronormativity can be discerned online:

> I knew a guy (lets call him Mr. X) in FFXI[1] who was hitting on this girl which was really a guy and myself and other guys knew that ... just for fun we told our friend (the guy who played the female char[acter]) to play along, 2–3 month Mr. X thought he was going out with her [in-game] ... and we found on vent[2] it was actually a guy ... Mr. X never showed up again since then ... lol [laugh out loud].
>
> In FFXIV [Final Fantasy XIV] we have another guy who thought he was going out with a girl but actually was a guy ... it last 4 month lol at least this guy didn't quite the game lol he changed LS [Linkshell: a social group in the game] and never talks to her (him) now lolol. (Posted on 29 July 2011)

This example divided players replying to this thread, with some finding it funny, whereas others disliked the level of deception. Both of the apparently male players believed that they were engaged in 'real' relationships with 'real' women, but were publicly humiliated by others who were 'in on the joke'. The players concerned were so humiliated that they felt compelled to shun their social circle. Such behaviour also makes players seek some form of 'proof' of gender. Valkyrie (2011) originally wondered if sexuality would become more pliable online, with less focus on 'true' gender, with the avatar providing an alternate focal point for sexual encounters rather than the body of the player. However, his findings suggested that this was not the case where heteronormative sexuality remains in place. Nevertheless, the link between offline and online norms can be seen, especially in terms of constraining sexuality, and a continuing emphasis on authenticity to avoid duplicity. This can be seen further in another thread.

When New York passed a law allowing same-sex marriage in July 2011, coincidentally, a thread suggested the addition of a wedding service to the game. Many online games offer a form of wedding service, including World of Warcraft and Second Life. In Final Fantasy XI, weddings were only possible between two avatars that were not of the same gender. The opening post of the thread proposed adding weddings, but only if an avatar could marry anyone they wished. Players do not always have an avatar whose gender matches their offline sex, thus potentially, weddings are less straightforward, such as an online marriage between a male player and female player with two male avatars, or two female players with two female avatars and so on. However, the thread quickly became argumentative as can be seen in the following post:

> I can see it now gay parade in ul'dah [a town in the game]:/its just all wrong in my view. […]
>
> My father brought me up to be if you say anti-gay and his father did the same. And i'll bring up my kids the same way, its just the way my family is. (Posted on 14 July 2011)

This player conflates a same-gender avatar marriage with the offline version. Despite the potential for more flexible attitudes towards gender and sexuality (Valkyrie, 2011), heteronormative approaches to both remain in online games and their forums, hence any type of marriage is subject to the same norms in the minds of players.

Such outright homophobic attitudes have come under scrutiny in the gaming media (e.g. Scimeca, 2012), yet academic research has neglected this problem. For example, despite being called 'fag' and 'homo' by other players while researching World of Warcraft, which was visible in the chatlogs he published, Bainbridge (2010) did not comment about the casual homophobia present in these remarks. One of the few examples can be found in Sundén's (2009) discussion of the debate around the advertisement of an LGBT World of Warcraft guild, and its developers' initially hostile reaction, though this was later retracted. Overall sexuality and sexual norms have been examined far less than gender in relation to gaming (Sundén & Sveningsson, 2012). The threads drawn from this forum thus represent an important means of studying this issue in greater depth. One further example demonstrates how levels of homophobia increased in this thread and how players seek to emphasise the game as a separate space to everyday life.

One player voiced their objection in a rather strange fashion. In a lengthy post, C. claimed that homosexuality is the result of promiscuity, childhood trauma caused by family breakdown and hormone problems. After a lengthy conservative, homophobic diatribe, the post closes with the following:

> For myself personally, I would rather not have to deal with homosexual issues while playing a game that I'm trying to relax and have fun with. Putting my practicality aside and going to my personal feelings, the very thought turns my stomach. If there is constant stomach turning by various players of various personal thoughts on the issue, there's always a chance it won't keep them playing long.
>
> Now I know you could say, 'well maybe heterosexuality turns mine', but the reality is that heterosexuality is the normal way of things. For the sake of humanity, it had better stay that way. I know it sounds mean, but it is the truth. (Posted on 15 July 2011)

Many players posted replies that can be divided into two broad themes. The first is that other players may not perceive game marriage as having the same meaning as offline marriage, so this player should not be so angry. The second stemmed from gay players attempting to debunk the post while expressing outrage. However, C. later replied by restating a belief in homosexuality as a genetic mutation, and denied the existence of evolution. Other players were quick to point out the existence of gay players on all servers regardless.

The majority of the thread continued in this manner, with a handful of players objecting to the inclusion of weddings, and the rest mostly in favour. Yet, only a few made posts like these:

> Though in [Final Fantasy] XI it's for opposite sex partners only and it pretty much sux. I'd hate to see them pull a bigoted move like that again, especially since [Final Fantasy] XIV is full of sexual references everywhere, straight or gay, and some of them are quite racy may I add >_> I'd rather have no marriage at all than witnessing this all over again.
>
> It screws over the whole community as people roleplaying an opposite sex of their real life get cut out too. (Posted on 16 July 2011)

However, the attitudes of players like C. on the forum encourage the reproduction of particular heteronormative opinions about sexuality from offline life in relation to the game. In Sundén's ethnographic study of an LGBT guild, which are social groups in the game, she notes the confusion of other players when told the guild was LGBT only (Sundén & Sveningsson, 2012). Other players who wanted to join could not see why LGBT players were trying to set themselves apart. Though Sundén felt the guild itself was constraining, such as how other members pressured her to define her sexuality away from being queer, she also noted that the guild enabled its LGBT players to interact in different ways, without so much heteronormative pressure. She suggests that such guilds can act as a safe haven for LGBT players in online games, in the face of the type of criticism outlined above (*ibid.*).

By looking at how views of sexuality are expressed on forums, the effect of heteronormativity online can be more clearly perceived. Where online games are framed as a form of immersive escapism separate to everyday life, such 'real' life matters are excluded discursively by players. Healy (1997) posited that online communities were not necessarily so diverse as their offline counterparts because users could easily walk away from a group if they disagreed with other users' views. However, Nardi (2010) stated that she was surprised at how many different backgrounds were represented among World of Warcraft players – indeed she doubted that she would have met them in any other situation. I suggest that the difference with this type of community is the game, which brings players together through shared enjoyment.

At times on the official forum especially with discussions around sexuality, the players put forward the notion that fantasy and gaming should not feature 'real' life considerations and debates. Grosz (2001) has noted a similar tension in discourses around virtual reality, which involves a user wearing a headset that projects a space directly into their field of vision. Furthering her earlier work on the relationship between mind and body (Grosz, 1994), Grosz (2001) later developed an approach towards virtual reality, emphasising the masculine approach towards embodiment enshrined in virtual reality research. She notes the way in which a masculine, liberal discourse promotes the separation of the mind from the body, with virtual reality enabling an escape from the messy, physical everyday. In effect, virtual reality and online games create a control fantasy for participants, which make them believe these spaces can be more easily controlled in comparison to their everyday lives. The online gamers who sought to exclude discussions of homosexuality are pursuing a similar agenda. In promoting gaming as a way of escaping the everyday, these online gamers feel able to try to control the game and discussions around it. However, this study has shown how this gap does not actually exist beyond the discursive efforts made by players to prevent such discussions from taking place. These tensions can be seen further in the 'missing genders' thread.

THE 'MISSING GENDERS' THREAD: HETERONORMATIVITY AND THE EMBODIED AVATAR

Cloud participated in the first round of interviews in January 2011. At this point, he mentioned his campaign to persuade the development team to add the so-called 'missing' genders prior to the game's release. He had also tried this in Final Fantasy XI, as well as other online games that had races with a single gender. Race is part of avatar creation and denotes a range of different types of humanoid appearances – indeed species could be just as applicable (Galloway, 2012). In an interview, Cloud mentioned having posted this request on as many fan forums as possible, so it was probably inevitable that he would do the same when the official, developer-run forum launched in March 2011. The missing genders thread became popular very quickly. Many players were supportive with many players posting supportive messages including the one below:

> I, too, would love to see male miquotes and female roegadyns[3] in game. I've never understood the mentality of providing only one gender, unless if the race itself only has one gender. However, as you state it's right there in the lore, that both genders exist. (Posted on 8 March 2011)

Many posts mentioned lore, which is written by authors in the development team as part of the game narrative, and alludes to the existence of female Roegadyn and male Miqo'te, but they never appear in the game. Cloud often referred to the lore argument suggesting it was odd that these races were mentioned, but absent. In Final Fantasy XI, Cloud was thwarted in his campaign since the lore claimed the Galka (the Roegadyn predecessor) were mono-gendered, and reincarnated instead of reproducing.

Similarly, the male Mithra (the Miqo'te equivalent) were said to be solitary and lived elsewhere. Yet, players who had spent a long time in Final Fantasy XI often conflated the narrative of both games in voicing their objections to Cloud's plan, along the lines of the following post:

> If a male Miqote is written into lore as a very rare thing, then I am against the addition of a male Miqote as a playable race/gender. It would make the lore seem very silly indeed. If it doesn't mention this, then I don't mind either way. If it means less gender-swapping in the game then I'm all for that as it's annoying to talk to a Miqote and then discover they're a guy. First impressions and all that – you go by what you see!
>
> Same thing for female Roegadyn. If the lore allows for it, great, if it's a reincarnation lore that says there are only males, no thanks.
>
> I don't think the world suffers from the lack of these gender/race options if there is lore to explain it, basically. (Posted on 19 March 2011)

Since the races look similar in both games, the players confuse the narratives, which is unsurprising as some of my respondents had played Final Fantasy XI for nearly ten years. The game's narrative can become a stronger reference point for players depending on the situation at different times. In Pearce and Artemesia's (2009) study of players from the defunct Myst online game, the players remained very attached to the narrative after the original game was closed. The Myst group had also played the offline games in the series in the past, which left a significant cultural contribution for them to consider. The lore of a game and any predecessors becomes internalised by the players who devote hours to it, over long periods of time. Consequently, the game's culture can have a similar effect to that of the culture the players have grown up in. The potential for change in the game itself is measured according to what the existing game culture permits.

Interestingly, the above post also discusses gender switching, which is a prevalent topic of discussion in much research around gender and gaming (Huh & Williams, 2010; Hussain & Griffiths, 2008). One of the most popular stereotypes in online gaming relates to self-defined heterosexual male players who have female avatars because they are 'nicer to look at' (*ibid.*). In some online games, there are certain races with curvaceous appearances, such as the female Night Elves in World of Warcraft, which are so associated with male players that anyone using them is perceived to be male (Nardi, 2010). Gender switching is generally deemed to be problematic and dishonest by other players, but continues regardless. Other players also believed that adding the missing genders could 'discourage' gender switching, especially with the Miqo'te, which were associated with self-defined male players. Yet, judging by many self-defined female supporters, this seems unlikely, as can be seen in the below post:

> I'd love to play as a male miqo'te, even though it doesn't reflect my gender irl [in real life]. I just wouldn't be able to resist the cuteness. The idea of it just makes me smile, especially if they end up being more boyish that RRRRRGH GRUFF MANLY MAN type of models. It would be a hard decision between male miqo'te and female roe [gadyn], especially if both of them are done well. (Posted on 16 March 2011)

Some self-defined female players writing in this thread were keen to play as male Miqo'te. Overall, the male Miqo'te is perceived as potentially more androgynous, so if anything, the addition of male Miqo'te could increase gender switching. Moreover, the male Miqo'te was often framed in a similar way to the female, with an underlying theme of self-defined female players objectifying a male Miqo'te. This perpetuates the notion of the Miqo'te as more sexual and attractive than other races. In the thread, some self-defined female players posted along the following lines:

> I am gonna make a harem of catboys for myself! yay for female gamers who finally have their objects of desires! (Posted on 14 April 2011)

Others countered this notion, rejecting a sexual aspect in favour of a more restrained version concerning a cute male Miqo'te instead.

> It's not that I have a ˜problem˜ with yaoi or cat boys, it's the attitude. The reason most people stay away from the idea of manthra [male Mithra/Miqo'te] is because of the ˜*LOLOL ANIME FANGURLZ*˜ [fangirls] who pretty much just want to fetish ... ize them/make them make out with each other.
>
> The reason I want the missing genders is equality and to play something that suits my personality better, not so I can stare at my model for hours and write terrible slash fan fiction about him. (Posted on 11 April 2011)

Yaoi is a particular form of hentai, or erotic comics, and involves two young men either embarking on a romantic affair, or having a sexual encounter (McLelland, 2006). These comics tend to be produced for and by young heterosexual female consumers, but they are denigrated in Japan through the nickname Fujoshi ('rotten women') leading to the concealment of Fujoshi identity unless amongst others (Okabe & Ishida, 2012). McLelland (2006) also notes a link with so-called slash fiction, written by fans of shows about sexual relationships between male characters, such as Kirk and Spock in the original Star Trek series. He also points out that such comics have spread online into English-speaking cultures, much like other forms of anime and manga. Final Fantasy players are often framed as fans of such cultures (Consalvo, 2012), which leads them to evoke such ideas. For some self-defined female heterosexual players, the male Miqo'te potentially represented as much of a sexualised avatar as the female Miqo'te for the self-defined male heterosexual players, yet the community framed such behaviour in different ways. Given the relatively common occurrence of self-defined male players who use female avatars, their behaviour was more readily associated with secure heterosexuality, even if they were also positioned as disrespectful, lonely, nerdy men. In this particular game, the relationship with Japanese culture meant that these self-defined female players were associated with yaoi, and a comparatively worse position than the self-defined male players. Excessive heterosexual desire in female players is portrayed as problematic. Valkyrie's (2011) study of cybersexual relationships in online games heavily suggested that prevailing norms around women's sexual behaviour were maintained where players perceived to be women would be stigmatised for participating in sexual behaviour with others. The expression of sexual desire was thus supposed to be contained and potentially shameful for female players, and this is perpetuated in regard to the avatar.

Such assertions regarding the Miqo'te as a sexualised race also point to how gender and sexuality cannot be viewed separately, thus researchers who suggest that sexuality should not be part of studies of online games are mistaken (e.g. Bainbridge, 2010). This point is further developed if the objections to the additions of the missing genders are included, which were homophobic in some instances due to the potential embodiment of these avatars, such as the below quotation:

> Female Rogs [Roegadyn] no sorry against it
>
> Male cats nope sorry not like the manthras [men who use Miqo'te avatars, or Mithra previously] that play will change to males anyways they play kitties for a reason ><
>
> Female Highlanders say what???? so yall wanna see big giant muscle woman running around? Jhmmmm no thx [thanks] leave em the way they are. (Posted on 11 March 2011)

One of the main objections to the female versions of these races concerned size. Muscular female avatars were perceived as repellent. Other users went as far as stating they did not think such a 'manly' female avatar would be very popular. In terms of the avatar's embodiment, many players believe female avatars should correspond to particular embodied norms. Slender female avatars are normative, and larger, more muscular female avatars are framed as unintelligible within a heteronormative environment. This echoes the treatment of female bodybuilders, who are accused of being too masculine in seeking to build muscle, and unattractive to heterosexual men (Shilling & Bunsell, 2011). Similar judgements are applied to larger female avatars in games.

However, there are other notions at work here that still need to be unpacked:

> First off, having male mi'qote are a BAD IDEA. You'd be stealing the gay race from elezens. Not to mention, it would gay up the whole server something fierce. I'm talking pride parades, rainbow-colored trees etc., And no, I'm not against homosexuality, I just don't think it fits for this type of setting.
>
> And don't go telling me I'm wrong, because you know, deep down, that I'm right.
>
> The only reason anyone would play male cat person like the ones in this game is because they're a flaming homosexual who wants to look *CUTE* for all his friends. My post might get deleted because some sensitive person will contact the mods and claim it's discriminatory, but I just want a game without rainbow trees and bass-beat dance bars. Is that wrong of me to ask? Really? (Posted on 15 March 2011)

This post is probably one of the more extreme objections and shows more blatant homophobia. The game is posited as a space where particular aspects of life ought to be excluded, much like the wedding service thread discussed above. Muscular 'masculine' female avatars and 'feminine' male avatars remain subject to heteronormativity, even online. Though players try to resist such norms, gender norms are constantly reinscribed. Gender still needs to be embodied along particular lines by the avatar itself. This thread illustrates how heteronormativity and homophobia operate in the game and its related spaces via players and their prejudices. In this way, particular dialogues around gender are foreclosed as players emphasise normative ways of both performing and embodying gender in online games.

CONCLUSION

This chapter has examined the process of studying a forum qualitatively over a period of time and how it can be incorporated into a larger dataset. Following the careful mapping of an online community, it is possible to learn much about the social values and norms that its users bring online. In my research, the forum complemented the interview data where it further illustrates the role of heteronormativity in the regulation of gender and sexuality. By necessity, the researcher may need to become a 'lurker' as a form of engagement with a forum and visit regularly to form a deep understanding of the group. While forums can seem straightforward to study given how unobtrusively one can 'harvest' data, it is much more beneficial to regularly visit a forum over a period of time. In this sense, a study of a forum can comprise an interesting part of an online ethnography. Nevertheless, there are some issues with the ethics of studying a forum that need to be addressed. One important ethical theme is the way in which users perceive the audience for their posts as automatically sympathetic without the expectation that a researcher is taking their posts. Such material ought to be handled sensitively by researchers, yet this does not mean that forums need to be excluded from research. Forums remain structured according to social norms and are very amenable to qualitative studies of social interaction. This chapter has shown how forum data can comprise an interesting and vivid part of an ethnographic study.

NOTES

1. Final Fantasy XI, the previous online game in the series.
2. Ventrilo, the Skype-like voice software for online games.
3. Miqo'te and Roegadyn are two of the five races in the game and were initially only available as single genders – female and male respectively.

REFERENCES

AoIR. (2002). *Ethical decision-making and internet research* [Online]. Retrieved from http://aoir.org/reports/ethics.pdf. Accessed on April 17, 2012.

AoIR. (2012). *Ethical decision-making and internet research 2.0: Recommendations from the AoIR ethics working committee* [Online]. Retrieved from http://www.aoir.org/reports/ethics2.pdf. Accessed on March 30, 2013.

Bainbridge, W. S. (2010). *The Warcraft civilisation: Social science in a virtual world.* Cambridge, MA: MIT Press.

Baym, N., & Markham, A. (2009). Introduction: Making smart choices on shifting ground. In A. Markham & N. Baym (Eds.), *Internet enquiry: Conversations about method* (pp. vii–xix). London: Sage.

Boellstorff, T. (2009). A typology of ethnographic scales for virtual worlds. In W. S. Bainbridge (Ed.), *Online worlds: Convergence of the real and the virtual.* London: Springer.

Bryson, M. (2004). When Jill jacks in. *Feminist Media Studies*, *4*(3), 239–254.

Butler, J. (1990). *Gender trouble*. London: Routledge.

Coffey, A., Rendd, E., Dicks, B., Soyinka, B., & Mason, B. (2006). Hypermedia ethnography in educational settings: Possibilities and challenges. *Ethnography and Education*, *1*(1), 15–30.

Consalvo, M. (2012). Cosmo-play: Japanese videogames and Western gamers. In D. G. Embrick, J. T. Wright, & A. Lukacs (Eds.), *Social exclusion, power, and video game play: New research in digital media and technology* (pp. 199–219). Plymouth, UK: Lexington Books.

Delamont, S. (2002). *Fieldwork in educational settings: Methods, pitfalls and procedures* (2nd ed.). London: Falmer.

ESRC. (2010). *Framework for research ethics* [Online]. Retrieved from http://www.esrc.ac.uk/_images/Framework_for_Research_Ethics_tcm8-4586.pdf. Accessed on April 21, 2012.

Eynon, R., Fry, J., & Schroeder, R. (2008). The ethics of internet research. In N. Fielding, R. M. Lee, & G. Blank (Eds.), *The Sage handbook of online research methods* (pp. 23–41). London: Sage.

Galloway, A. R. (2012). Does the whatever speak? In L. Nakamura & P. Chow-White (Eds.), *Race after the internet* (pp. 111–127). London: Routledge.

Grosz, E. (1994). *Volatile bodies: Towards a corporeal feminism*. Indianapolis, IN: Indiana University Press.

Grosz, E. (2001). *Architecture from the outside: Essays on virtual and real space*. London: MIT Press.

Hammersley, M., & Atkinson, P. (2007). *Ethnography: Principles in practice* (3rd ed.). London: Routledge.

Healy, D. (1997). Cyberspace and place: The internet as middle landscape on the electronic frontier. In D. Porter (Ed.), *Internet culture* (pp. 55–68). New York, NY: Routledge.

Hine, C. (2000). *Virtual ethnography*. London: Sage.

Hine, C. (2008). Virtual ethnography: Modes, varieties, affordances. In N. Fielding, R. M. Lee, & G. Blank (Eds.), *The Sage handbook of online research methods* (pp. 257–270). London: Sage.

Huh, S., & Williams, D. (2010). Dude looks like a lady: Gender swapping in an online game. In W. S. Bainbridge (Ed.), *Online worlds: Convergence of the real and the virtual* (pp. 161–174). London: Springer.

Hussain, Z., & Griffiths, M. (2008). Gender swapping and socialising in cyberspace: An exploratory study. *CyberPsychology and Behavior*, *11*(1), 47–53.

Jones, S. G. (1998). Information, internet and community: Notes towards an understanding of community in the information age. In S. G. Jones (Ed.), *Cybersociety 2.0: Revisiting computer-mediated communication and community* (pp. 1–34). London: Sage.

Kaigo, M., & Watanabe, I. (2007). Ethos in chaos? Reaction to video files depicting socially harmful images in the channel 2 Japanese internet forum. *Journal of Computer-Mediated Communication*, *12*, 1248–1268.

Kaolian. (2010). *Forum rules and sticky request information* [Online]. Retrieved from http://www.zam.com/forum.html?forum=3&mid=122844326723865525. Accessed on July 31, 2012.

Kivits, J. (2004). Researching the informed patient. *Information, Communication and Society*, *7*(4), 510–530.

Markham, A. (2005). The methods, politics, and ethics of representation in online ethnography. In N. Denzin & Y. Lincoln (Eds.), *The Sage handbook of qualitative research* (pp. 793–821). London: Sage.

McLelland, M. (2006, Online). Why are Japanese girls' comics full of boys bonking? *Refractory: A Journal of Entertainment Media*, *10*. Retrieved from http://refractory.unimelb.edu.au/2006/12/04/why-are-japanese-girls%E2%80%99-comics-full-of-boys-bonking1-mark-mclelland. Accessed on September 1, 2012.

Moinian, F. (2006). The construction of identity on the internet: Oops! I've left my diary open to the whole world! *Childhood, 13*(1), 49–68.

Nardi, B. A. (2010). *My life as a night elf priest: An anthropological account of world of warcraft*. Ann Arbor, MI: University of Michigan Press.

Okabe, D., & Ishida, K. (2012). Making fujoshi identity visible and invisible. In M. Ito, D. Okabe, & I. Tsuji (Eds.), *Fandom unbound: Otaku culture in a connected world* (Kindle ed.). New Haven, CT: Yale University Press.

Orgad, S. (2009). Question two: How can researchers make sense of the issues involved in collecting and interpreting online and offline data? In A. Markham & N. Baym (Eds.), *Internet inquiry: Conversations about method* (pp. 33–53). London: Sage.

Orton-Johnson, K. (2010, Online). Ethics in online research: Evaluating the ESRC framework for research ethics' categorisation of risk. *Sociological Research Online, 15*(4). Retrieved from http://www.socresonline.org.uk/15/4/13.html. Accessed on April 15, 2014.

Pearce, C., & Artemesia. (2009). *Communities of play: Emergent cultures in multiplayer games and virtual worlds*. London: MIT Press.

Rheingold, H. (1994). *The virtual community*. London: Secker and Warburg.

Scimeca, D. (2012). *The unquestioned homophobia in battlefield 3* [Online]. Retrieved from http://kotaku.com/5876445/the-unquestioned-homophobia-in-battlefield-3. Accessed on July 31.

Shilling, C., & Bunsell, T. (2011). The female bodybuilder as a gender outlaw. In D. Hobbs (Ed.), *Ethnography in context* (pp. 131–153). London: Sage.

Silver, D. (2000). Margins in the wires: Looking for race, gender, and sexuality in the Blacksburg electronic village. In B. Kolko, L. Nakamura, & G. B. Rodman (Eds.), *Race in cyberspace* (pp. 133–150). London: Routledge.

Strauss, A. C., & Corbin, J. M. (1998). *Basics of qualitative research: Techniques and procedures for developing grounded theory* (2nd ed.). London: Sage.

Sundén, J. (2009). Play as transgression: An ethnographic approach to queergame cultures [Online]. Breaking new ground: Innovation in games, play, practice and theory. In *Proceedings of Digital Games Research Conference*, London, UK, 1–4 September. London: Brunel University. Retrieved from http://www.digra.org/dl/db/09287.40551.pdf. Accessed on September 21, 2013.

Sundén, J., & Sveningsson, M. (2012). *Gender and sexuality in online game cultures: Passionate play*. London: Routledge.

Svenningsson Elm, M. (2009). Question three: 'How do various notions of privacy influence decisions in qualitative internet research?' In A. Markham & N. Baym (Eds.), *Internet enquiry: Conversations about method* (pp. 69–87). London: Sage.

Taylor, T. L. (2006). *Play between worlds: Exploring online game culture*. London: MIT Press.

Valkyrie, Z. C. (2011). Cybersexuality in MMORPGs: Virtual sexual revolution untapped. *Men and Masculinities, 14*(1), 76–96.

Williams, J. P. (2006). Authentic identities: Straightedge subculture, music and the internet. *Journal of Contemporary Ethnography, 35*(2), 173–200.

Williams, M. (2007). Avatar watching: Participant observation in graphical online environments. *Qualitative Research, 7*(1), 5–24.

PART III
DIGITAL, DIGITIZED AND PARTICIPATORY METHODS

MARKETING NARRATIVES: RESEARCHING DIGITAL DATA, DESIGN AND THE IN/VISIBLE CONSUMER

Mariann Hardey

ABSTRACT

Purpose – *This chapter critically evaluates the literature on digital consumer data and the ways in which it can be used in digital social research. The chapter illuminates how researchers have to conceptualise and negotiate digital data, focusing upon ethical and procedural challenges of employing digital methods.*

Approach – *The chapter draws upon and integrates a broad research literature from sociology, digital media studies, business and marketing, as these have opened up new directions for research design and method. It advocates interdisciplinary approaches to conceptualising what digital data is employing the concept of 'marketing narratives' to understand how the new visibilities of consumer data are shaped by related processes of branding and the interactivity of content.*

Big Data? Qualitative Approaches to Digital Research
Studies in Qualitative Methodology, Volume 13, 115–135

ISSN: 1042-3192/doi:10.1108/S1042-319220140000013008

Findings – *The chapter shows how the capacities of digital technologies present significant challenges for researchers and organisations that have to be carefully negotiated if the potentials of digital consumer data are to be harnessed. In addition, researchers should pay attention to novel issues of ethical responsibility in the context of the longer-term presence of data records.*

Value – *The chapter offers a set of guidelines for digital social researchers in negotiating the meanings of visible digital consumer data, the ethical and proprietary issues involved in utilising digital methods.*

Keywords: Digital; data; marketing; consumer; Generation C; relationships

Errors using inadequate data are much less than those using no data at all.
Charles Babbage

INTRODUCTION

This chapter makes a key contribution to the understanding of the pervasiveness of digital data as it is inherent in the daily life of consumers and marketers. In doing so, it illuminates how researchers may think about and negotiate digital data. It draws on a broad literature from sociology, business and marketing that has opened up new directions for qualitative research design and method by responding to digital data, and in particular the state of the digital consumer. This chapter is not a celebration nor a criticism of digital cultures. Instead, the discussion is formed around an understanding of the kind of research that is current to digital data, as well as the role of the researcher and their participants who are both users of the same technology, and who often share similar digital social and cultural settings.

The traditional lens of qualitative research informs us that data occupies a naturalistic state; at the moment of discovery the data comes without a codified or organisational structure. There is a temptation to repurpose traditional methodological design into digital settings and to let this alone inform the researcher about digital culture. Under these conditions it is important that digital data retain the 'messiness of real life', and that this may be analysed for thematic commonalities, patterns and contrast around a central organising concept (Braun & Clarke, 2013, p. 33). Whilst the researcher needs to respond to the dynamics of social media in particular, she/he must also allow data to inform them about wider social dynamics. Throughout this chapter, I draw on Rogers (2013) who, like myself, has been critical of digital methodology that overlooks the impact on sociality and social behaviour. There is also an alignment here with Niederer and van Dijck (2010) who underscore the importance of existing social settings in their research on networks and networking.

In my own research in the digital field I have made specific reference to digital consumer and marketing activities. Indeed, I have responded to the charm of digital data by consideration of the most appropriate approach to it and to the accompanying social media resources (for example, setting up an account on a user-review website that clearly stated my position as an 'academic and researcher ... interested in the content of user-reviews'). To secure ethical approval, I contacted the site's owners and, with their permission, openly linked to my research website and blog. Like others, I endorse a methodological approach that allows researchers to both use, and at the same time provide analysis of social media resources. To return to Rogers (2010, 2013), aside from examining data flows between various software and apps, there are also particular dependencies between the technologies that form the foundation for every kind of data ecosystem. The appreciation of this kind of social ecosystem was seminal to one of my first pieces of research into consumers and interpretation of their actions as led by co-created content and decision-making (see Hardey, 2011a). The interaction with digital and social media content is something that I have begun to identify as 'digital marketing narratives' (Hardey, 2011a, 2013, forthcoming). This provides the foundation for a framework for identifying specific digital consumer types and the condition of digital data. I have also found it helpful to have a critical awareness of the marketisation of digital data, and this is presented as a field for methodological techniques, analysis and tools.

Setting the Scene and Using Marketing Narratives to Explore Digital Data

One of the most compelling turns of the digital age has been the manner in which data has proliferated and converged as 'big data'. In marketing, this reflects the increasingly digital nature of the 'consumer journey' and of the consumers' introduction to, and interaction with, brands and marketing information. The collection of consumers' data on websites that publish customer reviews (TripAdvisor, Amazon) enables service providers to establish and promote a brand presence, and to integrate new modes of consumer content, data and analysis. Marketing composed of consumer narratives may be treated as a new form of social data. Identifying these as 'marketing narratives' allows the researcher to appreciate how brands seek to compulsively tell consumers stories about products and services to promote the brand (Hardey, 2013). Marketing narratives represent a new dynamic within digital culture and what is evolving as an active (though inconsistent) relationship between the users of technology and the recording of their consumer data. Digital data is treated as part of wider marketing narratives that can be used as organisational frames for analysis (such as an outline of typical digital consumer user types which we will look at later). This framing reflects the assemblage of digital data and the multiplicity of the digital consumer. Examples include brand communities that are built on top of SNSs (social networking sites), creating interactive worlds that offer an immersive experience for the consumer, as well as platforms that feature 'stories' and allow brands to weave together image, video, and interactive narratives into marketing packages. For qualitative methodology, these offer additional sources of data for researchers, as well as new experiences, and methods of data-cleansing and testing.

In terms of digital data capture and analysis, extracting 'clean' data has become considerably more complex. For example, by investigating marketing narratives it is relatively straightforward to identify a range of digital data trails that 'enable the accumulation of massive data sets which can be made productive by business, yet remain invisible to the vast majority of consumers' (Featherstone, 2014, pp. 6–7). The added complexity for the researcher on a quest for 'massive data sets' is the way in which the data-gathering generates a 'new architecture of visibility with social media such as Facebook, working off the fear of invisibility' (*ibid.*, 2014, p. 7). Whilst Featherstone's work focuses on the visual and visibility as the crucial fulcrum for everyday life, this type of self-disclosure (e.g. '*Liked*' brands and pages) provide useful points of data-generation and aggregation. As digital marketing narratives become more important, brands such as Virgin seek to occupy strong 'social media' territories and hold very visible profiles that allow them to interact and react in real time with customers on platforms such as Twitter and Facebook.

The temptation is to believe that consumer data simply extends the scope of research productivity and, therefore, the researcher's competence. Providing an overview of social media data under the analysis of data-driven scientists, Bik and Goldstein note that it is unfortunate that 'the majority of present evidence is anecdotal' (2013, p. 1). For these scholars, the inconvenience of the subjective nature of social media data presents its own challenges. To compensate for such difficulty, there are additional tools and services that any researcher can use and are provided by many social platforms. Twitter allows academics to prepare for data collection through the visibility of trending topics (i.e. those found with #hashtags) as well as additional data, such as geo-tagging and url links. This becomes infinitely more complex through the selection of applied methods of computation techniques to locate data, store it and prepare it for analysis. Tools and open APIs, such as Nodexl from Microsoft, allow users to map a network of influence without expert knowledge of computer coding. Other tools, such as TweetArchivist, enable researchers to download tweets by usernames. Programming languages such as Python[1] can be used to identify the emergence of relationships and reinterpret textual content, as well as deeper investigations into social, cultural and philosophical influences. It is worthwhile returning to Rogers (2013) to observe how digital data that is mashed up with other data produces visually attractive sets, as well as new interactive points of discovery that can be used to reflect a richer picture of sociality.

There are some practical perspectives on the types of knowledge and methods of analysis that are available. For detail on digital data-mining, Russell's (2013) overview of the analysis of Facebook, Twitter, Google+ and Linkedin with and without developer tools is excellent. These tools have a tendency to fragment the digital landscape into specific territorial areas. The digital consumer is treated as occupying only one territory at a time; for example, activities on Facebook, Amazon or TripAdvisor (for marketing management and consumer studies on social platforms see Hansson, 2013; Kang, Tang, & Fiore, 2014; Schulze, Schöler, & Skiera, 2014). In the traditional qualitative interview or focus group, it is relatively undemanding to establish a linear sequence of events that permit a quasi-temporal analysis of data and reconstruction of individual narratives. These procedures become considerably more challenging in a digital setting when the social and consumptive data is more abstract and diffuse. One task for the researcher is to select and unpick standardised points between which comparisons can take place, and these might be dependent on specific platform and related user information, such as location, age, relationship status, etc. Ruppert, Law, and Savage (2013) make two crucial observations in terms of comparative classifications; first, that social science methods depend on the social knowledge of the data; and second, that social network platforms and digitised sources of data constitute ongoing and dynamic movements that are pervasive and require the appropriate measurement and comprehension. In both cases the traditional demograph assembly of gender, age, income, and relationship status may or may not be available or reliable. Our user/s are distinct, unfixed and attached to interactive content.

Digital Interactive Content

The digital consumer is complex and changeable. A key characteristic is how the individual has entered into a set of relationships that are determined by 'prosumption' and crowd-sourced decision-making (see Beer, 2009; Beer & Burrows, 2013; Ritzer, Dean, & Jurgenson, 2012; Ritzer & Jurgenson, 2010). As a result, digital consumer data is underpinned by co-created activity and significant content (Hardey, 2011a, 2011b, 2012, 2013). Recognising and reading these activities as digital marketing narratives is one approach. However, it is ill-advised to ignore the wider consumer and social processes and activities that are already established, and how additional digital services adds to this mix. My argument is that digital data is co-produced through dynamic transactions and research intersections that draw the researcher towards their participants. Previous data analysis has focused on the isolated flow of transactional data but there is an important bridge between digital data and its trails. The latter forms a critical part of emerging informational infrastructures that is indexed by various technology, but also held together by networks of links (see, e.g. Beer & Burrows, 2013; Thrift, 2005).

It is not uncommon to read across literature how 'new' forms of digital data are transforming research and have merit because they are 'open' for researchers to track, analyse and investigate (Gurstein, 2011 has a valuable article on open data and effective data use; Halvais, 2013 on 'homemade' big data). A researcher might be interested in digital interactions, or seek to review mediated patterns of behaviour. In my own work is a desire to understand the digital consumer through a reassembly of desires, needs, requests, wants and codes of conduct that characterise their behaviour and link them to specific products and services. Digital networks, and the related activities of micro-consumption and mass communication, are often thought of as 'virtual' or 'elusive' as physical objects (Gitelman, 2008, p. 95), rather than understood as part of existing and more complex relationships. In short, the context of new technologies and data remain connected to the 'specific material and historical environments in which new media emerge and of the ways in which habits and structures of communication are naturalized or normalized' (Gitelman & Pingree, 2003, p. 10).

The digital age has provided access to data that in its crude form exists 'out there', waiting to be discovered and *simply* be turned into findings. However, let us side with Vis (2013), Ruppert et al. (2013) to critically deconstruct the simplicity of this process. There is a growing consensus that the researcher should appreciate the processes behind the construction of digital data before they choose which methodology and analysis to follow if they are to fully appreciate the productive and performative qualities of digital methods (see Lupton's, 2014; Roger, 2013 work on digital health records is especially useful). An interesting extension of this argument is posed by Ruppert et al. who say that digital devices and the data they generate are both the material of social lives and form part of the apparatus for *knowing* those lives (2013, p. 24, emphasis added). Focus should be the on the forms of sociality that give rise to digitally mediated practices and that set up relationships; this is especially true for general discussions about digital data (e.g. Atkinson et al., 2013), marketing and consumer research (e.g. Hardey, 2011a, 2011b, 2012, 2013), as well as journalism and commercial publications (Thurman, 2014; Thurman & Newman, 2014).

To understand digital interactive content, as researchers we need to view this as an extension of previous fields of research related to community and shared knowledge. Whilst it is important to note that there are distinctions between the 'cyberspace' of yester-year and today, one valid association is the shared structure of information. The familiarisation with data, and with communities as a network of links also holds commercial relevance. Writing in *Sloan Management Review*, McWilliam (2012) intensifies the way in which we can understand the popularity of online communities, as we have become familiar with from the work of (McEwen & Wellman, 2013; Wellman, 1999), into the presence of digital branded communities that has recently captured the attention of marketing professionals and academic researchers. Central to McWilliam's argument is the joining together of 'relationship' with 'community' as the newer buzzwords of marketing. This reflects how consumers are encouraged to be identified as brand members who share a 'common interest'. Disney, Bosch, Apple, Nike, Nescafe, Heineken and other well-known brands go beyond their conventional website to encourage community interaction and allow individuals to establish virtual bars and cafés, host play-dates and communicate with one another. Getting inside a brand community is an easy process for any researcher. Cova and Pace's (2006) article on 'my Nutella, the community' provides an exceptionally good outline on new forms of consumer dynamics, as well as the researcher's access to the 'virgin territory' of a branded online group.

Leading from Cova and Pace, the strategies that I have developed rely on 'open' online consumer groups that allow the researcher to lurk (I prefer loiter) and, if appropriate, to participate in a group's interaction. An important consideration in this scenario is the distance the researcher should establish in order to monitor and record the experience of participants. Indeed, the interaction amongst members of a brand community can produce other complexities, tensions and unexpected results. A two-year piece of research based on a user-review website revealed four types of members (see Fig. 1), characterised as:

Brand communities and user-review websites are sustained by the shared content from their users. At the same time, links into other social media (most websites allow a login through an SNS identity that acts as a 'key' to build a profile and access multiple web platforms), represent comparatively new forms of data that can be tracked to inform the researcher about the visibility of a brand. At the same time, these may be monitored to provide data on customer service dialogues (websites like John Lewis and Tesco include consumer reviews published alongside product overviews) and consumer recommendations about products and services. Smith's (2013) research into consumer experiences on Facebook is helpful to understand the needs of the researcher and preparation for data collection. His method places a 'value' on consumers' behaviour that can be directly related to the impact of online branded content. Drilling down to the microanalysis of textual content, the researcher has comparatively less control over how the

1. *The self-styled expert* – an individual who presents themselves to others as a true authority and credits themselves with providing first class information about a product/service/place;
2. *The extreme contributor* – someone who excessively creates content to prevent others from publishing as leading information providers or who explicitly restricts others comments and/or questions;
3. *Private participant* – publish limited content with little or no promotion of community membership or social media profile identifiers;
4. *Indifferent contributor* – someone who has membership of a community and/or who has only published a small amount of content, they have little interest in creating or replying to posts.

Fig. 1. Characteristics of User Type Common to Online Brand Communities. *Source*: Adapted from Hardey (2011c).

data is produced or its quality. Quantifiable survey data taken from users of brand communities can be an easy route to go from data collection to analysis. The freedom from conventional interview and focus groups, and the arduous transcription of this data, is very liberating. This does not mean a complete rejection of more established research techniques, and I have found it particularly helpful to combine a number of methodological routes. One of my most surprising results followed the content and textual analysis of a very negative reviewer on a number of user-review websites. A face-to-face interview revealed their profession as 'working in PR', holding a position as 'Marketing Director' for a well-known review-based community website – an important research note that was not revealed from a two-year open observation of reviews and user profiles.

The role of the researcher and their understanding of the *production* of data is key. This has an influence on the type of observation and capture of data (for example, if a SNS profile is required for access, should it be anonymous to protect the researcher/s?) as well as the analysis. In addition, the research budgets and timetabling should be integrated into the project planning; for example, one online user-group I researched began with open access before changing to a monthly subscription. The design elements may also be influenced by the presentation and marketing of the final researcher results – often proposals include social media and digital resources as part of impact outputs and dissemination.

Conditions of Digital Consumer Data

To establish the conditions of digital consumer data, let us visualise the swift upward curve (since, 2004) in the popularity of the use of social media, the concentrations of consumer content and smart mobile device ownership. PEW's American Life Project (2014), has recorded that 72% of online adults use SNS; young adults (18–29) are the most likely to say they use SNS, while women (over 30) and urban dwellers are more likely than men or rural users to be acting as consumers on the sites. The upward thrust of this curve can be observed to be slowing down and levelling out as a far more complex picture takes shape in terms of rate of use, time spent choosing products and services, types of platforms used, contribution to review sites and so forth. The key issue for qualitative researchers is *how we know about and trace these activities for analysis.*

The process of tracing consumer activities has a strong tradition in consumer and marketing literature (Womer, 1944 and applications of the 'continuous consumer panel'; Brown, 1950 and measurement of consumer attitudes towards products). For an overview of a critical history of marketing studies, I recommend the work of Tadajewski (2006, 2010, 2013). Most recently, the enlightenment provided by 'open data' (i.e. readily available) has added to the growing wealth of consumer knowledge. This is apparent in personal transactional data that includes the users' activities when they visit websites, the products they buy, as well as the commercial entities with which they interact. The assumption is that consumer activities and experiences provide compelling data that is ripe and disposed to exploration – it is, after all, published in a way that makes it available to anybody. However, the data may also hide some of the more complex and diverse patterns of behaviour, or encourage researchers to ignore important contextual and demographic information. No matter how open the data, there remain unexpected contexts and content of its conditions (a nod to my research participant from PR again).

The understanding of digital sociality as directly linked to material consumer conditions (i.e. the products that are purchased) are important for the interpretation of these forms of data, and represent a challenge when they are not necessarily directly relatable to class, gender, age, household income and other traditional demographic sources. Whether knowingly or unknowingly, consumers create and attract big data; from the conditions in which they make purchase decisions to how they share their experiences as user-reviewers. Related to this is the construct of 'postdemographic data' (Rogers, 2009, 2013) that explains how such activity is important for understanding sociality and the way in which this behaviour has impact on social conditions. Whilst a user profile carries a lot of social information, this can be distorted, and, if the user desires, can also be used to mislead or misinform. My own research has noted the rise of the digital PR content manager; those individuals whose role is to micro-manage digital content on community brand pages, websites and additional platforms.

The natural users of digital technologies have evolved into 'knowing' consumers who draw upon the knowledge and support of other consumers; I call it a form of *digital consumer data spectacle,* where transactions are open to others observation (Hardey, 2013). This has close associations, as noted by Ritzer et al., to the techniques of 'prosumption'. The most enduring commercial implications of digital data might lie in the how, what and why of commercial agencies seeking to capture consumer activities. Digital data enables companies to invite consumers *into* the commercialisation of marketing and product promotion, sometimes without the consumer being fully aware of the role they play.

Digital resources allow consumers to spend time and effort locating and deciding on a particular product and service. The replication of market segmentation (how the marketplace is divided up into divisions of a particular market) into digital 'spaces' is a key influence on consumer behaviour. This segmentation is often by population and into subgroups with similar motivations; common bases include geographic location, demographic type, use of product and psychological differences. For example, Simkin and Dibb's (2013) research into Customer Relationship Management (CRM) services and market strategy explores how the digital environment has brought a 'step-change to the marketing discipline. The interactivity, immediacy and individualisation made possible in the digital era have excited and challenged marketers', especially the influence of social media networks for data capture, testing of propositions and marketing communications (*ibid.*, 2013, p. 391–392).

Simply adapting empirical methods into a digital context would leave the researcher open to criticism, such actions being 'outdated' in the face of new systematic and collaborative approaches and the increasing utilisation of advanced digital data sets (Beer & Burrows, 2013; Savage & Burrows, 2007). The value of Marres (2012) methodological argument is particularly helpful in this context. Marres argues that understanding the nature of qualitative data and the influence of socio-cultural influences of digital is not enough. She proposes a redistribution of social research that has been opened up from the *'re-mediation'* (italics from original) of social methods as they are transposed into digital environments (2012, p. 140). What we can take away from Marres's discussion is the way in which these methods offer the opportunity for the digital social researcher to intervene critically and to 'actively pursue the re-distribution of social methods online' (2012, p. 139). Indeed this has raised not only the question of *what are the implications of technology* (Back, 2010, boyd & Crawford, 2011; Savage, Law, & Ruppert, 2010), but how we should be encouraged to ask: *what of the relationship to the social researcher herself?* (cf. Hardey, 2011a, 2011c).

Digital Ethics, Informed Consent and Anonymity

It is dangerous to deduce that digitisation simply makes the social more obtainable. For the researcher using 'open' and 'visible' data there is the added risk of exposing the participant and researcher on new and unexpected levels. The temptation for any researcher is to pursue data like a bounty-hunter, accruing evidence across multiple platforms. The abundance of content has additional challenges in terms of capture and interpretation, particularly around the complex issues of ethics and consent. Assuming that data and ethical consent is accepted because content is published in a 'public' setting might be questionable when we take into account the increasingly grey divide of public versus private. As this divide becomes muddier, and as digital users and consumers become more visible, the risks are greater to the researchers, as well as to the data acceptability and legitimacy. There are very specific threats (as well as opportunities) of which the researcher must be aware and which draws together the platform users, software creators and managers, as well as the market practitioners who curate and manage content in the same space/s.

From a reading of digital commercial marketing data, four facets emerge that are important to the understanding of the intersection of relationship between research participants and researcher. These are primarily concerned with informed consent and anonymity and may be summarised as follows:

From Fig. 2, we can appreciate that digital consumer activity can provide a very clean method of identifying and extracting data, whilst at the same time it masks the new complexities that encourage consumers to occupy multiple platforms with one, or various, digital profiles. Social geographer Nigel Thrift's (2005) observations about 'software sorting' (the way in which the software as a black box automatically sorts individual users by type, such as location, number of links in a network, etc.) enables us to appreciate how users are both automatically 'sorted' and at the same time encouraged to openly link a personal profile across multiple platforms. This raises important questions about privacy and ethical conduct; an example being how a user profile is visible and open on one platform, then

- First, the type of content, including textual, image-based, video, tagging, geolocation etc. and the nature and sensitivity of the content;
- Second, the digital resource and social media platform being used, as well as additional services and other open access;
- Third, the expectations the consumer had when posting, and;
- Fourth, the nature of the research, including the organisation (public, commercial etc.), and the international legislation and regulating bodies involved.

Fig. 2. Overview of the Considerations for Informed Consent and Maintaining Anonymity in Digital Research. *Source*: Adapted from the NetCen Social Media Report (2014, January).

the researcher has responsibility to protect and not disclose any personal identifiers that may be replicated on other platforms if they are not confident about the condition of the profile, and any privacy settings that may have been put in place. A return to traditional modes of methodology and the face-to-face interview is a reliable way to gain this consent.

To gain an overview of the appropriate procedures in 'targeting' digital consumers, I have drawn the above themes together in Table 1.

Table 1. Core Requirements of the Appropriate Actions for Digital Consent and Anonymity Inclusion in Research Design.

Consent and Anonymity are not Required	Informed Consent is Necessary	Anonymity is Necessary
(The consumer may be considered as fair game)	*(Otherwise the risk is as the unfair targeting of the consumer)*	*(It is essential that the consumer is anonymous to protect against unjust targeting and adhere to proper legislation)*
Responsibility lies with the consumer and their knowledge of the terms and conditions of the social media service provider. As a user they are responsible for how they choose to publish content, where, what and how privately to share.	Data deals with sensitive topics and consent is morally and legally required.	This is essential if informed consent has not been gained.
Digital platforms and social media providers make clear how public posts are micro-managed and the degree of visibility that each user may put in place.	Provides a key icebreaker between the researcher and participant/s and trust can be established to build into the research process. This allows the researcher to confirm that the user had intended to post publicly.	To preserve and protect both participant and researcher in order to avoid any potential harm, including bullying or ridicule.
	To quote a username alongside a post	If dealing with sensitive issues or vulnerable groups, for the research to be legitimate and to accommodate different consumer types.
	To gain permission to publish content, including photos or other imagery, etc. this is especially important if	The researcher/ team may also face risks. Researchers may abuse and be exposed to distressing information

Table 1. (*Continued*)

Consent and Anonymity are not Required	Informed Consent is Necessary	Anonymity is Necessary
	content could be considered particularly sensitive or personal.	that is publicly shared. If the researcher has a profile on any social media they may be more vulnerable to these risks as participants and may be targeted by participants and/or non-participants.
	For participants to be able to follow-up on the research and to determine the quality and potential outcomes from the research.	
	If content is not recent, to confirm the user has not changed their opinion.	

Source: Adapted from Report on Social Media Data Handling by Natcen (2014).

This more structured composition of the relationship and expectations that should be established by the researcher *before* they undertake any data collection and/or analysis of the consumer participants is helpful. It reflects current qualitative and social researcher guidelines from professional bodies (see Statement of Ethical Practice – *The British Sociological Association*[2] and *ASA Code of Ethics – American Sociological Association*[3]).

Informed consent, ethics and consumer group targeting require especially detailed scrutiny when applied in a digital setting. Whilst the researcher might be successful in securing the permission of research participants and trust of a targeted consumer group, the principles of integrity, research honesty and accuracy need to be taken forward from the core requirements of the project, into recruitment, through the analysis, and maintained throughout the publication and public dissemination. Digitisation, as Marres reminds us has '… special implications for the role and status of the social research methods in particular' (2012, p. 140). Marres's argument is particularly important as she (and others) seek to move away from the existing dichotomous diagnosis of digital methods, and to concentrate on the ways in which new methodologies open up new ways of redistributing research, and understanding shared accomplishments. Digital social methods resonate because of the nature of the data (changeable, in the flow of networks and holding multiple signifiers), and a key question to answer is how the researcher should adjust to these conditions.

Marketisation of Digital Data

One aspect of qualitative digital research methodologies that is crucial to social media and digital data is the commercial selling of consumer data. This is used to provide new indexes for analysis (e.g. social media sentiment analysis), to make forecasts and derive conclusions for investment, and predict the potential impact of data in the marketplace. Methodologically, the digital era has resulted in changes in how consumers build up relationships with brands (both on and offline), as well as through the interactions that consumers choose to enter into with other consumers. This shift has required a rethinking of how brands should be directed, and most notably the significance of co-created content and changing face of data insight (see Hatch & Schultz, 2010; Hipperson, 2010; Quinton, 2013). As consumers and brands increasingly inhabit digital territories, research methods begin to incorporate specific web-analytics that measure social media activity and digital reach.

The prevailing view of consumer data has been as a linear customer journey – an exchange-based set of activities that is part of a marketing paradigm (Louro & Cunha, 2001). There has been far less attention to the more complex and co-created digital consumer processes by which products and services may be discovered and how relationships can be built with brands. Whilst it is difficult to place a specific value on the content that is co-created by the digital consumer – who is (relatively speaking) still in her/his infancy (e.g. Arvidsson, 2006, 2008; Hardey, 2012; Prahalad & Ramaswamy, 2004; Thompson & Malaviya, 2013), there is without doubt a wealth of opportunity here. It is possible to observe how companies have increasingly involved consumers, and how they are using digital data to develop other marketing actions and promotion (Thompson & Malaviya, 2013). However, the proliferation of new technologies for recording, analysing and visualising digital consumer life masks an underlying trend.

Digital data are leading the researcher into relationships that encourage the privatisation of social research in that they enable the displacement of social research towards the corporate laboratories of big IT firms (Marres,

2012; Savage, 2013; Webster, 2013). The central proposition is that digital data are further employed not only to understand new knowledge, but also to provide multi-modal relationships with commercial companies and business. One potential change to the openness of digital data, is the gatekeeping and selling of user data. For example, Facebook markets and charges individuals who are interested in tracking and monitoring user data. Less a 'social network site', Facebook has become a *service network site,* promising new products for commercial companies, and identifying emerging services to target at its users.

There are some technical and legal challenges here for any researcher to take on board; principally, the ownership of consumer data and subsequent analysis. By way of illustration, let us look at one legal case in the United Kingdom; R v Paul Chambers (appealed to the High Court as Chambers v Director of Public Prosecutions), and better known as *The Twitter Joke Trial.* Chambers tweeted his frustration after the closure of the South Yorkshire Robin Hood Airport. His tweet was deemed as a 'hostile' public declaration of threat; '*Crap! Robin Hood airport is closed. You've got a week and a bit to get your shit together otherwise I'm blowing the airport sky high*!!' Prosecuted under the Communications Act 2003, Chambers' actions were interpreted as a 'public electronic message that was grossly offensive or of an indecent, obscene or menacing character'. The case was quashed only after a third appeal to the High Court. The distinction between a publicly shared sense of frustration about a private matter raises some interesting questions about the grey territory of digital privacy and user integrity, as well as the part of the platform provider; Twitter had no role in the defence or prosecution. More noteworthy was that the Crown Prosecution Service appeared to have no concept of the non-literal character of online public communications or dialogue, even though other areas of law, such as contract law, have long provided for 'mere' human exaggeration.

Suggestions for Improving Research Practices for Digital Data

Transparency is key to participant recruitment and building trust, and researchers must explicitly state the conditions of the research, including the intended outputs. Testing the *visibility* of digital content will also encourage confidence in the validity of the research. The overview below (Table 2) is intended as a suggestion for qualitative researchers to consider in the design of rigorous digital consumer data and social media research studies.

Table 2. Summarising the key Points of Consideration for Digital Methodological Procedures.

Sample and recruitment	to accommodate appropriately the consumer target group, and to target participants to the research ethically.
Generating and collecting data	to uphold the privacy of participants and protect (if required) the identity of the researchers involved the project.
Dissemination of results	to maintain the trust of the participants and continue over time to re-evaluate the visibility of the research project to ensure valued and risk-free reporting.

It is a relatively direct task to trace multiple aspects of the same social media post (e.g. using an online search engine to identify related content and users). These actions should be taken to ensure that after publication of the research material no user is identifiable and that they have understood that their participation means that their involvement is observable. Returning to the integrity of digital methods, part of the role of the digital researcher is the assimilation of content and context; the 'whom', and/or what group/s they are studying, as well as the platforms and software involved.

CONCLUSION

This chapter questions the existing methods of researching digital consumer data, the assemblages of content that are both visible and invisible in context, and finally, how data itself has become a by-product that may be marketed, commercialised and interacted with. Some have articulated this as a 'data deluge' (see Halford, Catherine, & Weal, 2013), whilst others have identified a new commercial industry opening up (e.g. data visualisation), and out of these, a desire by some for escape from social platforms completely (Beer & Hardey, 2013). Whilst these observations are valid in terms of comparison with traditional insights, tools for analysis and data artefacts, there is much to be gained from understanding the limitations of the seemingly unending territory of digital data.

While there are new and engaging challenges that arise in targeting specific consumer communities when data may be produced in real time, we must also consider the limitations. To this end, marketing narratives should accord with the 'social life of data' (see Beer & Burrows, 2013) that has significant consequences for the commercial industry, business and researchers. This is not just about the new sources of data in a digital form, but how the narrative is an appropriate metaphor for understanding how digital and social media have shifted research practices into more interactive and more visible territories for both researchers and research participants.

The capabilities of the technology will present significant challenges for researchers and organisations. Amongst the academe, there needs to be greater consideration in the practice of harnessing the potential offered by digital consumer data as well as the additional tools offered by social media for undertaking research. Quinton's (2013) work on the impact of social media on CRM embraces this practice of informed methodology, expressly arguing for the creation of new knowledge from which to develop new data and business strategy. For the forthcoming generation of digital scholars and qualitative researchers, the time for new methodological understanding and evaluation is now, and this urgency carries an added sense of responsibility about the longer-term presence of data records and the dissemination of such efforts in the public domain.

NOTES

1. For an excellent overview of the use of Python refer to 'Introduction to Data Science' by Bill Howe. Available at https://class.coursera.org/datasci-001/lecture/55
2. BSA Statement of ethical practice, download pdf from http://www.britsoc.co.uk/media/27107/StatementofEthicalPractice.pdf
3. ASA Code of ethics, available at www.asanet.org

REFERENCES

Arvidsson, A. (2006). Brands: A critical perspective. *Journal of Consumer Culture*, *5*(2), 235–258.

Arvidsson, A. (2008). The ethical economy of customer coproduction. *Journal of Macromarketing*, *28*(4), 326–338.

Back, L. (2010, August). '*Broken devices and new opportunities': Re-imagining the tools of qualitative research*. NCRM Working Paper Series.

Beer, D. (2009). Power through the algorithm? Participatory web cultures and the technological unconscious. *New Media & Society*, *11*(6), 985–1002.

Beer, D., & Burrows, R. (2013). Popular culture, digital archives and the new social life of data. *Theory, Culture & Society*, *30*(4), 47–71.

Beer, D., & Hardey, M. (2013). Talking about escape. In G. Lovink & M. Rasch (Eds.), *Unlike us reader: Social media monopolies and their alternatives*. (No. 8). Amsterdam, Netherlands: Institute of Network Cultures.

Bik, H. M., & Goldstein, M. C. (2013). An Introduction to social media for scientists. *PLoS Biology*, *11*(4), e1001535. doi:10.1371/journal.pbio.1001535 boyd, d., & Crawford, K. (2011). Six provocations for big data. Paper presented at Oxford internet institute's a decade in internet time, symposium on the dynamics of the internet and society, pp. 1–17.

Braun, V., & Clarke, V. (2013). *Successful qualitative research: A practical guide for beginners.* London: Sage.

Brown, G. H. (1950). Measuring consumer attitudes toward products. *The Journal of Marketing*, 691–698.

Cova, B., & Pace, S. (2006). Brand community of convenience products: New forms of customer empowerment – The case 'my nutella the community'. *European Journal of Marketing*, *40*(9–10), 1087–1105.

Featherstone, M. (2014). Preliminary reflections on the visible, the invisible and social regulation: Panopticism, biopolitics, neoliberalism and data consumption. *Journal of Critical Studies in Business & Society*, *4*(1).

Gitelman, L. (2008). Always already new: Media, history and the data of culture. Cambridge, MA: The MIT Press.

Gitelman, L. & Pingree, G. B. (Eds.). (2003). *New media* (pp. 1740–1915). Cambridge, MA: MIT Press.

Gurstein, M. B. (2011). Open data: Empowering the empowered or effective data use for everyone? *First Monday*, *16*(2).

Halford, S., Catherine, P., & Weal, M. (2013). Digital futures? Sociological challenges and opportunities in the emergent semantic web. *Sociology*, *47*(1), 173–189.

Hansson, L., Wrangmo, A., & Søilen, K. S. (2013). Optimal ways for companies to use Facebook as a marketing channel. *Journal of Information, Communication and Ethics in Society*, *11*(2), 112–126.

Hardey, M. (2011). Ubiquitous connecticity: User-generated data and the role of the researcher. In S. N. Hesse-Biber (Ed.), *The handbook of emergent technologies in social research.* Oxford: Oxford University Press.

Hardey, M. (2011a). Generation C: Content, creation, connections and choice. *International Journal of Market Research*, *53*(6), 749–770.

Hardey, M. (2011b). To spin straw into gold? New lessons from consumer-generated content. *The International Journal of Market Research*, *53*(1), 13–15.

Hardey, M. (2011c). Ubiquitous connectivity: User-generated data and the role of the researcher. In S. N. Hesse-Biber (Ed.), *The handbook of emergent technologies in social research.* Oxford: Oxford University Press.

Hardey, M. (2012). New visions: Capturing digital data and market research. *International Journal of Market Research*, *54*(2), 2–9.

Hardey, M. (Ed.). (2013). Re-asserting the social media contribution to the theory and practice of market research. *International Journal of Market Research*, (January), 751–754.

Hatch, M. J., & Schultz, M. (2010). Toward a theory of brand co-creation with implications for brand governance. *Journal of Brand Management*, *17*(8), 590–604.

Hipperson, T. (2010). The changing face of data insight and its relationship to brand marketing. *Journal of Database Marketing & Customer Strategy Management*, *17*(3), 262–266.

Kang, J., Tang, L., & Fiore, A. M. (2014). Enhancing consumer–brand relationships on restaurant Facebook fan pages: Maximizing consumer benefits and increasing active participation. *International Journal of Hospitality Management*, *36*, 145–155.

Louro, M. J., & Cunha, P. V. (2001). Brand management paradigms. *Journal of Marketing Management*, *17*, 849–875.

Lupton, D. (2014). The commodification of patient opinion: The digital patient experience economy in the age of big data. *Sociology of Health & Illness*, *36*(6), 856–869.

Marres, N. (2012). The redistribution of methods: On intervention in digital social research, broadly conceived. *The Sociological Review*, *60*, 139–165.

McEwen, R., & Wellman, B. (2013). Relationships, community, and networked individuals. *The Immersive Internet: Reflections on the Entangling of the Virtual with Society, Politics and the Economy*, 168.

McWilliam, G. (2012). Building stronger brands through online communities. *Sloan Management Review*, *41*(3).

NetCen Social Media Report. (2014). Retrieved from http://www.natcen.ac.uk/media/282288/p0639-research-using-social-media-report-final-190214.pdf. Accessed on September 20, 2014.

Niederer, S., & Van Dijck, J. (2010). Wisdom of the crowd or technicity of content? Wikipedia as a sociotechnical system. *New Media & Society*, *12*(8), 1368–1387.

PEW Research Centre. (2014, April). *Social networking use*. Report. Retrieved from http://www.pewresearch.org/data-trend/media-and-technology/social-networking-use/. Accessed on April 28, 2014.

Prahalad, C. K., & Ramaswamy, V. (2004). Co-creation experiences: The next practice in value creation. *Journal of interactive marketing*, *18*(3), 5–14.

Quinton, S. (2013). The digital era requires new knowledge to develop relevant CRM strategy: A cry for adopting social media research methods to elicit this new knowledge. *Journal of Strategic Marketing*, *21*(5), 402–412.

Ritzer, G., Dean, P., & Jurgenson, N. (2012). The coming of age of the prosumer. *American Behavioral Scientist*, *56*(4), 379–398.

Ritzer, G., Dean, P., & Nathan, J. (2012). The coming of age of the prosumer. *American Behavioral Scientist*, *56*(4), 379–398.

Ritzer, G., & Jurgenson, N. (2010). Production, consumption, prosumption the nature of capitalism in the age of the digital 'prosumer'. *Journal of Consumer Culture*, *10*(1), 13–36.

Rogers, R. (2010). Internet research: The question of method – A keynote address from the YouTube and the 2008 election cycle in the United States conference. *Journal of Information Technology & Politics*, *7*(2–3), 241–260.

Rogers, R. (2013). *Digital methods*. Cambridge, MA: MIT Press.

Ruppert, E., Law, J., & Savage, M. (2013). Reassembling social science methods: The challenge of digital devices. *Theory, culture & society*, *30*(4), 22–46.

Russell, M. A. (2013). *Mining the social web: Data mining Facebook, Twitter, LinkedIn, Google+, GitHub, and more*. Sebastopol, CA: O'Reilly Media, Inc.

Savage, M. (2013). The 'social life of methods': A critical introduction. *Theory, Culture & Society*, *30*(4), 3–21.

Savage, M., & Burrows, R. (2007). The coming crisis of empirical sociology. *Sociology*, *41*(5), 885–899.

Savage, M., Law, J., & Ruppert, E. (2010). *The double social life of methods*. CRESC Working Paper Series. No. 95. Retrieved from http://www.cresc.ac.uk/our-research/cross-theme-research/social-life-of-methods

Schulze, C., Schöler, L., & Skiera, B. (2014). Not all fun and games: Viral marketing for utilitarian products. *Journal of Marketing*, *78*(1), 1–19.

Simkin, L., & Dibb, S. (2013). Social media's impact on market segmentation and CRM. *Journal of Strategic Marketing*, *21*(5), 391–393.
Smith, S. (2013). Conceptualizing and evaluating experiences with brands on Facebook. *International Journal of Market Research*, *55*(3), 357–374.
Tadajewski, M. (2006). The ordering of marketing theory: The influence of McCarthyism and the cold war. *Marketing Theory*, *6*(2), 163–199.
Tadajewski, M. (2010). Towards a history of critical marketing studies. *Journal of Marketing Management*, *26*(9–10), 773–824.
Tadajewski, M. (2013). Promoting the consumer society: Ernest Dichter, the cold war and FBI. *Journal of Historical Research in Marketing*, *5*(2), 192–211.
Thompson, D. V., & Malaviya, P. (2013). Consumer-generated ads: Does awareness of advertising co-creation help or hurt persuasion? *Journal of Marketing*, *77*(3), 33–47.
Thrift, N. (2005). *Knowing capitalism*. London: Sage.
Thurman, N. (2014). Newspaper consumption in the digital age: Measuring multi-channel audience attention and brand popularity. *Digital Journalism*, *2*(2), 156–178.
Thurman, N., & Newman, N. (2014). The future of breaking news online? A study of live blogs through surveys of their consumption, and of readers' attitudes and participation. *Journalism Studies* (ahead-of-print), 1–13.
Vis, F. (2013). A critical reflection on big data: Considering APIs, researchers and tools as data makers. *First Monday*, *18*(10).
Webster, A. (2013). Afterword: Digital technology and sociological windows. *Digital Sociology: Critical Perspectives*, 227.
Wellman, B. (1999). *Networks in the global village, life in contemporary communities*. Boulder, CO: Westview.
Womer, S. (1944). Some applications of the continuous consumer panel. *The Journal of Marketing*, 132–136.

NOT BEING THERE: RESEARCH AT A DISTANCE WITH VIDEO, TEXT AND SPEECH

Angus Bancroft, Martina Karels, Órla Meadhbh Murray and Jade Zimpfer

ABSTRACT

This chapter examines the history and process of research participants producing and working with data. The experience of working with researcher-produced and/or analysed data shows how social research is a set of practices which can be shared with research participants, and which in key ways draw on everyday habits and performances. Participant-produced data has come to the fore with the popularity of crowdsourced, citizen science research and Games with a Purpose. These address practical problems and potentially open up the research process to large scale democratic involvement. However at the same time the process can become fragmented and proletarianised. Mass research has a long history, an exemplar of which is the Mass Observation studies. Our research involved participants collecting video data on their intoxication practices. We discuss how their experience altered their own subject position in relation to these regular social activities, and explore how our understanding of their data collection converged and differed from theirs.

Big Data? Qualitative Approaches to Digital Research
Studies in Qualitative Methodology, Volume 13, 137–153

ISSN: 1042-3192/doi:10.1108/S1042-319220140000013009

Crowdsourced research raises a challenge to the research binary as the work is done by participants rather than the research team; however it also reaffirms it, unless further work is done to involve participants in commenting and reflecting on the research process itself.

Keywords: Big data; mass observation; crowdsourcing; diary research; video ethnography; research binary

RESEARCH WORK

Our chapter examines distributed research methods, in which participants generate data and sometimes analysis for researchers. This has a long history with diary research such as Mass Observation, allowing for a potentially large volume of data with a relatively rapid response time. New technologies have reduced some of the technical and organisational barriers to this kind of research, lowering the cost and allowing new kinds of data collection. We discuss some of the epistemological, methodological and ethical challenges of this research. We draw on the history of research at a distance in the social sciences, the recent history of crowdsourced citizen science, and our own distributed video ethnography, defined as a collaborative research project where multiple participants collect naturally occurring observational video data. Our video ethnography allows us to examine features and challenges that are common to much crowdsourced research, its collaborative possibilities, and the way it challenges the research binary and exposes power relations and draws attention to social research as practical labour.

We examine social research as a set of practices that can be shared with participants, and in which sufficiently empowered participants can take the lead in setting the research agenda. Each of the research approaches we discuss draw on shared social practices and rely on shared understandings of what they are. Gaming, diarising, archiving and documenting are forms of work supported by material and cultural contexts. In each form of work the participant positions themselves differently, both in relation to the data collection method and to the setting they are reporting on. We use these examples to highlight how digital cultures shape the kinds of data collected and the work done on them. They draw on and reproduce shared tropes and knowledge about documenting and performing social life. We highlight the work research participants have done and are doing in creating the social through digital means. This has implications for research with Web

2.0, where the work done by participants in forming and reproducing their social worlds takes place on and off-line.

We are drawing on the history of diary research to show how sociology has and can still access the social at a distance. In the examples we have chosen, the researcher or the research team is absent. Their only presence is in the research instrument, the preparation, if any, they have given the research participant, and in digital research, the website or app design and prompts which the participant interacts with. There has been relatively little crowdsourcing of social science data, except in so far as geographical mapping data is also social science data. That is why in this chapter we want to excavate diary research as part of the history of crowdsourcing social science research. There is an opportunity to use crowdsourcing in new ways to create large qualitative datasets, involve participants actively in the process, and democratise our research practice. Our small project illustrates some of the problems and opportunities in doing this.

We have called our study a distributed video ethnography because of its open structure and its use of video recorded naturally occurring observations – 'documentary data'. It was conducted with 10 students at the University of Edinburgh. We asked student volunteers to collect video data on the themes of digital and intoxication cultures. Students were given a number of tasks to begin with, such as to record intoxication rituals they were involved in. We encouraged them to interpret the brief very openly. We asked them to record diary (talking to camera) and documentary video. Video took the form of diaries, observations, 'tipsy' confessions, freely recorded video of cameras left lying and interviews. Research meetings with the group reviewed what was collected and then each participant was interviewed around themes emerging from their video data. It seemed at first like a happy and straightforward circumstance that research technologies exist in the devices many use everyday, in mobile technology and web cameras routinely built into many computers, which allow our methods to flow with the technologies and techniques people employ to make social life happen (Savage & Burrows, 2007). We could make use of this to collect data on the topics. As we reviewed the data and discussed with the students it became clear that we were not just involved in a researcher–respondent interaction, but that both us and them were also interacting with a set of technologies, techniques, tropes and habits built into social interaction in Web 2.0 and real-world environments. So a key requirement for any researchers using this 'at a distance' method is to be aware of these material entities and practices that in crucial ways govern and filter what is produced and shared.

GAMING AND CROWDSOURCING

We have linked our chapter to crowdsourcing as this is an emerging model for digital research at a distance. The term covers a range of activities, covering fundraising, capital investment, content development, data collection and analysis, which are distributed among a large number of otherwise un-coordinated individuals who are operating in a semi- or non-professional role. It is an emerging structure for digital research. It has taken off rapidly in market research, partly because it relies on activities that participants are already used to. It has been used as a model to deal with some of the challenges of big data, in particular the volume of data outrunning the analytic capacity of the researchers, and the limits of computerised taxonomy. Although it existed as a practice long before it was named, and long before the internet came into being, the capacity of the internet and social media to facilitate crowdsourcing has made it common currency.

Crowdsourced research points us to the first kind of work participants do in research at a distance, which is gaming. A common method of crowdsourcing research is through Games with a Purpose. They divide tasks into collecting, validating and ranking data (Celino et al., 2012). *Zooniverse* is a platform for crowdsourcing scientific projects. This is a distributed analysis that addresses a longstanding problem in natural science and social science, the classification problem. One project, Galaxy Zoo, asks users to classify galaxies as part of a study of galaxy formation (Raddick et al., 2010). It is quite easy for humans to classify galaxies in terms of their features, but difficult to write an algorithm that allows a computer to do so. The Operation War Diary project involves users transcribing and classifying British Army war diaries from 1914 to 1922 using the Zooniverse platform. On its website, participants are addressed as 'Citizen historians'. They classify diary pages then tag them with names, places, unit information, weather, activity, casualties and other information. The project turns an unstructured archive into a sortable dataset.

Games with a Purpose overlap with an aspect of videogame culture which involves routine maintenance and time-intensive nurturing as a key aspect of the game. Users of social networking services are in many ways already used to engaging in 'playbour' (Goggin, 2011). Web 2.0 platforms could not exist without large-scale user-generated content, so this is a kind of labour that many are already familiar with. One effect of the growth of crowdsourcing, especially in the case of market research, is the commodification of data. Participants in crowdsourced studies when paid – or at least, poorly paid – tend to skew the sample towards the poor and developing countries (Norcie, 2011). Data gathering can be proletarianised – reducing the research to a sequence of atomised tasks. This has consequences for how we view the autonomy and agency of research participants. Feminist methodologists have long been critical of the disembedding of data in the research process. Elwood (2008) considers these critiques in the context of volunteered geographic information. Some crowdsourcing systems can submerge the process of identifying and classifying as a social process by making it just a matter of inter-rater agreement.

PRODUCING DIARIES

Diary research shares some characteristics of crowdsourced work. Diaries are individual documents of life, chronicles of both public and private events deemed important by the author, recorded and maintained in a regular and contemporaneous manner (Plummer, 2000). Diary writing and diary research has changed the traditional role of research participant from informant to collaborator more-or-less actively involved in both the creation of data and its interpretation. These personal records may take various distinctive forms: intimate journals filled with private thoughts and uncensored commentary, log entries listing activities and events of all sorts including their times and locations etc. (Allport, 1942), or memoires which, unlike intimate journals, are recounted in retrospect (Watson, 2013) and are produced with an intended audience (and possibly publication) in mind (Elliott, 1997). The practise of using diaries is an established component of social inquiry, although their forms, how they are produced and for what purposes, has evolved over time. Through the advancements in new media and readily available alternative recording tools, different incarnations of diary research are being introduced. Diaries can be differentiated by modes of production: they can be *kept*, are already *in existence* or are *solicited*, the latter being the focus of this section.

Historical diaries already in existence are essentially found objects that are explored and analysed. Scholars of social history have long relied on diaries and letters as primary research sources to discover and uncover the personal and social conditions and events of past times. Personal diaries might primarily contain the intimate details and desires of their authors, but they reveal more than autobiographic information or just the intimate details and desires of their authors. Personal journals also provide unique perspectives on local customs and etiquette, linguistic conventions and fashions, personal and public events, as well as both the geographical and social environment reflecting the time and space in which the document was produced. The popular diary of Samuel Pepys, who recorded his life's events from 1660 to 1669, offers exclusive commentary on the public, political and personal affairs of 17th century London. Pepys belonged to a class of elites: a wealthy, white and literate male. His descriptions and confessions reveal the habits and customs of this privileged group through the particular reference frames of Pepys' own social world (Alaszewski, 2006).

Diaries are both social artefacts and constructs determined by social, spatial and temporal contexts. As such they provide an opportunity to understand the diarists' viewpoints, and how social relations and structures were formed in their particular surroundings. Records kept by women have been of particular interest for social historians and scientists as they allow a glimpse into the day-to-day lives of the underrepresented non-elites. The at times cheeky diaries of Hannah Cullwick, a servant in Victorian England uniquely reveal the daily particularities of working-class servant women in an era defined by a national sense of middle class moral propriety (Cullwick & Stanley, 1984).

Both historical 'naturally occurring' diaries and diaries solicited through research are social and material products. Written diaries require a degree of literacy and literary confidence, and the time and space to maintain it on a regular basis. One of the first studies to solicit diaries as research tools was the *Mass Observation* project, which started as a social research organisation aiming to record everyday life in Britain. From 1937 to the early 1950s the group solicited a national panel of diarists, composed of both women and men, to record ordinary life across Britain. Diaries were kept and sent to the core research team in monthly intervals. As no particular record keeping instructions were given the diaries vary greatly in form, detail and length. The voluminous collection of records provides a view of life in Britain through the eyes of volunteer observers. The many women volunteers offer important female perspectives so often omitted in official records (Stanley, 1995). The writings of Nella Last, who maintained her diary for nearly 30 years, have gained particular attention of feminist scholars and were published in both original and edited form. In 1981 the project was revived and to this day is soliciting diaries from the general public.

Over the years the Mass Observation project has influenced studies that solicit data in the form of diaries and log entries. In 1965 Alexander Szalai commenced the *International Time-Use Study* which solicited 2000 participants between the ages of 18 and 64 from 12 different countries to keep time diaries, continuous logs of daily activities similar to surveys, to map how they spent their time over the course of one day (Szalai, 1972). The international study has expanded over the years (now including more than 25 countries) and has incorporated aspects of time/budget and spending, wages, transportation, leisure activities, etc. The Centre of Time Use Research holds large datasets of diaries providing empirical longitudinal resources for socio-economic inquiries, allowing for cross-national comparisons and considerations of variables like gender or age over time. Therefore, time-use/time-budget studies have been especially useful in quantifying analyses. Gershuny and Sullivan (2014) examined gender and children's time use through the analysis of existing datasets of the UK Office of National Statistics Time Use Survey of 2000/2001. Employing a representative sample of individuals in private households their findings include the conclusion that adolescent daughters do more domestic chores than adolescent sons, an argument that much of children's housework goes overlooked in studies of time-use and distribution.

A more recent study inspired by the Mass Observation team methods is the *Sharing Practice Project* (Fincher, 2013). The study solicited and collected diaries from academics in UK institutions of higher education over the course of one academic year to discover what academics find significant in their daily interactions with students, the institution and their own work. Once a month participants submitted electronically their private, at times candid diary entries and later received summarised feedback on collective emerging themes via a newsletter published by the researcher. The feedback established a sense of dialogue between participants and facilitators.

Diaries have been effective in gathering data on the minutiae of hidden practices around sex and drugs. Project SIGMA (1986–1994) was the largest study of gay men in Britain. Led by Tony Coxon the study solicited diaries from 1035 participants chronicling their social and sexual lifestyles including sexual risk behaviours and activities, especially the adoption of safe practices. The stigmatised and legally sensitive nature of the study made it difficult to collect data through traditional methods of observation and interviews. Journaling experiences and activities in intimate diary form allowed for a sense of privacy and protected anonymity (Coxon et al., 1993). Stopka, Springer, Khoshnood, Shaw, and Singer (2004) also worked with delicate data in their study of injection drug users in America. Participants recorded their drug using practises, especially those related to HIV risk behaviour, such as the acquisition, handling and disposal of syringes. They were asked to keep diaries for up to a week and to attend daily clarifying feedback sessions with a member of the research team, helping to ensure safety for the potentially incriminating diaries. These diaries allowed the research team an inside view into the closed groups of drug users.

Diaries present a great opportunity to collaborate with informants and participants because written accounts may be supplemented with other forms of data collection such as interviews. Zimmerman and Wieder (1977) are strong proponents of the solicitation of diaries as part of ethnographic field research and suggest the use of the 'diary, diary-interview method'. Informants are recruited to keep diaries and to record thoughts on routines and activities related to the subject of study that would otherwise not be accessible to the researcher or would be disturbed by an external observer's presence. Informants take on the role of a local stand-in, reporting back to the researcher initially in the form of the diary, then verbally in an in-depth interview setting in which they support, explain, develop, elaborate and reflect upon their written accounts of their own behaviours and observations.

Taking the diaries our participants produced we can see how the act of diarising changes their understanding of the activities they are involved in:

> I didn't go out last night because I had an essay due on Thursday. So I was a very sensible student. And the night started with a number of abusive texts to myself, trying to peer pressure me into going out such as [reads from mobile phone screen]: 'come out, please Alyssa. Poor show. Just come for a bit; 'Oi, oi, please . We will keep you on the right road'... the next day when there was a lot of chat going on our Facebook page, our shared Facebook page about what had happened the night before, it kind of made me wonder what the purpose of our ritual meeting up for drinks has on our friendship. (Alyssa, video diary)

In this case the group work of subjecting Alyssa to good natured abuse for her failure to join her friends on a night out drinking became apparent to her when she was recording it. Participating in the research resulted in changes in respondents' orientation to their activity. Alyssa went on in the interview to reflect on how she moved into the position of being a reflective insider, and more questioning of the activities that were the norm in her friendship group:

> I'm thinking about it, that's the difference. Before it was just a case of 'I'll go out and come back' and have a headache because I'm hungover but now I'm thinking about, you know, why I go out, why I had a drink there, what it means. It has made me think a lot more about why I'm doing stuff so that is interesting. When I was filming I guess I was the insider as I knew all the group. So then I could film them and they were acting normally. And it meant I could ask them questions which they would answer which maybe they wouldn't if I'd come from an outsider situation. (Alyssa, interview)

For Alyssa, as for Pepys and Cullwick, producing a diary meant taking a subject-position as a peripheral insider. The last quote from Alyssa shows her more of an active researcher, probing and questioning her friends to give accounts of themselves. This account producing can take place between the diarist and others, and this is a possibility opened up by the video ethnography method. The fact of recording video as part of a research project helped to give Alyssa the status and confidence to quiz her friends.

The method of soliciting research diaries and logs is an effective way of gathering large datasets from and about the activities. While some big privately held datasets and spending habits of ordinary members of the public are possible to solicit, it would be logistically unattainable for researchers to be physically present and to follow hundreds or even thousands of participants. Similarly, research diaries are particularly suitable for studying and accessing closed or intimate environments, situations in which the researcher's mere presence would disrupt typical behaviours under investigation or sensitive subject matter. Some of these apparent benefits of diary research – the large scale, the recording of mundane activities – might be superseded by big data. However, our contention is that the uncritical acceptance of big data methods can submerge political, ethical and epistemological questions about data production and ownership, and also submerge the subject position of participants.

DOCUMENTING AND MOBILITY

> It was strange to take a step back as I was involved myself. When I was in there it was more 'this is really funny, I'm going to film it'. Then a few days after, what was that like and speaking to them. (Millie, interview)

Crowdsourcing, in past years solely found on the fixed internet, has evolved into a heavy reliance on mobile platforms. Our research project aimed to take advantage of the fact that many people in the United Kingdom possess video recording devices in the form of their mobile phones. By using this method for our study we were able to draw from a large pool of participants without being overly concerned about equipment costs. We found that by employing these methods two of the key strengths were fluidity and flexibility. A mobile device is small, lightweight, portable, and does not seem threatening or obtrusive like a large video camera might. Additionally, many applications that are found on mobile devices today, such as an audio recorder, camera, and note pad, allow the opportunity to gain consent without loading the student down with paperwork for the participant to sign. It also allows the participant to make notes to him or herself, save questions or key prompts which they might want to use in order to guide the conversation, and also capture the audio and visual data in whichever format they choose; for example, deciding between taking a single shot photo or capturing a video.

The project leveraged students' familiarity with social media. Many would take photographs and sometimes short videos of nights in and out and events and post them on social media sites. This practice of documenting social life, textually via Twitter, by photo via Instagram and with video through Vimeo and other sites was a regular feature of life for the participants. Being sociable meant documenting and being documented. The mobility of connected technology was crucial in sustaining that. As one of our participants reflected, the act of documenting the event affirms it as a positive and worthwhile occasion:

> They sense if they are documented having fun among many other people that would be a positive sign for them outside the party increasing their social status … When they were filmed, people try to act as if they are having more fun than they are actually having. They want to look as good as possible. They are just being filmed for a few seconds and want to symbolise everything they have been doing so far. (Simon, interview)

For us, documenting was a different activity. Together with the participants, we were engaged in reconstructing social scenes. In the interview below Cassie recalls some of the footage she had submitted to us:

> I don't really remember some of the footage. Was there a pub scene as well? My flatmate and I had gone to the pub for a few drinks beforehand. We filmed that as well. It was a Friday night and it was absolutely heaving. It was just everybody who had finished work for the week and needed wind down time. You chose them because they were things you were doing anyway. (Cassie, interview)

Though her account initially suggested a fairly random selection of video was submitted, when reviewing it together we pieced together a 'story' of the evening, from meeting in a pub to attending a surprise party, to herself and her friends secluding themselves within it. The party itself was not one they were very keen on being at. The videos recorded some of their activities in trying to shape the evening in ways that they would enjoy more. This context was not apparent until we reconstructed it with Cassie using the videos and interview. The reconstruction was temporal at first. The videos were put together in time sequence. Cassie's reconstruction produced another sequence of events, that of varying sociable engagement with the party.

> It changed the interaction a little bit maybe. I was aware of what I was doing so if I was recording friends I was aware of holding back and that you probably didn't want me shouting from behind the camera. It made me think about what I would be doing in that situation. (Alyssa, interview)

The data highlighted how respondents should be involved in the work of narrating and commenting, but also the limits of their own role as observer participants. For example, the same party or drinking space can be classified very differently by observers depending on their positioning in relation to it. It might be threatening, exhilarating, risky, all and more at once. Women's experience was often dualistic in this way, as they responded to the demand and the desire to be sociable through drinking but also to avoid risk to themselves as women.

SHARING AND PERFORMING

> There's usually photos before actually. If we're predrinking we'll take group photos or someone will have a camera. Someone will liaise beforehand: 'someone bring a camera', and make sure someone is bringing one. So there is usually photos beforehand and we all have phones with cameras on them so we tend to take those out now and take pictures of each other on the night. (Alyssa, interview)

We found that most students were used to sharing photography and sometimes video on social media so the project took advantage of their already developed skills – in fact, some of these skills had to be unlearned so that students were able to take up the role of researcher-participant. In particular, people naturally filter material they gather according to its shareable qualities. These can be aesthetic and also social. Embarrassing or socially awkward material might get binned, as does indistinct, blurred, underexposed photography or video. However, that was often the material we were most interested in.

There was a tension between relying on participants' established practices of social media self-presentation and performance, and our desire to have unvarnished, naturally occurring video data. On reflection, the latter does not exist. Selecting a scene to record, letting others know you are doing so, then choosing it to share with others, is all part of a performance.

> The next day it's the worst part. Especially on someone's 21st or 18th. I always take my camera out with me anyway and it's kind of a ritual when everyone's hung over. To turn my camera on and look through the photos and videos. It's amazing what you'd don't remember. And what you wish you didn't. Things start coming back. Some of what we ask students to do is what we do anyway? It's a given, my friends constantly have a camera in hand, taking photos.
>
> Do you share them?
>
> Yes, especially since moving away from home. I like my friends back home and my family to see what I've posted online. Some are too explicit. There's usually a message saying 'take that down it's too embarrassing'. There's a digital trail. So you have to be careful with some of the stuff. You have to be careful what footage you make available or create. (Cassie, interview)

The digital trail was something Cassie was aware of mainly through the activities of others trying to censor what she shows online. Sharing memories and photos was part of maintaining her family and friendship relationships between Edinburgh and her hometown.

This video ethnography recorded the performance of drinking and being drunk:

M1: you know you want to, it's, it's alright

F1: how about finishing the ring of fire, it's fun

M1: you want to play? (inaudible discussions and fingerpointing)

F2: I don't know if I want to

F3: no, I'm not falling for your crap (more laughter) (inaudible conversation, but people appear to be trying to get others to partake in the game)

F1: yup you did, but I don't know who changed it

F2: I'm tired (inaudible conversation)

F1: OMG!! it's not me who started it (more laughter and yelling)

F2: Ok, I did drink (people are passing around a mug and drinking from it)... wait a minute, wait a minute (inaudible yelling and camera focuses on the drink, the rest of the screen is dark)

M1: No, omg!

F2: oh no, it's in my cup (disgusted noises)

F3: omg! I can hear my voice, it is drunk already (inaudible conversation in the background)

M2: you are not drunk

F3: yup, yes I am!' (Misty, documentary video).

There is a process going on in this recording where one woman tries to perform being drunk and persuade another male participant that she is drunk. The video captures the mutual construction of social interaction and the agency of one participant in insisting on the correct interpretation of her drunken comportment.

THE RESEARCHERS AND THE RESEARCHED: JUST ANOTHER FALSE BINARY?

In connection with Savage and Burrows' (2007) argument, social researchers do not have privileged methods but we do have a privileged position. Crowdsourcing in research challenges the traditional researcher/researched binary in which the two are seen as distinct, discrete categories and the assumption is that the researcher holds much more power than the researched. However, research encounters are more nuanced than this and power is rarely so unidirectional, even without officially crowdsourcing data or analysis.

In crowdsourced research, the researched can become researchers whereby they go out and conduct interviews, capture videos and write diaries, producing research texts and then using digital technologies, data can be widely distributed and collectively analysed. In such a situation the only difference between the 'official' researchers and the crowdsourcing participants is the lack of formal expertise amongst these 'citizen sociologists'. As briefly discussed in relation to our video ethnography, the expertise such participants contribute is their experiential knowledge, unique access and skills they might have that are transferable to social research projects. However, a power dynamic between these participants and the official researchers still remains and it is unclear if this can be overcome.

It is perhaps useful to think of crowdsourcing as an expansion of the research team approach, whereby a large, diffuse research team is assembled with many non-academics. In a research team of any size or make-up, the output is co-constructed and a hierarchy of status positions exists within it; for example the principal investigator, research assistants, transcribers or interviewers, administrative staff and participants. Often the 'official' research team consists only of the principal investigator and research assistants, with participants and other people involved seen as relatively passive contributors. However, in appreciating the co-construction of knowledge between researchers and participants (Mauthner & Doucet, 2003) and acknowledging the important role played by transcribers, interviewers and administrators in producing knowledge and interpreting what is ‘relevant’ information or who are ‘appropriate’ participants, and other such questions, which are often left out of the official write-up, the research team becomes a much larger entity than just the official academics involved. Often the difference in status and thus in presumed expertise is the basis of inclusion and exclusion of those officially in or out of the research team.

Indeed, feminist researchers have long discussed the unequal power dynamic in researcher interactions, whereby the researcher holds the position of power; organising, structuring and controlling the interview and the write-up. Letherby (2003) discusses the material and status differences between those in each role but also acknowledges the nuances of identity and social position in such an encounter. Research participants will often experience barriers to fully participating in research, for example linguistic, time, and expected knowledge, alongside their assumed position as the answerer of questions rather than co-constructer of knowledge in the interview setting for example. However, participants hold particularly interesting forms of power in their encounter whereby they are essential to the project. The different social positions of individuals involved in research shifts the power dynamic, for example, if the participant is a senior male police officer giving an interview to a young female PhD student, there are broader power dynamics at play than just the roles of researcher/participant, which are often underexamined in discussing the impact on knowledge produced.

Ultimately, the research team writes up and controls the final research output, for example academic papers, Youtube videos, etc., as was the case in our video ethnography project. This often means that those with status and material means, namely academic researchers, have the final say. Hence, even if the data collection and analysis was crowdsourced, the project cannot be said to be fully participatory and informal power dynamics might go unacknowledged. It will be exciting to see how crowdsourcing research develops, particularly with the emphasis of user-generated content in Web 2.0 and the ease of sharing information and collaborating with digital technologies. Perhaps the future of crowdsourcing will be academic researcher(s) setting up projects and getting the ball rolling before groups of citizen researchers continue them.

CONCLUSION

Research at a distance has the potential to dislocate social research from particular expert domains and make social research a more continuous and open-ended process (Law, 2004). These studies draw attention to the work done by the research subjects. Responding to a survey, answering interview questions, completing a diary or helping to snowball a sample, are structured activities calling on the emotional, intellectual and sometimes physical resources of respondents. The effect of crowdsourcing may be on how we value research labour, both financially, and in that the terms of the emotional and intellectual resources that respondents put into it are made apparent by the mechanisms of crowdsourcing. We noted in our study the amount of work put in by participants at each stage – in gaining others' consent to film a scene, recording social occasions when they could be participating, and reviewing the data before passing it on to us. The rise of crowdsourcing reflects a historic shift from the early internet with its open-sourcing, which involved distributed webs of experts working on shared coding tasks. In contrast, expertise and barriers to entry in crowdsourcing are kept low. However, ownership of the project is more concentrated. The activity may be an instance of the digital 'redistribution of methods' (Marres, 2012), and at the same time be a form of research labour that is commodified and monetised, and likewise, proletarianised and atomised.

What social science questions might be addressed through these means? There is potential for crowdsourcing data activism, which has been used by the Missing Sisters project, which maps missing and unsolved murders of indigenous women in the United States and Canada. Attempts to use crowdsourcing data to leverage political positions or novel ontological claims also have a long history (Sidgwick, Johnson, Myers, Podmore, & Sidgwick, 1894). Indeed Mass Observation could be seen in some ways as a social movement as much as a research organisation (Summerfield, 1985). Questions emerge around whether and in what ways social life is becoming data-mediated in a qualitatively different fashion in the digital era. Feedback loops from crowdsourced, continually updated, datasets can create rapid, semi-automatic reflexivity in human behaviour. Sociologists might naturally follow the crowd; now 'the crowd' is potentially a global agglomeration of millions of actions and tasks being updated in real time (Beer & Burrows, 2007). However, our study questions the 'automatic' characterisation of the activity we scrutinised. Our participants worked at being present on social media, at representing themselves, at making social occasions enjoyable, or at least bearable. We have shown how social research can draw on this kind of work as it intersects with research work in many ways. So a model for research at a distance can enhance many of the qualities of in-depth social research, where it can be attentive to the social and material contexts of data production, and the agency of individual participants in making the social world theirs.

REFERENCES

Alaszewski, A. (2006). *Using diaries for social research*. London, UK: Sage.

Allport, G. W. (1942). *The use of personal documents in psychological science*. New York, NY: Social Science Research Council. Retrieved from http://psycnet.apa.org/psycinfo/1942-02314-001

Beer, D., & Burrows, R. (2007). Sociology of, and in, Web 2.0: Some initial considerations. *Sociological Research Online*, *12*(5), 17.

Celino, I., Cerizza, D., Contessa, S., Corubolo, M., Dell'Aglio, D., Valle, E. D., & Fumeo, S. (2012). Urbanopoly: A social and location-based game with a purpose to crowdsource your urban data. *Privacy, Security, Risk and Trust (PASSAT), 2012 international conference on social computing (SocialCom)*, pp. 910–913.

Coxon, T., Davies, P. M., Hunt, A. J., McManus, T. J., Rees, C. M., & Weatherburn, P. (1993). Research note: Strategies in eliciting sensitive sexual information: The case of gay men, *The Sociological Review*, *41*(3), 537–555.

Cullwick, H., & Stanley, L. (1984). *The diaries of Hannah Cullwick, Victorian maidservant*. London, UK: Virago.

Elliott, H. (1997). The use of diaries in sociological research on health experience. *Sociological Research Online*, *2*(2). Retrieved from http://www.socresonline.org.uk/2/2/7.html

Elwood, S. (2008). Volunteered geographic information: Future research directions motivated by critical, participatory, and feminist GIS. *Geo Journal*, *72*(3–4), 173–183.

Fincher, S. (2013). The diarists' audience. In L. Stanley (Ed.), *Documents of life revisited: Narrative and biographical methodology for a 21st century critical humanism*. Avebury, UK: Ashgate. Retrieved from http://kar.kent.ac.uk/id/eprint/34033

Gershuny, J., & Sullivan, O. (2014). Household structure and housework: Assessing the contributions of all household members, with a focus on children and youths. *Review of Economics of the Household*, *12*(1), 7–27.

Goggin, J. (2011). Playbour, farming and leisure. *Ephemera: Theory & Politics in Organization*, *11*(4), 357–368.

Law, J. (2004). *After method: Mess in social science research*. London, UK: Routledge.

Letherby, G. (2003). *Feminist research in theory and practice*. Buckingham: Open University Press.

Marres, N. (2012). The redistribution of methods: On intervention in digital social research, broadly conceived. *The Sociological Review*, *60*(S1), 139–165.

Mauthner, N. S., & Doucet, A. (2003). Reflexive accounts and accounts of reflexivity in qualitative data analysis. *Sociology*, *37*(3), 413–431.

Norcie, G. (2011). Ethical and practical considerations for compensation of crowdsourced research participants. *CHI WS on ethics logs and videotape: Ethics in large scale trials & user generated content*.

Plummer, K. (2000). *Documents of life 2: An invitation to a critical humanism*. London, UK: Sage.

Raddick, M. J., Bracey, G., Gay, P. L., Lintott, C. J., Murray, P., Schawinski, K., Szalay, A. S., & Vandenberg, J. (2010). Galaxy zoo: Exploring the motivations of citizen science volunteers. *Astronomy Education Review*, *9*(1), 010103.

Savage, M., & Burrows, R. (2007). The coming crisis of empirical sociology. *Sociology*, *41*(5), 885–899.

Sidgwick, H., Johnson, A., Myers, F. W. H., Podmore, F., & Sidgwick, E. (1894). Report on the census of hallucinations. *Proceedings of the Society for Psychical Research, 10*, 25–394.

Stanley, L. (1995). Women have servants and men never eat: Issues in reading gender, using the case study of mass-observation's 1937 day-diaries. *Women's History Review, 4*(1), 85–102.

Stopka, T. J., Springer, K. W., Khoshnood, K., Shaw, S., & Singer, M. (2004). Writing about risk: Use of daily diaries in understanding drug-user risk behaviors. *AIDS and Behavior, 8*(1), 73–85.

Summerfield, P. (1985). Mass-observation: Social research or social movement? *Journal of Contemporary History, 20*(3), 439–452.

Szalai, A. (1972). *The use of time: Daily activities of urban and suburban populations in twelve countries*. Den Haag, the Netherlands: Mouton. Retrieved from http://www.cabdirect.org/abstracts/19821888623.html. Accessed in May 2014.

Watson, C. (2013). Between diary and memoir: Documenting a life in wartime Britain. In L. Stanley (Ed.), *Documents of life revisited: Narrative and biographical methodology for a 21st century critical humanism*. Avebury, UK: Ashgate.

Zimmerman, D. H., & Wieder, D. L. (1977). The diary: Diary-interview method. *Journal of Contemporary Ethnography, 5*(4), 479–498.

USING SOFTWARE FOR QUALITATIVE DATA ANALYSIS: RESEARCH OUTSIDE PARADIGMATIC BOUNDARIES

Jonathan Tummons

ABSTRACT

Purpose – *This chapter aims to explicate the use of computer software for qualitative data analysis. Drawing on both a review of relevant literature and a reflexive commentary on an ongoing ethnography, this chapter argues that the use of computer software for qualitative data analysis facilitates rigour and reliability in research, whilst also contributing to wider debates regarding the distinctions made between different research paradigms.*

Design/methodology/approach – *The chapter is divided into two sections. In the first, a review of literature pertaining to the use of computer software for qualitative data analysis is reported. The key themes to emerge from this review are then explored in the second section, which consists of a reflexive commentary on the use of computer software for qualitative data analysis within an ongoing three-year Canadian/UK research project.*

Big Data? Qualitative Approaches to Digital Research
Studies in Qualitative Methodology, Volume 13, 155–177

ISSN: 1042-3192/doi:10.1108/S1042-319220140000013010

Findings – *The chapter concludes firstly by foregrounding the methodological benefits of using computer software for qualitative data analysis, and secondly by commenting on wider debates relating to the historical distinctions between quantitative and qualitative research paradigms.*

Practical implications – *The chapter suggests that the uptake of computer software for qualitative data analysis should be considered as an integral element of the research design process.*

Originality/value – *The originality of this chapter rests in its focus on methodology rather than method, on a reflexive discussion of the place of computer software within the research process rather than a technical description of how software should be used. This chapter is of value not only to researchers who are using or considering using software for their research, but also to researchers who are engaged in wider methodological discussions relating to qualitative and quantitative research paradigms, and to research quality and generalisability.*

Keywords: Qualitative research; Atlas-Ti; computer software; methodology; ethnography

INTRODUCTION

What is the current condition of the use of specialist computer software for qualitative data analysis? Is it indeed the case that it has now become so (relatively) common for a researcher or a team of researchers to use software such as Atlas-Ti or Nvivo to manage their projects that it does not need to be mentioned in the methods section of a research article (Seale & Rivas, 2012)? Or is it in fact the case that the use of such software continues to be contentious, somehow causing losses in some aspects of the research process or otherwise generating problems of theory and/or method for the researcher (King, 2010)? Does the lack of reference to software in methods sections denote a greater familiarity with and consensus regarding the use of such software, or does it simply reflect the fact that the writing up of much qualitative research is instead characterised by scant regard to method and theory (Tight, 2004; Trowler, 2012; Tummons, 2012), whether or not qualitative data analysis software has been used?

In this chapter I provide an account of the use of specialist software for the analysis of qualitative data that rests on both theoretical/methodological and empirical perspectives. The theoretical/methodological perspective is derived from a discussion of current and recent literature relating to the use of software. In this section of the chapter, I argue that whilst some of the critiques of such software to have emerged within the literature during the last (almost) thirty years continue to make valid points that should be of concern to the reflexive researcher, other longer-standing critiques have outlived their usefulness and their applicability. Following this, I provide an empirical perspective through an account of the ongoing work that I am currently involved with as a co-investigator on a three-year institutional ethnography, *Higher Education in a Digital Economy*. Through providing an account of the use of Atlas-Ti by the research team, I argue that this software provides us, as researchers, with ways of working that can serve to problematise the so-called paradigmatic distinctions between qualitative and quantitative research in terms of not only how data analysis is *operationalised* (Sin, 2008), but also in terms of the *transparency* of the research work being done as an element of research quality (Hammersley, 2008).

A BRIEF NOTE ON NOMENCLATURE

The term CAQDAS is commonly used within the literature. Somewhat confusingly, this acronym can be arrived at in two slightly different ways. Firstly, there is *C*omputer *A*ssisted *Q*ualitative *D*ata *A*nalysi*S*, leading to constructions such as 'CAQDAS software'. Secondly, there is *C*omputer *A*ssisted *Q*ualitative Data *A*nalysis *S*oftware, the term that is employed here. The term QDAS (*Q*ualitative *D*ata *A*nalysis *S*oftware) is also in use.

USING SOFTWARE FOR QUALITATIVE DATA ANALYSIS: SOME RECENT (AND NOT SO RECENT) PERSISTENT CONCERNS

A number of themes emerge from a review of literature pertaining to CAQDAS. Some of these – as might be expected when discussing ICTs – have receded or changed over time and new issues have emerged: this can be seen in, for example, the changing emphasis on CAQDAS as a tool for helping with the analysis of not only textual data, but audio and video as well. The ways in which discussion around CAQDAS has shifted over time will be considered. At this time, I also want to unpack and respond to those other themes that have entrenched themselves within CAQDAS literature and that have been reiterated and revised over time but that CAQDAS communities, it would appear, cannot quite shrug off: a straightforward example of this can be seen in the recurring notion that the use of CAQDAS might in some ways serve to distance the researcher from her or his data. I suggest that these kinds of issues can be conveniently if not quite perfectly considered in four ways (acknowledging that there is some overlap between these and that these are not intended to be discrete classifications), in terms of: closeness to the data; driving the research process; theory-building using CAQDAS; and attitudes towards CAQDAS.

Closeness to the Data

It might at first seem rather odd to discuss the researcher's relationship to her or his data using some of the terms that reoccur frequently within the CAQDAS literature. Terms such as 'separation' (Smith & Hesse-Biber, 1996) 'closeness' (Weitzman, 2000) 'distance' (Gibbs, 2007) and 'reduced proximity' (Roberts, Breen, & Symes, 2013) are used to describe the first aspect of CAQDAS to be unpacked here, namely the notion that the use of CAQDAS in some way serves to separate or distance the researcher from her data. There is something inherent in the use of a computer, as distinct from reams of paper that have (one assumes) been sifted, cut up, colour-coded, stuck onto notice boards and so forth, that prevents the researcher from achieving the required level of 'closeness' to their data (whatever that might actually mean).

Where does this aversion to the use of computers to do work (research is, after all, a form of work) come from? The current ubiquity of ICTs at conferences, in offices and in workplaces more generally would seem to render such an aversion somewhat idiosyncratic at best. One of the earliest statements regarding this concern over closeness in the use of computers to assist in qualitative research can be found in a research paper from 1988, when Tesch (1988, p. 179) argued that researchers suspected that using computers might distance them from their research material. Certainly, early adopters of computers for qualitative data analysis (including, but not restricted to, the use of early specialised software programs such as The Ethnograph) were choosing to do their work in a very different manner from those researchers who were continuing to use needles to sort their edge-notched cards into piles for the purposes of theory-building. At the same time, these latter researchers could, quite correctly, point to the fact that the hardware and software of the time posed restrictions (in comparison to current CAQDAS) in terms of the number of interview transcript files that they might be able to manage within their software programs or the maximum permitted length of a coded segment of text. And yet despite these restrictions (to which I shall return), early users of computers for qualitative research were under no illusions as to the labour-saving potential that computers offered, closeness to the data notwithstanding, highlighting a number of mechanical tasks that might be ameliorated through the use of computers, such as searching notes for specific passages (Brent, 1984).

Driving the Research Process

Recent commentators have stressed the ways in which CAQDAS can, for example, allow the researcher to search very quickly for specific segments within large bodies of text (Lewins & Silver, 2007). But the claim (above) that using CAQDAS might dictate the process of data collection and analysis is more serious, and perhaps might get us closer to understanding the concern for closeness. The notion that the software drives the research process in some way therefore becomes the second aspect of CAQDAS to be unpacked here. According to these concerns, CAQDAS provides a series of methodological straightjackets that hamper the work of the researcher. Examples include the ways in which particular software packages impose particular coding structures on the researcher. The two most frequently cited examples of this phenomenon are the imposition of coding hierarchies in Nvivo, and the flat coding structures within Atlas-Ti that promote a grounded theory approach by the researchers who use it (Coffey, Holbrook, & Atkinson, 1996; Weitzman, 2000; Willis & Jost, 1999). Certainly it would be an undesirable consequence of CAQDAS uptake if particular forms of or approaches to qualitative research were to be lost sight of.

But to what extent does any social practice (research is, after all, a form of social practice) shape or get shaped by the tools and artefacts that are used by practitioners? Consider the facilities offered by current CAQDAS in terms of the different file formats that they support. The most recent version of Atlas-Ti (version 7 – this is the version used by the *Higher Education in a Digital Economy* research team) can support not only Microsoft office files but also pdf files and web pages, all the time maintaining the format and colour of the original files as they are loaded into an hermeneutic unit (HU – the name given to a project in Atlas-Ti, which acts as a kind of digital 'container' for all of the primary documents being used). Sound, picture and video files in a variety of formats (.wav, .mp4, .jpeg and so forth) can also be loaded into Atlas-Ti. All of these documents can be coded and searched. This is in stark contrast to early iterations of CAQDAS, which could only support plain text files. Facilities for collaborative work have also been greatly expanded in recent software releases. In Atlas-Ti it is now a simple task to bundle an entire HU (primary documents, codes, memos and all) and email it to a colleague. And both Atlas-Ti and Nvivo can – after that the correct software licenses have been purchased, be installed on network servers, allowing for the simultaneous reading, coding, analysis or memoing of a document by multiple researchers.

Of course, not everyone will use her or his software in quite the same way. Some researchers will make use of only a relatively small number of CAQDAS features in order to perform relatively simple 'code-and-retrieve' functions – arguably the most ubiquitous of all CAQDAS features (Kelle, 1997). Some will perform searches using Boolean operators in a manner akin to conducting library catalogue searches (OR, XOR, AND, NOT) – for example, by searching a data set for quotations that have been tagged with both one code AND another, or for quotations that have been tagged with either only one code or only another, but not both (XOR) (Friese, 2012). Others will create network views in order to visualise their data (Lewins & Silver, 2007). As with any technology, there will be some users who operate at an instrumental level, only drawing on a small number of available functions, and other users who operate at a more fluent or expert level, who use a wider range of functions in a more systematic and critical manner (Mangobeira, Lee, & Fielding, 2004; Odena, 2013). And software functions are just one issue to consider when reflecting on the practices of the researcher: what about the methodological assumptions upon which the software rests? Is it indeed the case that CAQDAS in some way implicitly supports and promotes a grounded theory approach to qualitative research (van Hoven & Poelman, 2003)? Certainly, the predominance of code-and-retrieve functions in early iterations of CAQDAS might be seen as encouraging a predominantly 'grounded' approach to data analysis (Coffey et al., 1996).

Such concerns are in fact robustly countered in CAQDAS literature. The perception of a grounded theory bias within CAQDAS is countered not only by a reminder that the functions offered by CAQDAS are employed within other methodological frameworks (Kelle, 1997) but also by a reminder that grounded theory is an ambiguous methodology at best that has only ever been attached to CAQDAS on an erroneous basis

(MacMillan & Koenig, 2004; Roberts et al., 2013; see also Thomas & James, 2006). Indeed, the theoretical vagueness that troubles qualitative research more generally can be seen as contributing to the conceptual confusion that surrounds the use of CAQDAS (MacMillan & Koenig, 2004). CAQDAS users also remind us that software is just a tool, not a methodology: the software does not do the analysis; it simply facilitates the analysis done by the researcher. Therefore, the fact that many CAQDAS users have chosen to draw on grounded theory should not be considered as consequent to the use of the software (Dormady & Byrne, 2006; Van Hoven & Poelman, 2003). CAQDAS does not drive the researcher towards grounded theory, therefore.

Theory-Building Using CAQDAS

The term 'theory-building' originates in an early classification of types of CAQDAS, which were divided up into categories such as 'text-retrievers' (used for operations such as frequency counting), or 'code-and-retrieve programs' (Weitzman, 2000). A further category, 'code-based theory builders', was used to describe those programs that offered functions such as hyperlinking or graphical network modelling to help the researcher draw links between text segments, codes and memos, although such classifications were by no means accepted by all CAQDAS users (Kelle, 1997; Lewins, 2001). And although the increasing sophistication of CAQDAS has over time rendered these categories obsolete, it can be argued that the term 'theory-building' has over time been the victim of conceptual slippage, with software being given an undue prominence in the processes of analysis and theorisation, leading to the (so-called) *mechanism* (García-Horta & Guerra-Ramos, 2009, p. 163) or *mechanisation* (Roberts et al., 2013, p. 280) of qualitative data analysis through a perceived over-reliance on software tools, in particular auto-coding tools. But to assume that the software somehow does the thinking for the researcher is a mistake and the literature reminds us time and again that CAQDAS can provide the tools, but it cannot do the analysis – a concern that has been dismissed by one commentator as a form of slight paranoia about technology more generally (Seale, 2005, p. 197).

I shall return to this theme of 'paranoia' shortly. At this time, it is important to stress that the tools and opportunities offered by CAQDAS are a reflection of software construction, not methodology, and that what is being constructed are tools to help the researcher do her or his work and nothing more. Atlas-Ti no more 'does' the analysis within *Higher Education in a Digital Economy* than Adobe Acrobat (one of the other programs that we use) does. It is therefore necessary to cut through the hyperbole that has sometimes surrounded CAQDAS in the past, hyperbole that has had the effect of using computers to add a 'sheen of scientific rigour' to the analysis of qualitative data (Darmody & Byrne, 2006, p. 123), or a 'wow factor' of mystique surrounding the use of software that serves to generate unrealistic expectations (MacMillan & Koenig, 2004, p. 180).

The possible impact of auto-coding functions is more problematic, however. The use of auto-coding is described as debateable at best by Lewins and Silver (2007), who argue that it risks limiting the analytical process and lowers the status of any text excluded by the process, thereby echoing earlier concerns that an excessive focus on coding at the expense of other methodological tools risks decontextualising data (Kelle, 1997; Seidel & Kelle, 1995). Such criticisms rest on the notion that the use of CAQDAS might lead researchers to do too much coding because it is so straightforward to accomplish, leading to 'data-fetishism' (Garcia-Horta & Guerra-Ramos, 2009) or a 'coding trap' (King, 2010) in which the researcher is surrounded by an excess of codes which distort the rest of the research process. However, it is the researcher and not the computer who defines auto-coding parameters (Odena, 2013). Auto-coding is a function like any other within CAQDAS that needs to be used properly and carefully a part of a well thought through methodology, for which CAQDAS cannot provide a substitute.

Attitudes towards CAQDAS

The fourth and final concern that I wish to unpack is what might be termed attitudinal responses towards CAQDAS. By this I mean to draw attention to the ways in which CAQDAS 'sceptics' (Odena, 2013, p. 355) are positioned in relation to the use of software for qualitative data analysis. To some extent, the underlying concerns that will lead to some researchers being seen as apprehensive (Tesch, 1988, p. 179) or cautious (Bathmaker, 2004, p. 175; Van Hoven & Poelman, 2003, p. 114) can be understood in the light of the kinds of issues already unpacked – the concerns that proximity to data will be affected, that software design affects methodological choices, and that computation might lead to automation.

It is also important to acknowledge the historical context of CAQDAS usage. Seale and Rivas (2012), Smith and Hesse-Biber (1996), Tesch (1988), and Willis and Jost (1999) all note that early adopters of CAQDAS were working at a time where prevailing attitudes towards the use of computers in social research might be seen as resting within a positivist paradigm, aligned to the early predominance of software for statistical data analysis in relation to software for qualitative data analysis. In such a climate, the scepticism that can surround the use of computers in the 'naturalistic, phenomenological' realm of qualitative research can all too easily be seen as distancing researchers from real-world ethnography or other forms of qualitative work, a sentiment added to by the functions of those CAQDAS programs categorised as 'text retrievers' and 'textbase managers' (Weitzman, 2000), which were used for functions such as word frequency counting or string searching that general statistical outputs which appeared to 'belong' to a quantitative paradigm. I shall return to the notion that CAQDAS might serve to blur the boundaries between qualitative and quantitative work later, but for now I wish to stress that the personal preferences of the researcher should be acknowledged and that these preferences will have in part been shaped by that researcher's history, prior research experiences, and so forth: a history in which the distinctions between qualitative and quantitative work will almost certainly have been reified within training programmes, methods textbooks and the like (Cooper, Glaesser, Gomm, & Hammersley, 2012, p. 2–3).

USING SOFTWARE FOR QUALITATIVE DATA ANALYSIS: PERCEIVED ADVANTAGES

A number of themes emerge repeatedly from a review of literature pertaining to CAQDAS. There is, arguably, a strong consensus in literature relating to the advantages or benefits of using CAQDAS for qualitative research. Where there is some variation is in the extent to which some of these advantages can be seen as operating at a more than technical level. That is to say, there are some advantages to using CAQDAS that might be seen as producing positive effects that go beyond being related to efficiency or productivity, for example, and instead produce effects that have a meaningful impact on research method and quality, for example. I shall discuss each of these in turn (again, mindful of the fact that these two categorisations are loose and not intended to be discrete). At the same time, it is important to remember that this discussion rests on the assumption that the nature of research work or analysis being done is such that the use of

CAQDAS is meaningful and worthwhile – some forms of qualitative analysis such as conversation analysis or discourse analysis where quite small data sets are used being examples of research work that would not particularly benefit from using CAQDAS.

The advantages that can be gained from using CAQDAS include: the convenience of being able to store and manage data sets in one digital location (which has been further facilitated in recent years as updates to CAQDAS have included support for an increasingly wide variety of file formats); quick and easy access to data; systematic and consistent data management; greater speed in searching and re-searching texts; increased and more convenient access to both whole data files and segments of files; simple and convenient tools for keeping track of developing ideas during the research process; the gradual incorporation of new documents within existing data sets; and portability (further facilitated in recent years as laptop computers have become more powerful – in addition, a version of Atlas-Ti for ipad has also been announced). All of these facilities in turn make it relatively straightforward for teams of researchers to work on the same data sets: the ability to easily and quickly export and share bundles of data, graphical representations or networks, groups of memos or code families (or, indeed, all of these) allows for multiple researchers to work on the same project without the need for physical proximity. In turn, these tools also afford such collaborative work a high degree of consistency and hence reliability, which will be discussed in more detail below.

However, whilst the efficiency and productivity effects of using CAQDAS can be seen as being relatively uncontested and certainly uncontroversial, other aspects of using CAQDAS can be seen as having a more profound impact in terms of firstly, method and secondly, quality (once again, with overlap between these two categories). I shall discuss four key issues: system closure; visibility and transparency; rigour and reliability; and qualitative/quantitative blurring.

System Closure

System closure is the term used to refer to the practice of including not only primary documents but also secondary documents such as memos, graphical representations, search results, notes or other working papers within the analysis process. The use of CAQDAS makes it a simple task for the researcher to search and then code her or his ongoing analytical or explanatory material using the same coding structure as has been used for the primary data (Bathmaker, 2004, p. 168; Richards & Richards, 1994, p. 449; Weitzman, 2000, p. 809).

Visibility and Transparency

The idea that using CAQDAS renders the work of qualitative research more transparent and more visible runs strongly through the literature (Gibbs, 2007). This is not due to any nebulous 'wow factor' that CAQDAS can – erroneously – be seen to apply to the research process. Using CAQDAS to do qualitative research requires the researcher to engage in careful and thorough research design and in precise conceptual thought and analysis to the exact same degree as the researcher who chooses not to use CAQDAS (MacMillan & Koenig, 2004). We should not therefore be fooled by any 'sheen of scientific rigour' that CAQDAS might – equally erroneously – be seen to apply (Darmody & Byrne, 2006, p. 123). Rather, the use of software provides the technical means by which different elements of the ongoing research process – such as memoing or coding – can be straightforwardly captured and made visible to research users. As such, it becomes more straightforward to describe and illustrate the work of qualitative data analysis in greater detail, which in turn enhances the robustness of the claims that arise from the research (Odena, 2013). This straightforwardness can be seen as being equally applicable to different members of a research team, and to the end users of a research project. It is also applicable to research participants. Although respondent validation, as a discrete topic, is under-represented in CAQDAS literature it can be argued that CAQDAS, as a tool that helps make the processes of data management and analysis more visible, would thereby enhance respondent validation through making the analytical steps taken by the researcher more straightforward for the researched to scrutinise.

Rigour and Reliability

Greater visibility and transparency can in turn be seen to lead to greater rigour and reliability in qualitative research. More detailed accounts of qualitative data analysis become more straightforward to produce, as a response to the persistent claims that too much qualitative research pays insufficient attention to methodology and theory (Sin, 2008; Trowler, 2012). It becomes easier (assuming that permissions have been agreed) for users to view and reflect upon research materials (Davidson & di Gregorio, 2011). Specific aspects of the research process such as coding can be audited (Gerson, 1984; Roberts et al., 2013). But it is important to note that just as CAQDAS cannot compensate for poor research design, so CAQDAS cannot in and of itself generate greater reliability and rigour during the research process. Rather, it is through the use of CAQDAS that tools are made available to the researcher that will make it simple for her to demonstrate and describe her research work in such a way that the claims or warrants that are being made for the research are robust.

Qualitative/Quantitative Blurring

The extent to which the boundaries that are said to exist between and hence to distinguish and define qualitative and quantitative research paradigms lie outside the scope of this chapter. They have been extensively and convincingly discussed elsewhere in terms of issues ranging from the extent to which one paradigm or the other is more or less positioned on an inductive or deductive mode of inference or the extent to which one is more objective and the other is more subjective, to whether or not the research in question primarily uses numbers rather than words or the nature and scope of the sample size used in the research. Put simply, paradigmatic debates such as these rest on both methodology and method (Bryman, 2008).

The emergence and development of increasingly sophisticated forms of CAQDAS can be seen as contributing in some way to the broader debate as to the applicability and desirability of the maintenance of such paradigmatic distinctions. In part this is a consequence of the construction of some of the earliest CAQDAS programs such as 'text-retrievers' (Weitzman, 2000), which provided researchers with the tools to, for example, compile frequency counts which might then be exported to statistical software packages such as Excel (Weber, 1984; Willis & Jost, 1999). As such, one of the characteristic features of CAQDAS can be seen as providing tools for the construction and analysis of numerical as well as textual data. Typical examples of the kinds of numerical data that might be derived from a predominantly text-based data set include frequency counts of a particular word or phrase (e.g. the use of a key word or phrase within a policy document or across a number of documents if a comparison is being sought) as well as frequency counts of code usage (e.g. in order to compare the prevalence of one code or theme in relation to another, within and/or across different documents). A second characteristic feature of CAQDAS, albeit one that is a more recent phenomenon consequent to ongoing technological innovation, is the capacity for CAQDAS to manage increasingly large and more diverse sets of data drawn from correspondingly larger and more diverse sample populations (Friese, 2012; Seale, 2005; Smith & Hesse-Biber, 1996). In this way it can be argued that the use of CAQDAS contributes to wider debates around the qualitative/quantitative divide through encouraging the very kind of movement both among and across so-called research paradigms that have been entrenched by the politics of method (Cooper et al., 2012, p. 8). I shall return to this theme later.

USING SOFTWARE FOR QUALITATIVE DATA ANALYSIS: *HIGHER EDUCATION IN A DIGITAL ECONOMY*

Higher Education in a Digital Economy (HEDE) is a three-year institutional ethnography, funded by the Social Sciences and Humanities Research Council of Canada (SSHRC). Institutional ethnography is a framework for qualitative inquiry derived from the work of Dorothy Smith (2005) that focuses on everyday activity – work – as a way of investigating the organisation of social life, with a particular focus on the ways in which work is mediated or ordered through text-based artefacts (Tummons, 2010). The broad aims of the project are to explore issues that surround the implementation of a new medical education curriculum that is enacted simultaneously across two locations in Canada (New Brunswick and Nova Scotia) that are approximately 300 miles or 480 kilometres apart. This new Distributed Medical Education (DME) curriculum has been designed to rest on information and communication technologies (ICTs) 'from the ground up': that is to say, the use of technology (digital video, digital learning platforms, e-learning devices and such like) functions as a means to enact synchronously a curriculum across two distinct locations, as distinct from the use of technology as an 'additional' feature within a curriculum that could still be delivered were the technology not present. Thus, instead of simply designating a curriculum as being an example of 'blended learning' through the post-hoc provision of e-learning resources alongside or on top of an existing 'real world' curriculum delivery model, this new medical education curriculum can be understood as only being possible through the affordances offered by ICTs. Without ICTs, this curriculum could not have been written and enacted in the ways that it has been.

The project is approaching the halfway stage, having been active for about eighteen months. Much has been accomplished in this period. The literature relating to distributed medical education has been reviewed. The theoretical tenets of institutional ethnography and actor–network theory (the two significant theoretical foundations for the project) have been debated, critiqued and sometimes disagreed with during the research team's online meetings (which have ranged in style from informal discussions to formal presentations by individual members of the team). Policies and protocols for the analysis of paper-based and online textual documents, including photographs and videos (one of the major sources of primary research data for the project) have been discussed, piloted and then rolled out across the research team. Thus far, 60 different texts ranging from institutional policy documents to YouTube videos have been analysed by 11 different members of the research team. The first tranche of semi-structured observations has also been carried out. At the time of writing, 108 observations of lectures, seminars, and staff meetings have been conducted by five members of the team across the two research sites and a framework for analysis based on Spradley (1980) has been discussed, piloted and then operationalised. Data from the observations is, at the time of writing, being analysed as part of the preparation of two distinct papers being written by different members of the research team. Protocols relating to access and use of the data developed by the team are close to being finalised: an 'open access' approach has been established in order to allow shared access to and ownership of the data across the research team (and which in itself is the focus of a third paper being prepared by some of the other team members). And finally, and perhaps most importantly, the members of the research team have got to know each other, to talk, joke and share frustrations with each other as we discuss issues such as data access, the analysis of online as opposed to paper-based texts, or the desirability or otherwise of anonymity in research.

Mindful of the distributed nature of this new curriculum, it is perhaps appropriate that the research team that is exploring this new curriculum – both its adoption and the ongoing experiences of the staff, students and faculty who are enrolled within it – should be similarly distributed, and thus similarly reliant on ICTs for their work together. The research team consists of eighteen people: the majority of the team are in Canada (distributed across three provinces), and two are in the United Kingdom. The research team uses a number of different technologies in order to facilitate working together. Project documentation is stored online using *Mindmeister*, an online mind mapping tool which can also be used for data management and storage. Through the Mindmeister portal, any member of the research team can access any of the materials that have been collected or generated thus far, ranging from the initial grant documents to working papers written by members of the research team, from PowerPoint slides generated by team members for conference presentations to copies of the minutes from research team meetings. It should also be noted that access to the Mindmeister portal is open, in keeping with the open access policy of the project, although some sections (such as those containing raw project data) are password protected. Team meetings are facilitated online using GoToMeeting, a video-conferencing and web meeting tool. As well as allowing for virtual face-to-face communication through webcams and headsets, GoToMeeting facilitates the sharing of documents across the team, in a manner akin to the tabling of hard copy documents at a 'real world' meeting. Thus, PowerPoint slides or PDF files can be 'tabled' and discussed during the meeting. A pop-up screen allows users to toggle their microphones and cameras on and off, and also contains a messaging function that allows the user to send a text-based message to one or more of the other attendees. Finally, entire meetings can be saved and then stored online for future reference.

It can clearly be seen that the new DME curriculum and the research team that is exploring it are accomplished through and because of ICTs. Both the curriculum and the research team rely on technology and are mediated through technology: spoken words and written texts (lectures, curriculum documents, teaching resources, faculty team meetings, students' assignments, slides, prospectuses and so forth) are distributed or stored online. As such, it is perhaps unsurprising that the research team has chosen to use CAQDAS.

CHOOSING AND USING SOFTWARE FOR QUALITATIVE DATA ANALYSIS: THE AFFORDANCES OF TECHNOLOGY

After some discussion, the HEDE team decided to use Atlas.Ti version 7. Whilst the majority of the team is quite comfortable with using ICTs more generally, the choice of CAQDAS required a little more thought. In part this was because only a small number of the team had used CAQDAS previously (both Atlas-Ti and Nvivo/NUD*IST), and in part because some of the team had not conducted ethnographic research before and this relative lack of methodological experience (it should be pointed out that they are experienced in other forms of research work) resulted in a lack of familiarity with qualitative data analysis more generally rather than the facilities offered for analysis by software. It was decided to proceed with Atlas-Ti primarily because it was felt by the research team that this CAQDAS offered superior and more straightforward tools for the sharing of research work (data, codes, memos and so forth) across the team. The future possibilities of both native mac (at the moment the research team are using Atlas-Ti with Windows emulators on Apple mac laptops) and ipad versions of the software are also attractive to the team, reflecting once again the importance of personal preferences when using CAQDAS (King, 2010).

A reflexive account of the work of the HEDE team would find it difficult to unpack, exactly, the relationship between the research team, the research project being undertaken, and the role of CAQDAS in the project. At one level it seems right to acknowledge that the specific nature of the field being studied – a field that consists of both the physical and the virtual – is ideally suited to research facilitated by CAQDAS. Many (though by no means all) of the interactions, social practices and artefacts used by the staff and students who are enrolled within the curriculum exist in virtual rather than physical spaces, and often across both. The experience of a plenary lecture, delivered in one location (it could be either Nova Scotia or New Brunswick, although the majority take place in the former, which is also the larger of the two faculties) but simultaneously streamed in the second, provides a good example. The lecturer is required to stand or walk only in a very narrow space, marked out on the floor, so that her or his image and speech can be reliably captured. Whilst attending to the students who are present in the same physical lecture room, the lecturer also has to be mindful of the students who are present in the remote location: s/he has to observe the remote students who only appear on screen whilst also paying attention to her/his teaching materials that will appear on a different screen. Something as simple as walking around the lecture room in order to gain students' attention or to emphasise a point becomes impossible. In order for students at both sites to take part in question-and-answer sessions, a push-button system has been introduced. Students – at both sites – push a button next to an adjacent microphone when they wish to raise a point, and the lecturer pushes a button at the podium in order to 'activate' the next question in the queue. Questions are answered in the order that they are 'asked', not in any order of relevance or logical progression to a preceding point or theme.

A variety of technologies (webcams, laptops, software, web browsers, ipads) change how the students and the lecturers talk, look, act and even write. How they behave, the kinds of artefacts that they use, how they talk and how they make meaning – all of these social practices are mediated to some degree by technologies, by the virtual. It makes sense, therefore, to use CAQDAS to capture these online as well as physical practices. Field notes can be transcribed and loaded into the software, where they can sit alongside the pdf files or PowerPoint slides that were used by lecturers, which in turn can sit alongside both audio recordings and transcriptions of interviews with staff and students. All of these different modes of data can be gathered in a single repository, which can in turn be easily distributed across the research team (Sin, 2008).

At the same time, it could be argued that doing research within this field is only made possible in the first place by the affordances of technology, without which some of the research goals of the project would be impractical at best and impossible at worst (Mangabeira, Lee, & Fielding, 2004). By this I mean to stress that it is only because Atlas-Ti has the functionality that it has that the HEDE research project can seek to explore the questions that it is seeking to explore. Indeed, it is doubtful whether an earlier iteration of the software would have been able to operationalise the HEDE research in a similarly comprehensive manner. The combination of the physical and virtual that resides within the research team is matched by the field being researched, and the many physical as well as virtual artefacts that the research team are working with could be explored 'off-line' only with extreme difficulty. The presence of two transatlantic members of the research team would certainly be impossible without ICTs, including CAQDAS; and the cooperation between the two faculty sites in Canada would be rendered impracticable at best. It might just be possible to distribute copies of the different primary documents across physical as opposed to virtual spaces, but it would require a considerable amount of printing, copying and posting. Opportunities for offline collaborative coding would be so difficult as to be impossible without significant amounts of time and resources to facilitate travel and accommodation so that the team could meet and talk: it is hardly surprising that opportunities for facilitating research within teams is highlighted as one of the benefits of using CAQDAS (Friese, 2012; Lewins & Silver, 2007).

There are several distinct, though overlapping, themes at work here, therefore, when considering how the HEDE project might be and is being accomplished or operationalised. Both the researchers and the researched are distributed across physical and virtual boundaries, and both the field of research and the artefacts that enrich that field are similarly distributed across and reified within both physical and virtual forms. So how do we theorise the position of CAQDAS within this complex research field? As an enabler that affords us, as researchers, the tools to conduct our research? Has the shape of our research project been driven in some way by the facilities that Atlas-Ti provides for us? If we had used Nvivo, would the final shape of the research be different? Could this research be done without Atlas-Ti? There are no simple answers to these questions because of course they are hypothetical. Instead, as a crucial component of the reflexivity that ought to accompany any ethnography (and not just an ethnography that is saturated with technology), we need to be aware of the ways in which our choices – including our choice to conduct observations in some locations and not others, or our choice to conduct content analysis on some documents and not others, or our choice to use Atlas-Ti and not Nvivo – have shaped our research as a whole.

CHOOSING AND USING SOFTWARE FOR QUALITATIVE DATA ANALYSIS: RELIABILITY, GENERALISABILITY AND THE POLITICS OF METHOD

Whilst the exact relationship between our research questions, our research field and our research tools remains to some extent problematic, the possible consequences for research reliability and generalisability of our decision to use Atlas-Ti are relatively more straightforward. By this I do not mean that they lack complexity or difficulty; rather I mean to counter the notion of the *problematic* as it is understood within institutional ethnography, as describing problems or questions that may not yet have been posed but which are nevertheless latent in the experiences of a social actor (Campbell & Gregor, 2004; Smith, 2005). That is to say, the relationship between our research questions, our field and our tools is problematic: it is latent in our work as researchers but is only gradually emerging as a theme for discussion and analysis within the research team. But the impact of those tools – to be precise, of one tool in particular, namely Atlas-Ti – can be theorised with more certainty. There are two elements to this theorisation: reliability and generalisability, and the politics of method (and as before, these should be understood as complementary, not competing).

Reliability and Generalisability

I have already established that CAQDAS allows a researcher or a team of researchers to work to a high degree of consistency and accuracy. With CAQDAS, document searches are likely to be comprehensive as well as fast, and this speed facilitates searching and re-searching, coding and re-coding. Memos can be coded in turn and all of the data sets – video, audio, text, image, web – are searched, coded and memoed in exactly the same way. Code families, memos or even entire research projects can be easily shared, compared, updated and merged. And CAQDAS allows all of the steps taken by us, as researchers, to be clearly documented for the scrutiny of other research users. The data management and analysis processes are transparent, consistent, accurate and rigorous – and these four qualities are, arguably, all ameliorated by the use of software. I have also already established that CAQDAS allows a team of researchers to draw on data sets of significantly greater size as well as modality than would normally be possible with a research team who chose not to use software, because these same functions – of speed, of capacity of storage, of sharing – make managing large data sets more practicable. The first aspect of using CAQDAS that I wish to posit here, therefore, is that using CAQDAS allows for more consistent and more thorough analysis of larger data sets, meaning that larger research samples can be explored. These two elements – consistent analysis and cross-analysis by a team of researchers who are working with qualitative data sets of significant size – combine to refute one of the claims that is often made against qualitative research, namely that qualitative research is partial, excessively subjective and lacking in robust generalisability. CAQDAS allows teams of researcher to test and retest their ideas (or hypotheses?) in ways that can be traced and then demonstrated to other research users, across large-scale data sets that can equally easily generate textual and/or numerical (mindful of my earlier discussion relating to 'text-retrievers') outputs.

The Politics of Method

I subscribe to the arguments that are both reiterated and expanded by Cooper et al. (2012), namely that many of the distinctions that are drawn between quantitative and qualitative research paradigms are both artificial and unhelpful. I also subscribe to the arguments made by MacMillan and Koenig (2004), Sin (2008) and Odena (2013), amongst others, namely that the impact of qualitative research – the robustness of the claims made by qualitative research – needs to be persuasive and credible. The use of CAQDAS, as explored in literature and as illustrated by the HEDE project – reinforces both of these lines of argument. Whilst it is not an a priori necessity to use CAQDAS for any research project, to do so allows the researcher or researchers to draw on significantly large sample sizes and a variety of modes of data, to analyse and re-analyse this data quickly, efficiently and reliably, to open up the data to entirely new patterns of analysis and to revise existing patterns, and to share the data, code families, memos and so on conveniently and comprehensively. All of these operations can be done with an enhanced transparency, ameliorating the visibility of the research process, in turn aiding credibility and rigour. CAQDAS software does not discriminate between numerical or textual outputs: it can generate reports of both kinds. As such, I suggest that a reflexive consideration of qualitative research that uses CAQDAS embodies the need to take a different attitude towards the so-called qualitative/quantitative divide, instead providing a focus on the research questions to be answered and the credibility of those answers, rather than sustaining a focus on spurious distinctions between, or characteristics of, qualitative and/or quantitative research.

CONCLUSIONS: RESEARCH OUTSIDE PARADIGMATIC BOUNDARIES

Attitudes towards CAQDAS have, of course, changed over time. Whilst it may still be a matter of debate as to whether the use of CAQDAS is now 'routine' (Seale & Rivas, 2012, p. 432) or 'contentious' (King, 2010, p. 6), or 'critical' or 'instrumental' (Mangabeira et al., 2004), it cannot be denied that CAQDAS has changed how qualitative research might be done. However, these changes are rather different to those envisaged by early commentators. CAQDAS has not generated homogeneity amongst researchers, with grounded theory crowding out other forms of analysis. Nor has it 'quantified' qualitative research by promoting positivist research at the expense of the interpretivist or constructionist traditions (although these are in themselves troublesome concepts), or generated distance between researchers and their data. But what CAQDAS has done, and continues to do, is to facilitate ways of doing research work that are fast, transparent, and auditable, capable of encompassing ever larger numbers of respondents and artefacts derived from both physical and virtual spaces, in formats that are convenient, easy to share and straightforward to work with, revise, re-code and overlay with new and different analytical frameworks. Within CAQDAS, 'there are *not* two quite distinct quantitative and qualitative ways of thinking' (Cooper et al., 2012, p. 8, original emphasis): what there are, are ways of doing research that are thorough, robust, and trustworthy, capable of generating conclusions – and perhaps theories – that will stand up to rigorous scrutiny, even if the conclusions remain as points of disagreement.

REFERENCES

Bathmaker, A-M. (2004). Using NUD*IST. In C. Opie (Ed.), *Doing educational research*. London, UK: Sage.

Brent, E. (1984). Qualitative computing: Approaches and issues. *Qualitative Sociology*, *7*(1–2), 34–60.

Bryman, A. (2008). The end of the paradigm wars? In A. Alasuutari, L. Bickman & J. Brannen (Eds.), *The Sage handbook of social research methods*. London, UK: Sage.

Campbell, M., & Gregor, F. (2004). *Mapping social relations: A primer in doing institutional ethnography*. Lanham, MD: AltaMira.

Coffey, A., Holbrook, B., & Atkinson, P. (1996). Qualitative data analysis: Technologies and representations. *Sociological Research Online*, *1*(1). Retrieved from http://www.socresonline.org.uk/1/1/4.html. Accessed on May 4, 2014.

Cooper, B., Glaesser, J., Gomm, R., & Hammersley, M. (2012). *Challenging the quantitative-qualitative divide: Explorations in case-focused causal analysis*. London, UK: Continuum.

Darmody, M., & Byrne, D. (2006). An introduction to computerised analysis of qualitative data. *Irish Educational Studies*, *25*(1), 121–133.

Davidson, J., & di Gregorio, S. (2011). Qualitative research and technology: In the midst of a revolution. In M. Denzin, & Y. Lincoln (Eds.), *The Sage handbook of qualitative research* (4th ed.). London, UK: Sage.

Friese, S. (2012). *Qualitative data analysis with Atlas-Ti*. London, UK: Sage.

García-Horta, J., & Guerra-Ramos, M. (2009). The use of CAQDAS in educational research: Some advantages, limitations and potential risks. *International Journal of Research & Method in Education*, *32*(2), 151–165.

Gerson, E. (1984). Qualitative research and the computer. *Qualitative Sociology*, *7*(1–2), 61–74.

Gibbs, G. (2007). *Analysing qualitative data*. London, UK: Sage.

Hammersley, M. (2008). *Questioning qualitative inquiry*. London, UK: Sage.

Kelle, U. (1997). Theory building in qualitative research and computer programs for the management of textual data. *Sociological Research Online*, *2*(2). Retrieved from http://www.socresonline.org.uk/2/2/1.html. Accessed on May 4, 2014.

King, A. (2010). 'Membership matters': Applying membership categorisation analysis (MCA) to qualitative data using computer-assisted qualitative data analysis (CAQDAS) software. *International Journal of Social Research Methodology*, *13*(1), 1–16.

Lewins, A. (2001). CAQDAS: computer assisted qualitative data analysis. In N. Gilbert (Ed.), *Researching Social Life*. London: Sage.
Lewins, A., & Silver, C. (2007). *Using software in qualitative research: A step-by-step guide*. London, UK: Sage.
MacMillan, K., & Koenig, T. (2004). The wow factor: Preconceptions and expectations for data analysis software in qualitative research. *Social Science Computer Review*, *22*(2), 179–186.
Mangabeira, W., Lee, R., & Fielding, N. (2004). Computers and qualitative research: Adoption, use and representation. *Social Science Computer Review*, *22*(2), 167–178.
Odena, O. (2013). Using software to tell a trustworthy, convincing and useful story. *International Journal of Social Research Methodology*, *16*(5), 355–372.
Richards, T., & Richards, L. (1994). Using computers in qualitative research. In M. Denzin, & Y. Lincoln (Eds.), *Handbook of Qualitative Research*. London, UK: Sage.
Roberts, L., Breen, L., & Symes, M. (2013). Teaching computer-assisted qualitative data analysis to a large cohort of undergraduate students. *International Journal of Research and Method in Education*, *36*(3), 279–294.
Seale, C. (2005). Using computers to analyse qualitative data. In D. Silverman, *Doing Qualitative Research* (2nd ed.). London, UK: Sage.
Seale, C., & Rivas, C. (2012). Using software to analyse qualitative interviews. In J. Gubrium, J. Holstein, A. Marvasti, & K. McKinney (Eds.), *The Sage handbook of interview research* (2nd ed.). London, UK: Sage.
Seidel, J., & Kelle, U. (1995). Different functions of coding in the analysis of textual data. In U. Kelle (Ed.), *Computer-aided qualitative data analysis: Theory, methods and practice*. London, UK: Sage.
Sin, C. H. (2008). Teamwork involving qualitative data analysis software: Striking a balance between research ideals and pragmatics. *Social Science Computer Review*, *26*(3), 350–358.
Smith, B., & Hesse-Biber, S. (1996). Users' experiences with qualitative data analysis software: Neither Frankenstein's monster nor muse. *Social Science Computer Review*, *14*(4), 423–432.
Smith, D. (2005). *Institutional ethnography: A sociology for people*. Lanham, MD: Altamira Press.
Spradley, J. (1980). *Participant observation*. London, UK: Holt, Rinehart and Winston.
Tesch, R. (1988). The qualitative researcher and the computer. *Qualitative Studies in Education*, *1*(2), 179–183.
Thomas, G., & James, D. (2006). Reinventing grounded theory: Some questions about theory, ground and discovery. *British Educational Research Journal*, *32*(6), 767–795.
Tight, M. (2004). Research into higher education: An a-theoretical community of practice? *Higher Education Research and Development*, *23*(4), 395–411.
Trowler, P. (2012). Wicked issues in situating theory on close-up research. *Higher Education Research and Development*, *31*(3), 273–284.
Tummons, J. (2010). Institutional ethnography and actor-network theory: A framework for researching the assessment of trainee teachers. *Ethnography and Education*, *5*(3), 345–357.
Tummons, J. (2012). Theoretical trajectories within communities of practice in higher education research. *Higher Education Research and Development*, *31*(3), 299–310.

Van Hoven, B., & Poelman, A. (2003). Using computers for qualitative data analysis: An example using NUD.IST. *Journal of Geography in Higher Education*, *27*(1), 113–120.

Weber, R. (1984). Computer-aided content analysis: A short primer. *Qualitative Sociology*, *7*(1–2) 126–147.

Weitzman, E. (2000). Software and qualitative research. In M. Denzin, & Y. Lincoln (Eds.), *Handbook of qualitative research* (2nd ed.). London, UK: Sage.

Willis, J., & Jost, M. (1999). Computers and qualitative research. *Computers in the schools*, *15*(3–4), 21–52.

PART IV
VISIBILITIES, ROUTINES AND PRACTICES

MISSED MIRACLES AND MYSTICAL CONNECTIONS: QUALITATIVE RESEARCH, DIGITAL SOCIAL SCIENCE AND BIG DATA

Robin James Smith

ABSTRACT

Purpose – *This chapter critically discusses implications of working with 'big data' from the perspective of qualitative research and methodology. A critique is developed of the analytic troubles that come with integrating qualitative methodologies with 'big data' analyses and, moreover, the ways in which qualitative traditions themselves offer a challenge, as well as contributions, to computational social science.*

Design/methodology/approach – *The chapter draws on Interactionist understandings of social organisation as an ongoing production, tied to and accomplished in the actual practices of actual people. This is a matter of analytic priority but also points to a distinctiveness of sociological work which may be undermined in moving from the study of such*

Big Data? Qualitative Approaches to Digital Research
Studies in Qualitative Methodology, Volume 13, 181–204

ISSN: 1042-3192/doi:10.1108/S1042-319220140000013011

actualities, suggesting an alternative coming crisis of empirical sociology.

Findings – *A cautionary tale is offered regarding the contribution and character of sociological analysis within the 'digital turn'. It is suggested that 'big data' analyses of traces abstracted from actual people and their practices not only miss and distort the relation of social practice to social product but, consequentially, can take on an ideological character.*

Originality/value – *The chapter offers an original contribution to current discussions and debates surrounding 'big data' by developing enduring critiques of sociological methodology and analysis. It concludes by pointing to contributions and interventions that such an empirical programme of qualitative research might make in the context of the 'digital turn' and is of value to those working at the interface of traditional and digital(ised) inquiries and methods.*

Keywords: big data; ideology; Interactionism; practices; qualitative methodology

The increasing digitalisation of areas of social life has resulted in a significant proportion of our everyday practices, movements, communications and interactions leaving a digital footprint, sometimes knowingly and intentionally, sometimes not. This upsurge in 'transactional data' is producing change and challenges for the social sciences and, perhaps in particular, for the role of 'qualitative' methodologies and traditions. The more or less constant activity of online transactions and communications produces data at a previously unimagined scale – hence the need for new descriptors such as Petabytes and Exabytes or, simply, 'big'. The use and 'mining' of this 'big data' seam by commercial and state agencies prompted, in part, the oft cited concerns of Savage and Burrows (2007) with the 'coming crisis of empirical sociology' and their wider uptake within and across the social sciences. The availability of such powerful data sets to those outside of the discipline, often with better suited statistical skills to deal with them (Uprichard, 2013), was seen to threaten the marginalisation of empirical sociology; sociologists were warned to adapt their theoretical assumptions and methodologies, and fast. Those who heeded this call, pioneers on the digital mountain of transactional and social media data and innovators in 'computational sociology', have claimed that the prevalence and preponderance of digital data is transforming social relations and organisation and, thus, 'the digital turn' entails a necessary paradigm shift for the science of society. The degree to which these claims are to be realised is, as yet, a matter of debate. What is certain is that 'big' digital data and its sociology are here to stay. The nature of that relationship is, again, yet to be decided, but, despite claims that due to the sheer scale of the data, the numbers are able to 'speak for themselves',[1] it is social scientists who are in the position of bringing a much needed sophistication and complexity to the analyses and, at times simultaneously, providing an equally needed effective critical voice.

Digital social science – and in particular in relation to the current hype surrounding the potential and potency of 'big data' – brings with it many issues of application and use, theoretical framing(s) and, of course, research ethics (see Boyd & Crawford, 2012 for some useful provocations in these areas). Many of the issues that are yet to be resolved in the emergent digital social science – to continue using that unhelpfully broad label for now – bring in to sharp focus opportunities and challenges for ethnographic traditions of research, Interactionist sociology (Atkinson & Housley, 2003; Reynolds & Herman-Kinney, 2003), and 'qualitative research' more generally. This chapter aims to contribute to current discussions and debates relating to digital social science and 'big data' by recognising some of the specific challenges, complexities and cautionary tales that these traditions, focused as they are upon the specificity of practice and the empirical detail of interaction, institutions and everyday life, bring to the table. The key point made in this chapter, then, is that the fullest contribution that can be made by 'qualitative research' is found in an attention to the practices, routines and activities in and through which 'patterns', 'traces' and 'correlations' (for example) are brought in to being, in actual settings by actual peoples' actions. Consequently, it is shown how analytic work in which this contribution is compromised, overlooked or ignored, obscures the very resources with which the observable order of society is produced. In noting the sensibly available ways in which social order can be found (Sharrock, 1995, cited by McHoul, 2008) 'at all points' (Sacks, 1995), I draw, in part, on proto-ethnomethodological work by Aaron Cicourel (1964) and ethnomethodology's topicalisation of sociology's 'fundamental phenomena' (Garfinkel, 1967[2007], 2002). This chapter is not, however, written from an ethnomethodological perspective, nor offers an analysis, but adopts a 'theoretical attitude' (Laurier, 2001) in applying lessons from that perspective within a wider Interactionist frame to draw out some of the analytic difficulties with and within 'big data' and digital social science. One does not, necessarily, have to adopt the 'alternative, asymmetrical and incommensurate' approach of ethnomethodology (EM) to prioritise practice over patterns, aggregates and the 'residue' left by activities of social organisation (Livingston, 1987). In developing the significance of moving away from this analytic priority, I draw on a critique provided by Dorothy Smith (1974) whose words, forty years later, point to a continuation of what she described as the 'ideological character' of much theoretical and methodological work in sociology. Indeed, there is cause to suggest that contemporary developments in sociology – and, particularly those within the suggested 'digital paradigm' – have amplified some of these prior concerns with the status, priority and broader politics of sociological analysis. In a broader sense, the recognition of this 'ideological character' is important in developing a social scientific critique of the treatment of 'big data' both within and without academia; not least because a key change heralded by 'big data' is a blurring of the boundaries between sociological analysis and social research conducted by commercial analysts producing a (potential but by no means guaranteed) marginalisation of sociological research more generally, and perhaps qualitative research particularly. As argued in this chapter, it is more important than ever to retain, and promote, that which is *distinctly sociological* about our work.

This chapter thus seeks to offer a cautionary tale against the continued separation of method from methodology and discipline (see Atkinson, Delmont, & Housley, 2008; Housley & Smith, 2010) in subsuming qualitative 'methods' and reducing, re-using or recycling them in attempting to deal with 'big data'. The current digital moment has, in some of its constituent parts, seen the continuation of a trend recognised some time ago (Housley & Smith, 2010) in which innovation strategies are increasingly driven by reduction, reification and specialisation within a disciplinary and methodological vacuum (Atkinson, 2009). Here, disciplinary logics are obscured enabling methods to be slipped from their disciplinary moorings with the consequence of facilitating 'analytical accounts for phenomenon for which there are no questions' (Housley & Smith, 2010). In many ways 'big data' are the phenomenon for which there are no questions, produced in this instance not by methodological innovation within the social sciences but, rather, in and through technological developments in society. 'Big data' is thus akin to the Everest of contemporary social research. 'Because it's there', so massively there, is sufficient rationale to tackle it. Figuring out what to do with it is the problem and here qualitative approaches and traditions may have a contribution to make (Edwards, Housley, Williams, Sloan, & Williams, 2013).[2] The fate of qualitative research within this moment is, nevertheless, uncertain and how qualitative research will contribute to and contest the 'big data' challenge poses many questions. One possible issue is identified in this chapter; an issue that makes for a different view of a 'coming crisis' of empirical sociology in which the distinctive contribution of an attention to the practices which produce the phenomena viewed from the impossibly lofty vantage point of 'big data' is obscured.

The chapter begins by, briefly, discussing some of the ways in which the relationship between qualitative research and digital data and devices is presently being realised, practiced and re-considered. I suggest here some of the incommensurabilities between an ethos of attentiveness and careful and care full research and analysis that underpins much of qualitative social science and some of the ways in which, within the wider 'digital turn', qualitative methods are being reduced, re-used and recycled. To illustrate and describe some of the tensions that arise from and within an uncritical integration of qualitative analysis within 'big data social science' I draw on some humble examples; the analysis of people crossing the road (Livingston, 1987) and ethnographic fieldwork documenting the circulations of outreach workers who work with the homeless (Hall & Smith, 2014; Smith & Hall, 2013). These examples serve to demonstrate the significance of divergences in analytic priorities in relation to what it is that the analysis 'sees' and how possible 'findings' can become inverted when there is a distance between the analysts' view and the everyday practices of actual people. This analytic distance is then considered, following Smith (1974), as a space in which analysis and theorising can take on an ideological form; an issue present in (commercial) 'big data science' that the social sciences and perhaps especially qualitative methodologies are well suited to resist. Finally, I consider some of the ways in which ethnographic and qualitative methods and studies might contribute to the 'big data moment' in ways which do not obscure, lose or overlook what makes such approaches distinct and significant in their own right.

REDUCE, RE-USE, RECYCLE

As described in various ways throughout this book, 'digital sociology' is somewhat of a catch all term covering a multitude of sins and triumphs. To simplify matters, and to gloss distinctions made more finely in this collection and elsewhere, the 'digital turn' finds qualitative methodology affected in two primary ways. The first is in and through the enhancement of 'traditional' forms of sociological inquiry (ethnography, for example) via the affordances of digital technology employed in generating, capturing and representing data. In the sense of 'enhancement', digital technology is understood to develop new field relations and possibilities of data generation and capture. Such research also includes the study of the ways in which people themselves use and employ digital technology and social media in the course of their everyday lives. Indeed, one challenge for qualitative research is keeping abreast of widely available technological developments, and finding critical, appropriate and sensitive uses for such innovations within ethnographic and qualitative research. In this broad category of digital research, social media and the availability of ubiquitous mobile computing and communication in the form of smartphone technology, for example, is being critically and sensitively explored as a means of creating an 'enhanced sociality' of field encounters, relations and data. Here technology is found employed in creative ways of doing sociology, for example to conduct 'live' ethnographies where the 'now' is represented and accessible in a number of new ways which are no longer tied to the 'here', enabling the researcher, *with* their participants, to listen and look with more care (see Back, 2007; Back & Puwar, 2013). In other areas of inquiry – EM and conversation analysis (CA), especially – technology has long been at the heart of the business. Definitional, even. As is well known, Harvey Sacks, 'inventor' of CA, was only 'incidentally' concerned with conversation due to the affordances of talk as available to be reliably recorded, replayed and treated in a systematic manner (something Sacks saw as a prerequisite for a science of society (Sacks, 1995, LC2: 26)). Today multi-angle synchronised cameras, omni-directional microphones, and advances in video analysis and transcription have enabled those with serious intent to deal with the details of social interaction to develop analyses of the multimodal character of situated practice and action (e.g. Mondada, 2009) where, following the recommendations of Husserl (e.g. 1970[1936]; and see Liberman, 2013) and, later, Garfinkel (1967[2007]) and Sacks (1995), the analysis remains with what actual people are actually doing and the actualities of how whatever it is they are doing gets done. Whatever the particular analytic orientation, such technological enhancements bring in to view important questions of field relations, the nature and limits of 'participatory research', the role of analysis and interpretation and, of course, ethical considerations new and old. Qualitative research, and EMCA and ethnographically inspired work in particular, have long represented the leading edge of the integration of technology with and within research and is well placed to respond to some of the challenges described in this chapter.

The second sense of what 'digital sociology' might mean in relation to qualitative research is the one that primarily concerns this chapter: the much hyped 'population level', 'near real time', analyses of 'big data' streams mined from social media interactions and communication conducted within 'computational social science'. Spurred, in part, by the recognition of Mike Savage and Roger Burrows (2007) of the potential marginalisation and obsolescence of sociological analysis and research, social scientists have, over the past five years or so, been developing means of dealing with 'big data'. This chapter does not intend to critique such approaches per se, and certainly not specific cases; there is much good and critical methodological and substantive work been done in that regard. It does, however, concern itself with the ways in which 'qualitative research' is constructed and positioned within the 'digital paradigm'. One of the dangers that come with claims to paradigmatic shifts are that 'paradigm' suggests 'the Kuhnian notion of normal science being transformed by sudden revolutions where what went previously is unceremoniously tipped into the junkheap of academic history (Kuhn, 1996)' (Cresswell, 2010, p. 18). What chance the local, slow methods and 'small data' of ethnographic and qualitative research in the face of all that data?

The potential demise of traditional qualitative methods within the digital paradigm is, of course, an extreme formulation. The relationship between qualitative research and the digital is currently being considered, rethought and contested in far more nuanced ways. Indeed, it is widely recognised, and across this book, that there are many good reasons to resist such unsustainable actions. There is no (real) suggestion (at present) that big data analyses and digital sociology can completely do away with traditional 'terrestrial' methods. In most discussions of how the social sciences might deal with 'big data' there is a recognition of the role of established methods, although this is often couched within a relationship that finds 'big data' analyses 'augmenting' or 're-orientating' traditional, 'terrestrial' methods such as the interview and the survey (Edwards et al., 2013). It is this relationship that this chapter considers in detail.

In an article describing the relationship of 'big data' social science, and specifically the analysis of (an actually 'small' proportion of) the vast amounts of data produced by social media transaction, Edwards et al. (2013) provide a measured account of the relationship of 'big data' to what they term 'terrestrial' methods (exemplified by the survey and the interview). Building, cautiously and not uncritically, on Savage and Burrows' (2007, 2009) prediction of the 'coming crisis of empirical sociology', Edwards, Housley, Williams, Sloan and Williams consider the potential of 'big data' social media analysis (SMA) to act as surrogate for, to augment, or to re-orientate existing 'terrestrial' research methods. They do not, to follow Creswell's phrasing, consign extant methods to the junkheap of academic history, but, instead, point to a number of reasons why the 'surrogate' contribution of big data digital social science will not be realised. Issues such as the low fidelity of the data – a prevalence of 'misinformation, pranks, rumour and sarcasm' – identified in previous social media research (Procter, Viz, & Voss, 2013), and difficulties in determining demographic characteristics of the people behind the communications caused, for example, by people inconveniently leaving locational functions on their devices turned off, produce a need for digital and terrestrial methods to be integrated.

One way in which the digital and the terrestrial might usefully (if not unproblematically) compliment and combine with the other is in the development and use of 'signature proxies' (best estimates of social characteristics) that (may) allow some degree of connection between digital traces and transactions and questions of social group processes and identity formation. Thus, one relationship proposed between computational sociology and traditional methods, finds SMA augmenting traditional research in addressing conventional questions but, also, potentially re-orientating social research and inquiry. In the commentary of Edwards et al. (2013), SMA might best serve to augment traditional understandings of social action and process produced in and through terrestrial methods in relation to the 'classic questions' (Mills, 1959[2000], p. 6–7) of social organisation, change and identity. Here access to 'hard-to-reach' populations[3], and the possibility of understanding social change and identity at a far larger scale is realised through 'proxy' readings of the demographics of 'Tweeters' (the people) tied to the actual content of their tweets (the traces of their activities), thus extending the coverage of the traditional survey and the scope of specifically contextualised qualitative methods. An interesting development in this regard is the use of 'conventional' approaches and their findings – in this instance CA and Membership Categorisation Analysis (MCA: Housley & Fitzgerald, 2002; Sacks, 1995) – to provide analytic strategies for the interrogation of the content of 'big data' itself. This proposes a sophisticated relationship between traditional and digital approaches to the integration of 'mixed' methodological approaches but is, of course, not without difficulties in relation to the established problem of turning findings in to analytic strategies (see Button, 1990 for a related discussion of the use of CA in programming computers to 'converse' with humans). The final scenario proposed by Edwards et al. (2013) finds traditional sociological concerns and associated categories of social identities and groups re-oriented within a 'signature science' concerned with the analysis of 'digital proxies' for 'terrestrial attributes' and which may or may not map on to the 'digital publics' captured, represented and created within 'big data streams' and associated mining operations. Whilst offering a resolution to some of the analytic troubles facing big data analysts, this scenario, as discussed below, can also be seen to open up a virtual ideological space in which to 'make up' populations (Ruppert, 2013) and, moreover, poses difficult and sensitive questions relating to the categories usually prioritised by sociology such as race and ethnicity, gender, and class in online networks and flows of communication.

Moving away from the commentary by Edwards et al. (2013), a central issue in discussions of SMA and 'big data' is an apparent ambiguity concerning, and at times an absence of concern with, the disciplinary moorings of particular methods such as the survey, the interview, and ethnography; that is to say, the ways in which particular methods and data sets *construct*, and are understood to construct, the social as tied to particular disciplinary and social histories and trajectories. In their recognition of the potential crisis of empirical sociology, Savage and Burrows (2007, 2009) argued for the need for the social sciences to focus upon methodological innovation – rather than rehearsing rather narrow dominant forms and frames of social theory – yet, if the social sciences and sociology are to retain their analytic 'jurisdiction' over the social then there is also a sense that such innovations need to, necessarily, retain a connection to the disciplinary context in which they developed. There are several consequences of considering 'methods' in this broader sense; as emergent from and tied to particular philosophical, theoretical and empirical traditions and, as such, framing the world they often claim to study neutrally in specific ways. One particular issue that is raised when considering the relationship between 'qualitative research', particularly as practiced in Interactionist sociology, with 'big data' is a tension, and sometimes a total disconnect, between analytic priorities and understandings of what 'the social' is and where it might be found and how it might be observed. Methods, such as the interview and field and participant observation, taken simply as tools and treated in isolation from philosophical and theoretical constructions and understandings of social action, order and organisation can (be made to) appear neutral and consequently available for repurposing as one sees fit. Yet an attention to the ways in which methods are, necessarily, tied to traditions of inquiry and wider disciplinary concerns (Atkinson et al., 2008; Housley & Smith, 2010) points to deeper and less readily avoided difficulties with the enrolling of 'qualitative methods' within the 'big data' project within or without social scientific inquiries. In the reducing, re-using and recycling of qualitative methodologies to and as neutral 'tools', whether through enhancement through digital technology or in augmentation and re-orientation through SMA and 'big data', the distinctive (and distinctively sociological) contribution of the interview, ethnographic fieldwork and working with naturally occurring ('terrestrial') data risks being obscured or lost; thus, perhaps ironically, further contributing to a crisis of empirical sociology.

MISSED MIRACLES: THE IMPORTANCE OF ACTUAL PRACTICES AND 'SMALL DATA'

Critically engaging with some of the ways in which 'qualitative research' might engage and interact with digital social science (of the 'big data' variety) leads us to the significance of disciplinary questions, sociological traditions and, perhaps most significantly, the philosophical and theoretical grounds upon which our claims are made. These questions, whilst certainly unfashionable, might equally be seen to be of renewed significance in the contemporary moment. These questions were elucidated some fifty years ago by Aaron Cicourel (1964) in the classic text, *Method and Measurement*. Of the many insights provided by that proto-ethnomethodological survey of research methods, particularly relevant is the critique of the recourse of sociology to measurement by fiat (Cicourel, 1964; Torgerson, 1958) in which theoretical constructs are assigned a priori significance, and translated in to research questions, design and findings despite the social scientist lacking a sufficiently sophisticated theory of measurement or the precise nature of any causal relationship between attributes and variables. The significance of this observation is not to dismiss measurement as impossible but to demonstrate how, ultimately, measurement practices are practical decisions and, as such, available for study (Lynch, 1991). For Cicourel (1964) this critique did not only apply to quantitative and statistical measurement, but also to qualitative and ethnographic work which lapses into introspective interpretations and accounts which find the analysis concerned simply with 'meaning' and operating with a thin sense of subjectivity. In any case, such an approach to method and measurement finds that 'qual' and 'quant' analyses, when topicalised as product of and reliant upon practical reasoning, have much in common; an observation empirically described in recent 'methodographical' work (Greiffenhagen, Mair, & Sharrock, 2011).

The traditions of sociological inquiry that influenced Cicourel, which might be broadly labelled as Phenomenology and Interactionism (Blumer, 1969[1998]; Garfinkel, 1967[2007]; Schutz, 1967) have long stood as a critique of a formal theoretical sociology that operates by fiat, assuming and 'discovering' connections, priorities and significances that may or may not have anything to do with the participants' perspective, their modes and frames of perception and their methods for doing, communicating and producing the reflexively accountable social order that forms the resource of the sociologist in the first instance. The analytic distance from which 'big data' analyses operate from actual people's practices might mean that such considerations are merely inconvenient. Yet, 'big data' might also seen to be an increasingly powerful, prevalent and popular way through which sociologists might continue to procedurally 'miss the point'. As outlined in this section, there are at least two potential problems produced by an analytic distance from what actual people are actually doing. The first is that precisely that which is social in the first instance (the practice, rather than the aggregate) is missed or lost; the second is that a prioritisation of aggregate over practice can lead to a distortion or an inversion of the social organisation of a given phenomenon, setting or scene.

To draw out this analysts' problem in less abstract terms we might borrow an example from Eric Livingston originally developed to introduce and explain the work of ethnomethodology (EM). Again, I am not, necessarily, proposing an ethnomethodological critique here, nor am I simplistically positioning EM as belonging with 'qualitative research' (it does and it does not …). Rather, I intend Livingston's example to indicate an elementary, underlying difficulty with the view of social organisation produced by 'big data'.

In demonstrating the EM approach to the study of actually occurring, empirically observable and socially organised mundane practices over and above the generalisation, abstraction and theorisation characteristic of 'formal sociology', Livingston (1987) asks the question of *how* it is, and with what local methods, people do crossing the road. To address this seemingly trivial question, something that gets done by a good deal of people everyday, in relation to sociological method and analysis, Livingston constructs a thought experiment of a sort. Representing the formal analytic impulse, Livingston's sociologist[4] proceeds to address the organisational problem of the crossing of the intersection by climbing to the top of a conveniently located and sufficiently high building to produce (video) data of the persons involved. From up there, above the rush of people, the business of crossing the road initially appears chaotic. The only formal rules identifiably 'in play' are the lights indicating the apportioned interval for crossing the intersection and painted lines indicating where this should be done. Even the queuing system as people wait on the pavement is hard to determine. Here, technology can come to the aid of the sociologist. The ability to capture the stream of people crossing the road allows the analyst to review and replay the action, to begin to filter, arrange and 'clean up' all that data, to better focus on the question at hand. By reviewing the data something begins to emerge. The sociologist begins to find patterns in the aggregate of persons crossing the road, formations in the data. These patterns and formations are then coded and tested against other data to see if the observation holds. The sociologist, after a time, becomes more confident in what they are seeing. They have found, in the data produced from the lofty vantage point, patterns in the activity. They proceed to label these patterns as concepts: 'wedges' and 'fronts' that form behind and follow 'point people'. Here, then, we have a coherent explanatory mechanism for the business of crossing the road, described in and through the sociologist's concepts. A finding that might be tested for reliability and validity when the analysis is repeated in different places and at different times with the same results.[5] Yet, for Livingston and for the wider argument being developed here, a question remains; a question produced by the analytic enterprise of the sociologist. The question relates to the 'missing what' (Garfinkel, 2002), the practical methods in and through which people orientate to each other and co-accomplish the crossing of the intersection, and to matters of relevancy. The question, the analytical question, is not whether the analysis of front, wedges and point people is 'valid' or 'correct' or not; it is the product of empirical analysis after all, and is verifiable through further study. The question, ultimately, is has the sociologist accessed the contingencies, competencies and conditions that are 'in play' for the people at the intersection? That is to say, do people actually employ 'wedges', 'fronts' and 'point people' as concepts in the business of crossing the road? The answer, of course, is no they do not. In Livingston's (1987, p. 22) words:

> The perspective of 'wedges', 'fronts' and 'point people' is, of course, from a vantage point that none of the participants have or could have. Pedestrians do not use these documented, geometrically described alignments of physical bodies; they are engaged in

> a much more dynamic forging of their paths. They are engaged in locally building, together, the developing organisation of their mutual passage.

The resultant order is visible to the sociologist atop the building at the expense of access to the 'local building' practices of members and is, as Livingston notes (p. 25), 'at best a documented residue of the naturally organised, lived-work of getting through traffic'. Yet, this example is not proposing an alternative 'answer'. It is not an analysis of the problem of the intersection in its own right, but is a re-orientation (if you will) of for whom, and in what sense, the crossing of the intersection is a problem. Livingston's re-orientation is thus an invitation to discover and describe actual cases of the ways in which actual people do crossing an intersection (see, e.g. Liberman, 2013). The relevance of which for the argument developed across this chapter is summarised neatly by ten Have (2004, p. 160): 'Filming from above, one gains access to social life as a *product* but at the same time the lived-work of *production* is hidden from view'.

Here, and in the numerous examples provided by studies of the accomplishment of local order (e.g. Bröth, 2008; Hester & Francis, 2004; Laurier & Brown, 2008; Liberman, 2013; McHoul & Watson, 1984; Mondada, 2006; Ryave & Schenkein, 1974) we are again reminded of a fundamental distinction of the targets, priorities and aims of our analysis; of differences in finding social life as product or ongoing production and in addressing social organisation as noun or verb. Taking seriously the knowing, competent and skilled actions and activities of actual people does not, necessarily, belong solely to ethnomethodological studies. Ethnographies of skilled craftsmen, professional practices, institutional life and mundane activities also reveal something of the work in and through which social organisation gets done. The significance, here, is that rather than attending to the traces of social, the residue of people's activities, such approaches attend to how such sociology's phenomenon is bought in to being by the actual persons involved in its doing.

Some might dismiss the significance of finding out what actual people are actually doing in actual settings as a somewhat trivial pursuit. People go on doing stuff all the time. People just *do* cross the road, drive on the motorway, hold conversations, queue in shops, buy and sell stuff, cook and eat food, use computers and smartphones and interact with and through social media. Again, the point being made here is not simply a matter of disciplinary dogma, but the recognition of the significance of matters of analytic priority. It seems one either takes the foundational phenomenon of situated, practically organised interaction seriously, or takes it for granted or cannot see it. And perhaps this distinction is being exacerbated in that, as noted by Ruppert, Law, and Savage (2013), digital devices and the transactional data that they produce – which is, in that view, not always and not necessarily related to persons – do much to challenge the ways in which the social sciences understand, conceptualise and study society. We will return to this challenge below, but for now we might consider a further analytic difficulty that comes in working with traces of what people do, rather than the people and practices involved in the doing.

As argued in a previous article (Hall & Smith, 2014),[6] the problem with the analytic absence of the social organisational and socially organised practices and actions of people involved in the production of whatever it is that is being studied is not only that a 'layer' of understanding is missed[7] but that the absence produces a gap in the analysis which, in turn, can create an 'analytic inversion'. The (potential) inversion was found in a project concerned with analysing and describing the knowing and knowledgeable movements of outreach workers employed to locate and work with the homeless as they made their way through the city centre of Cardiff. In addition to prolonged field observations, we also captured the movements of the outreach workers with Global Positioning System (GPS) devices. This, as has been discussed in Livingston's example above, gave us an impossible perspective – not belonging to the ethnographer, nor the outreach workers – from which to view the practice. And, again, the temptation is to look to pattern, density and repetition in recognising a 'finding'. As such, the GPS traces revealed a regularity of movement, 'uniformity' even, that could be taken as evidence of expertise (when experts are taken to be people who know what they are up to and, as such, tend to deviate rarely from an efficient execution of the practice in which they can be taken to be experts in). The GPS traces can then be made to demonstrate what it is that these professionals know about homelessness and about Cardiff city centre: knowledge in the head, enacted through the feet (Hall & Smith, 2014; Ingold, 2007). The 'analytic inversion' caused by this impossible perspective of outreach work and in a more foundational sense, the relationship between mobility, experience, perception and knowledge, produced by the impossible perspective of the GPS data, is precisely that it positions knowledge (and the 'knowledgeable practitioner') ahead of the activities in and through which the 'knowledge' of homelessness and of the city centre might be said to be achieved. The further the analysts' perspective from where the action is, the more likely a distorted view of what it is that people are up to, the contingencies that they face and the significance that the practices have for those involved in their accomplishment. And this distance, as well as producing potential analytic distortions can open up a space in which the analysis not only relies on 'measurement by fiat' (Cicourel, 1964) but takes on an ideological character in forming 'mystical connections' (Marx & Engels, 1970) between the data and the actual people and their phenomena.

MYSTICAL CONNECTIONS: 'BIG DATA' AS IDEOLOGY

The characterisation of social science inquiry and methodology pursued in this chapter has, clearly, being drawn from a 'traditional' and 'terrestrial' perspective. Commentators such as Ruppert et al. (2013) have noted the 'extent to which digital data sources relate to people or indeed to populations of people is limited' and that the 'humanist conceptions of society are being eclipsed' (p. 36); thus, the expertise of the social scientist as intervener and mediator in the production and interpretation of knowledge are called in to question and re-orientated (Edwards et al., 2013). The authors, in outlining something of the networks, transactions and digital communications that are seen and said to increasingly constitute, disassemble and re-assemble 'the social' are not, of course, proposing that this state of affairs is not without its politics and its problems. And, in some ways, the observation opens up a space for the existing expertise of the social sciences. For whilst (some of) the expertise of the social scientist may no longer be (necessarily) necessary for the production and interpretation of (some forms) of data, there is, certainly, a role for the social sciences in making critical interventions and empirical studies of the ways in which such social data are organised, interpreted and applied. Indeed, the upshot of some of the (traditional) analytic problems that I have been outlining thus far in this chapter is a contribution to an understanding of the ways in which we might consider such matters not only as technical or methodological but as political too. This is recognised by Ruppert et al. (2013) in their description of how social relations are, arguably, returning to an 'older, observational kind of knowledge economy' tied to the 'political power of the visualisation and mapping of administratively derived data about whole populations' (p. 35). Indeed, as noted above, the discussions of relations of knowledge and power, seen to be shaped by the mechanisms brought in to being in and through transactional 'trace data', might prompt us to go on to consider the ways in which the role of analysis within this space might take on an ideological character and, furthermore, how it is that the task of the social scientist – to describe the mechanisms, situations and practices in which such 'relations' are realised – might be more important than ever.

Such a critique was developed by Dorothy Smith (1974) in response to previously dominant 'terrestrial' modes of inquiry and theory building in which she proposed that the operation of abstracted sociological theory and method was akin to the production and workings of ideology as outlined by Marx and Engels in *The German Ideology*. An unexpected source, perhaps, but the writings of Marx and Engels (1970) on the production of 'mystical connections' by the bourgeoisie, led Smith (1974, p. 41) to note that sociological theory building can 'look uncomfortably like this recipe for making ideology'. The recipe is as follows:

Trick 1: Separate what people say they think from the actual circumstances in which it is said, from the actual circumstances in which it is said, from the actual empirical conditions of their lives and from the actual individuals who said it.

Trick 2: Having detached the ideas, they must now be arranged. Prove then an order among them which accounts for what is observed.

Trick 3: The ideas are then changed 'into a person', that is they are constituted as distinct entities to which agency (or possibly causal efficacy) may be attributed. And they may be re-attributed to 'reality' by attributing them to actors who now *represent* the ideas.

Smith's complaint was with the ways in which (theoretically driven) interview studies (as an example – although other methods are, of course, capable of the same moves) operate by taking 'something which actual people actually said [and] making it over so that it can be treated as an attribute of an aggregate' producing an 'end product' for the theoretical analyst, from which the identified 'social beliefs', 'social valuations' and 'social norms' can then be assigned to a constructed personage and, moreover, 'treated as causing behaviour' (p. 42). In current debates relating to big data analysis by commercial analysts, the fact that 'correlation does not prove causation' is well known, and, as outlined above, poses one of the main issues for social scientific analysts being worked with and around in the handling of big data. In building on the previous cases provided by Livingston (1987) and the mapping of outreach work (Hall & Smith, 2014), the critique provided by Dorothy Smith points to the ways in which the analyst might not only potentially, confidently, be seeing something that is only a residue of what it is that is actually going on, or might be led to see something that is not there but, more significantly, that the distance from what actual people are actually doing presents an ideological space in which said actual people are assigned beliefs, motives and perspectives that were never 'theirs' in the first instance.

It seems fair to note that big data, produced by the ubiquity and pervasiveness of social media 'communication' and 'interaction', finds Trick 1 achieved as a signature function of the technology in and through which the data are produced. The available streams of digital data produce an unavoidably de-situated, de-personalised view of social action and social process and, as noted above, produce traces of transactions that sometimes can be seen to have little to do with people at all (Ruppert et al., 2013). Just as the social scientist atop the tower block struggles to see the detail of interaction, the big data scientist can see nothing (or very little with any certainty) of the actual people behind the laptops, smartphones and tablets. Trick 2, also, is taken care of by technology and becomes all the more efficient for it. Patterns, correlations, spikes and trends are identified and arranged by computer and algorithm: detached ideas amongst which an order is found and then, in Trick 3, re-assigned actors that the exercise itself has 'made up' as a population (see, e.g. Ruppert, 2013). As noted by Smith (1974, p. 42) a key characteristic of this (sociological) ideological recipe was that the sociologist would 'take a concept such as social class or power and locate it in the real world by creating indicators for it'. Sloan et al. (2013) usefully describe some of the complex steps that are necessary in working out 'who' (in terms of social scientifically meaningful categories of gender and geographic location) these data 'belong' to in (re)turning the data in to 'real' persons – necessary work for the sociologist but not, perhaps, for others. Analysts working outside of the social sciences may not be so very concerned with these matters at present, although 'commercial sociologists' (Savage & Burrows, 2007) are undoubtedly turning their attention to the ways in which qualitative and ethnographic approaches might provide greater insight in to consumer action and some of the meanings behind the 'prosumption' activities (Ritzer & Jurgenson, 2010) on Web 2.0 sites and networks. The analytic and ideological troubles outlined in this chapter remain and are likely to be exacerbated.

Again, these issues are both instructive for the emergent practices and landscape of digital social science and in relation to the spaces in which the social sciences are positioned to make critical interventions. Ultimately, for Smith (1974, p. 42) and the argument developed across this chapter, it is the task of the sociologist to recover what it is that people do to produce social phenomena in the first instance in 'preliminary inquiries'. A task distinct from the ways in which such observations are potentially obscured within the commercial digital 'paradigm' and the forms of potential analytical abstraction, inversion and ideological apparatus that come with it. Her description of this task seems particularly pertinent:

> Contemporary sociology commands techniques for transforming concepts into currency which were unheard of in Marx's time. If they are to be reclaimed and made to stand as the preliminary formulation of inquiry, then they must be anchored back into an actual analysis of actual living people. The sociologist must begin to discover what people do to bring into being the phenomena which its concepts analyse and assemble.

ATOP THE HIGHEST BUILDING: OR, SO WHAT FOR DIGITAL SOCIAL SCIENCE?

As Ruppert et al. (2013) eloquently describe, the landscape of social science research has been changed by the development and ubiquity of digital devices in a manner that suggests a reworking of some of the long held foundational theoretical assumptions of social science. Often data is being produced as signatures of the devices and the transactions they facilitate within networks in their own right. As the majority of commentators are currently asking, what, then, is the role of social science – and in the context of this chapter, qualitative methodologies – within this new landscape? Savage and Burrows (2007) were not simply encouraging social scientists to 'join in' with the rush to explore and exploit 'big data' simply 'because it is there', but, rather, to pay attention to the ways in which the jurisdiction of the social sciences over the analysis of the social was being eroded and undermined by external forces. And one of the ways in which this might be achieved is a re-emphasis of the task of sociological analysis as defined by Dorothy Smith and co-travellers. This is not to suggest a simply defensive move, nor a withdrawal from the debates. Rather this chapter has argued for a recognition of a distinct and strong contribution of qualitative approaches to understanding contemporary social organisation, focused on practice and people, which should not be thought of as simply put to service in the production of more sophisticated automated means of reading, measuring and interpreting 'big' aggregates of 'small' practices but as having much to offer to social sciences' attempt to 'keep up' with what people do to bring the phenomena of online transactions and big data in to being. I want to suggest that in dealing with the complexity that big data brings to social scientific analysis the distinct modes of inquiry and analytic priorities that characterise qualitative methodologies need to be retained *as distinct*, rather than simply reduced, re-used or recycled. This contribution may be seen in two forms (although there are and will be others). The first contribution and perhaps most effective intervention that might be made for 'qualitative sociology' is not essays such as this but actual studies of the actual activities of the actual people working with big data. This has been a fertile furrow ploughed by those who have analysed the everyday practices of physicists, air traffic controllers, or CCTV operators for example, focusing on their professional and occasioned ways of seeing, doing and talking what they are up to. Here, then, we recover something of the ordinary reasoning practices employed by those in the business of creating and applying (for example) algorithms that incorporate and automate existing social scientific approaches in the treatment of big data. Moreover, such ethnographically orientated work might also 'follow the data' and observe and describe the ways in which what is known (and constructed as knowable) about 'X' population and is handled and treated in, for example, decision making processes and the ways in which such processes are made accountable in situ, thus describing the consequences of 'big data' profiling and predictions for people in the course of their everyday affairs. Moreover, we might, again following the recommendations of Smith (1974), produce studies which are concerned with documenting and describing the ways in which technologies are produced, appropriated and distributed to and by 'socially organised entities', institutions and agencies which have use for them. And this is to say nothing of the myriad practices found in the mundane, overlooked and undervalued work of maintenance workers, engineers and other agents employed in repairing the networks, exchanges, and servers which ensure the continued stream of transactional data (Graham & Thrift, 2007).

The second contribution is to continue to develop a programme of studies concerned with the interaction order of online and offline communications and the complexity of the interaction between the two, in empirical descriptions of the ways in which people engage with digital devices in the course of particular social activities in particular settings. Some of this work is, of course, being done, for example examinations of interactional troubles in Skype communication (Rintell, 2015); the use of smartphones and particular apps 'in the wild' (Brown, McGregor, & Laurier, 2013) or in the use of digital technology in relation to 'digital memorisation' (Hand, 2014). The impulse here, as with the example of crossing the road is to switch, or at least hold back, from the attraction of the 'God's eye view' atop of the building and, instead, access the work that gets done at street level, both physically and virtually, and how digital devices and online communications become socially salient for people in the course of their daily round.

Both forms of contribution position qualitative methodologies well to ameliorate the ideological character of big data analyses conducted beyond and outside of disciplinary concerns and first principles within and without the social sciences and, moreover, to retain an underlying ethos of research that connect the qualitative and ethnographic traditions drawn on in this chapter: an impulse of respect for competencies and practices employed in the accomplishment of what it is that actual people are actually up to, and, perhaps most strongly, an ethos of attentiveness and a patience and care with analysis. Moreover, they point to challenges to, or at least critically investigations of, the ways in which technological change is – still and increasingly since Marx and Engels first made the observation – presented as an irresistible force independently and inexorably shaping social organisation, change and identity.

In and through the course of this chapter I have pointed to some of the challenges posed to and posed by the relationship between big data and digital social science from the perspective of qualitative methodology. After sketching out some of the ways in which 'digital social science' is currently being organised, I drew on two small and humble examples to point to some of the difficulties that arise from an analytic vantage point that moves one too far away from the actual practices of actual people. Here we considered what is missed in working only with the residue of practice and how the view of the analyst atop the building, peering down at people on the street, can lead to a distortion which conflates concepts with findings and produces a potential analytic inversion. Finally we moved to consider this analytic distance as, potentially, opening up a space in which analysis and theorising can take on an ideological form before considering the ways in which the social sciences and 'qualitative methodologies' in particular can resist the potential ideological character of 'big data' and computational analysis by producing 'preliminary inquiries' and descriptions of the small, practical things that get done by people involved in the production, distribution, use and application of digital devices and big data.

NOTES

1. Taken from an (in)famous provocative essay published in *Wired* magazine (Anderson, 2008). The full quote has much to do with what this chapter argues qualitative social science might challenge as regards big data analytics: 'Who knows why people do what they do? The point is they do it, and we can track and measure it with unprecedented fidelity. With enough data, the numbers speak for themselves'.

2. It is worth noting that these famous three words spoken by Mallory were originally part of a critique of the idea that an activity and a challenge as 'pure' and 'spiritual' as mountaineering should need to be rationalised or justified through notions of economic or scientific gain. We might also note how simply climbing Everest has been much reduced to an economic 'challenge' and is the subject of much controversy relating to commercialism and exploitation, the use of assistance (human and technological) and, of course, ethics.

3. This claim is common, as is the claim that social life has 'gone digital'. Both overlook the fact that the experience of most of the most vulnerable and marginalised social groups remains, and looks set to remain, 'terrestrial'.

4. The methodological and analytical problem posed by 'street-level' social order is further explored in an instructional case provided by ten Have (2004).

5. Anyone can repeat this experiment by heading to an intersection or by simply searching for images on the Internet: we can crowdsource the analysis, if you will. If you stick to Western(ised) cities then you will likely confirm the theory and the finding. Try it in other cities and you might find something else going on. Of course, the usual recourse of sociology is to explain differences such as this as 'cultural'. Nevertheless, there remains order at all points.

6. I apologise for not being able to develop this case in more detail here. Accounts of the work of outreach in Cardiff can be read elsewhere (Hall & Smith, 2013; Smith, 2011; Smith & Hall, 2013).

7. For some, and some ethnomethodologists in particular, the local, situated, constitutive actions and practices of members are not to be understood in relation to or explained via other 'layers' of social organisation but, rather, *is* the very grounds of immortal society.

REFERENCES

Anderson, C. (2008). The end of theory: The data deluge makes the scientific method obsolete. *Wired*, *16*(7). Retrieved from http://archive.wired.com/science/discoveries/magazine/16-07/pb_theory

Atkinson, P. (2009). Illness narratives revisited: The failure of narrative reductionism. *Sociological Research Online*, *14*(5), 16. Retrieved from http://www.socresonline.org.uk/14/5/16.html

Atkinson, P., Delmont, S., & Housley, W. (2008). *Contours of culture: Complex ethnography and the ethnography of complexity*. Plymouth, UK: AltaMira Press.

Atkinson, P., & Housley, W. (2003). *Interactionism*. London, UK: SAGE.

Back, L. (2007). *The art of listening*. Oxford: Berg.

Back, L., & Puwar, N. (Eds.). (2013). *Live methods*. Oxford: Wiley-Blackwell.

Blumer, H. (1969[1998]). *Symbolic interactionism: Perspective and method.* London: University of California Press.

Boyd, D., & Crawford, K. (2012). Critical questions for big data: Provocations for a cultural, technological, and scholarly phenomenon. *Information, Communication & Society*, *15*(5), 662–679.

Bröth, M. (2008). The studio interaction as a contextual resource for TV-production. *Journal of Pragmatics*, *40*(5), 904–926.

Brown, B., McGregor, M., & Laurier, E. (2013). iPhone in vivo: analysis of mobile device use. *Proceedings of the SIGCHI Conference on Human Factors in Computing Systems*. pp. 1031–1040.

Button, G. (1990). Going up a blind alley. In P. Luff, N. Gilbert, & D. Frohlich (Eds.), *Computers and conversation* (pp. 67–90). London: Academic Press.

Cicourel, A. (1964). *Method and measurement in sociology*. Oxford: Free Press of Glencoe.

Cresswell, T. (2010). Toward a politics of mobility. *Environment and Planning D: Society and Space*, *28*, 17–31.

Edwards, A., Housley, W., Williams, M., Sloan, L., & Williams, M. (2013). Digital social research, social media and the sociological imagination: Surrogacy, augmentation and re-orientation. *International Journal of Social Research Methodology*, *16*(3), 245–260.

Garfinkel, H. (1967[2007]). *Studies in ethnomethodology*. Cambridge: Polity Press.

Garfinkel, H. (2002). *Ethnomethodology's program: Working out Durkheim's aphorism*. Lanhm, MD: Rowman & Littlefield Publishers.

Graham, S., & Thrift, N. (2007). Out of order: Understanding repair and maintenance. *Theory, Culture & Society*, *24*(3), 1–25.

Greiffenhagen, C., Mair, M., & Sharrock, W. (2011). From methodology to methodography: A study of qualitative and quantitative reasoning in practice. *Methodological Innovations Online*, *6*(3), 93–107.

Hall, T., & Smith, R. J. (2013). Stop and go: A field study of pedestrian practice, immobility and urban outreach work. *Mobilities*, *8*(2), 272–292.

Hall, T., & Smith, R. J. (2014). Knowing the city: Maps, mobility and urban outreach work. *Qualitative Research*, *14*(3), 294–310.

Hand, M. (2014). Digitization and memory: Researching practices of adaption to visual and textual data in everyday life. In M. Hand & S. Hillyard (Eds.), *Big data? Qualitative approaches to digital research* (Vol. 13, pp. 205–229). Studies in Qualitative Methodology. Bingley, UK: Emerald Group Publishing Limited.

ten Have, P. (2004). *Understanding ethnomethodology and qualitative research*. London, UK: SAGE.

Hester, S., & Francis, D. (2004). Analysing visually available mundane order: A walk to the supermarket. *Visual Studies*, *18*(1), 36–46.

Housley, H., & Fitzgerald, R. (2002). The reconsidered model of membership categorisation analysis. *Qualitative Research*, *2*(1), 59–83.

Housley, W., & Smith, R. J. (2010). Innovation and reduction in qualitative methods: The case of conceptual coupling, activity-type pairs and auto-ethnography. *Sociological Research Online*, *15*(4), 9. Retrieved from http://www.socresonline.org.uk/15/4/9.html

Husserl. (1970[1936]). *The crisis of the European sciences and transcendental phenomenology*. In D. Carr (Trans.). Evanston, IL: Northwestern University Press.

Ingold, T. (2007). *Lines: A brief history*. London, UK: Routledge.
Kuhn, T. (1996). *The structure of scientific revolutions*. Chicago, IL: University of Chicago.
Laurier, E. (2001). Why people say where they are during mobile phone calls. *Environment and Planning D: Society and Space*, *19*, 485–504.
Laurier, E., & Brown, B. (2008). Rotating maps and readers: Praxiological aspects of alignment and orientation. *Transactions of the Institute of British Geographers*, *33*, 201–221.
Liberman, K. (2013). *More studies in ethnomethodology*. Albany, NY: State University of New York Press.
Livingston, E. (1987). *Making sense of ethnomethodology*. London, UK: Routledge.
Lynch, M. (1991). Method: Ordinary and scientific measurement as ethnomethodological phenomena. In G. Button (Ed.), *Ethnomethodology and the human sciences: A foundational reconstruction* (pp. 77–108). Cambridge: Cambridge University Press.
Marx, K., & Engels, F. (1970). *The German ideology*. In R. Pascal (Ed.), International Publishers London: Lawrence and Wishart.
McHoul, A. (2008). Questions of context in studies of talk and interaction: Ethnomethodology and conversation analysis. *Journal of Pragmatics*, *40*(5), 823–826.
McHoul, A. W., & Watson, D. R. (1984). Two axes for the analysis of 'commonsense' and 'formal' geographical knowledge in classroom talk. *British Journal of Sociology of Education*, *5*(3), 281–302.
Mills, C. W. (1959[2000]). *The sociological imagination*. Oxford: Oxford University Press.
Mondada, L. (2006). Participants' online analysis and multimodal practices: Projecting the end of the turn and the closing of the sequence. *Discourse Studies*, *8*(1), 117–129.
Mondada, L. (2009). Emergent focused interactions in public places: A systematic analysis of the multimodal achievement of a common interactional space. *Journal of Pragmatics*, *41*(10), 1977–1997.
Procter, R., Viz, F., & Voss, A. (2013). Reading the riots on Twitter: Methodological innovations for the analysis of big data. *International Journal of Social Science Research Methods*, *16*(3), 197–214.
Reynolds, L. T., & Herman-Kinney, N. J. (Eds.) (2003). *Handbook of symbolic interactionism*. Oxford: Alta Mira Press.
Rintell, S. (2015). Omni-relevance in technologised interaction: Couples coping with video calling distortions. In R. Fitzgerald & W. Housley (Eds.), *Advances in membership categorisation analysis* (pp. 213–256). London: Sage.
Ritzer, G., & Jurgenson, N. (2010). Production, consumption, prosumption the nature of capitalism in the age of the digital 'prosumer'. *Journal of Consumer Culture*, *10*(1), 13–36.
Ruppert, E. (2013). Not just another database: The transactions that enact young offenders. *Computational Culture*, 1–13. Retrieved from http://computationalculture.net/article/not-just-another-database-the-transactions-that-enact-young-offenders
Ruppert, E., Law, J., & Savage, M. (2013). Reassembling social science methods. The challenge of digital devices. *Theory, Culture & Society*, *30*(4), 22–46.
Ryave, A. L., & Schenkein, J. N. (1974). Notes on the art of walking. In R. Turner (Ed.), *Ethnomethodology. Selected readings* (pp. 265–274). Middlesex: Penguin.
Sacks, H. (1995). *Lectures in conversation*. Oxford: Blackwell.
Savage, M., & Burrows, R. (2007). The coming crisis of empirical sociology. *Sociology*, *45*(5), 885–889.

Savage, M., & Burrows, R. (2009). Some further reflections on the coming crisis of empirical sociology. *Sociology*, *43*(4), 762–772.

Schutz, A. (1967). *The phenomenology of the social world.* Evanston, IL: Northwestern University Press.

Sharrock, W. (1995). Ethnographic work. *The Discourse Analysis Research Group Newsletter*, *11*(1), 3–8.

Sloan, L., Morgan, J., Housley, W., Williams, M., Edwards, A., Burnap, P., & Rana, O. (2013). Knowing the tweeters: Deriving sociologically relevant demographics from twitter. *Sociological Research Online*, *18*(3), 7. Retrieved from http://www.socresonline.org.uk/18/3/7.html

Smith, D. (1974). Theorising as ideology. In R. Turner (Ed.), *Ethnomethodology* (pp. 41–44). Middlesex: Penguin Education.

Smith, R. J. (2011). Goffman's interaction order at the margins: Stigma, role, and normalization in the outreach Encounter. *Symbolic Interaction*, *34*(3), 357–376.

Smith, R. J., & Hall, T. (2013). No time out: Mobility, rhythmicity and urban patrol in the twenty-four hour city. *The Sociological Review*, 61(S1), 89–108.

Torgerson, W. S. (1958). *Theory and methods of scaling.* Oxford: Wiley.

Uprichard, E. (2013). Big data, little questions? *Discover Society*. Retrieved from http://www.discoversociety.org/2013/10/01/focus-big-data-little-questions/

DIGITIZATION AND MEMORY: RESEARCHING PRACTICES OF ADAPTION TO VISUAL AND TEXTUAL DATA IN EVERYDAY LIFE

Martin Hand

ABSTRACT

Purpose – *To discuss two research projects, illuminating the ways in which digital technologies are both enfolded into people's lives and open up new possibilities for practice that, in turn, have to be* managed. *To revisit this material to reflect on the benefits and limitations of in-depth interviewing for understanding the dynamics of new textual and visual forms of data in everyday life.*

Approach – *A broadly relational approach to technology and practice was employed, pursued through in-depth interviewing in two research projects about digitization and memory making.*

Findings – *In employing the qualitative method of in-depth interviewing to focus upon what people regularly do, the chapter shows how the*

Big Data? Qualitative Approaches to Digital Research
Studies in Qualitative Methodology, Volume 13, 205–227

ISSN: 1042-3192/doi:10.1108/S1042-319220140000013013

material and mediating *capacities of networked digital technologies such as cameras and smartphones are enacted and actively negotiated in relation to expectations and conventions about the temporality and visibility of personal life through diverse memory practices. These can be considered multiple 'practices of adaptation'.*

Value – *The research reported on provides some novel ways of thinking about devices and data in relation to practice.*

Keywords: Smartphones; memory; digital photography; social practice; visual data

INTRODUCTION

In this chapter I discuss one previous and one ongoing research project aimed at situating debates about digitization and memory in the context of people's everyday engagements with their digital devices and the visual and textual data produced and circulated. As discussed in several of the chapters in this collection, digital data and the multiple devices through which it is relayed have become enfolded into the fabric of ordinary life. The combination of the increased *routine* production and *visibility* of digital data presents novel challenges for both researchers and participants. This chapter discusses explorations of *how* digital data is routinely produced, negotiated, recursively worked upon and circulated, or in other words, how digital data is *socialized* in daily practice. It is seen as both the outcome and visualization of intersecting practices, making them available for self-reflection in ways that also need to be addressed during the research process.

After a brief review of the key issues in 'digital memory', the first part revisits a previous study of the digitization of personal photography, pulling out two key themes relating to memory practices. First, the reconfiguration of album making in the domestic sphere; second, the emerging practices of managing image circulation in social media. The second part reflects upon in-depth interviews with smartphone users to show how combinations of digital devices, software and social media facilitate practices of coordinating and managing intersecting schedules of work and leisure; altering conceptions of conventional temporalities; and enabling novel temporalities to emerge through the *visualization* of social practices that seem to require continual monitoring.

The chapter has two aims. The first is empirical, in illuminating the ways in which digital technologies are both enfolded into people's lives (domesticated in Silverstone's, 1994, sense) and open up new possibilities for practice that, in turn, have to be *managed.* In employing the qualitative method of in-depth interviewing to focus upon what people regularly do, the chapter shows how the *material and mediating* capacities of networked digital technologies such as cameras and smartphones are enacted and actively negotiated in relation to expectations and conventions about the temporality and visibility of personal life. The second is methodological, in revisiting this material to reflect on the benefits and limitations of in-depth interviewing for understanding the dynamics of new textual and visual forms of data in everyday life. The chapter argues for the explanatory potential of in-depth interviewing and observation in understanding the *multiple practices of adaptation* occurring in relation to new forms of visual, textual and geolocational data. It is argued that in order to understand such practices, researching the specific ways in which people *negotiate* their use of devices, connected systems and data can be particularly helpful in evaluating some of the claims made about the impacts of digitization on memory and temporality.

Digital Devices, Data and Memory Practices

Digitization and the global proliferation of networked media technologies have precipitated a great deal of scholarly interest in how personal and collective memories are constructed, commodified and mediated (Garde-Hansen, 2011; Sturken, 1997, 2007). The storage capacities of digital infrastructures and systems, and the new means of classification and retrieval facilitated by relational databases, have been the subject of a wide range of scholarly debates (see Bowker, 2005; Van house & Churchill, 2008). In the context of digital data in personal life, some have argued that a new culture of informational instantaneity precipitates 'the end of forgetting' (Mayer-Schonberger, 2009) as established practices of memory making in modernity are displaced by transient and 'confessional' traces of lived experience (Bauman, 2007; Gane, 2006; Lash, 2002). Some of this concerns the rapidity of data flows in a broader 'culture of speed' combining fast capitalism with ubiquitous media that in turn reshapes the everyday experience of temporality in terms of 'immediacy' (Tomlinson, 2005). It also involves the ways in which flows of personalized and public digital data through connected devices and systems appear to deconstruct prior distinctions between private and public, personal and collective, active and passive memories, producing what Hoskins calls a 'continuously networked present' (2012, p. 101).

In this scenario (e.g. Twitter), the past appears to be permanently accessible through the expanding digital archives of everyday life (Featherstone, 2000), but as Hoskins (2011a, 2011b) argues this 'connective memory' is not so straightforward in practice. Images, text and other traces produced and stored in digital media may or may not be retrieved, may remain present or have decayed, and most importantly, retrieval may be 'accidental', out of context, and instantaneous, creating novel anxieties for individuals 'entered' into the dataverse (Bowker, 2013) or the 'media everyday' (Grusin, 2010). Hoskins' (2011a, 2011b) concept of the 'connective turn' is especially useful in capturing the convergence between new digital technologies that are with people at all times and thus continually generate and visualize data about the self, with the postwar turn towards 'memorialization' (re-consuming the past).

A further dimension is that visual and textual objects produced and stored in digital formats are somewhat ephemeral: sometimes fluid, often re-workable and as many have argued, less 'durable' than their print equivalents (Bowker, 2005; Garde-Hansen, 2009; Hoskins, 2012; Murray, 2008; van Dijck, 2007, 2011). Some of this fluidity is the outcome of the continual algorithmic classification and reordering discussed in recent scholarship on sociotechnical agency (Gillespie, 2010; Schwarz, 2014). This has been well documented in relation to digital images: how images and the contexts of their interpretation are subject to continual reconfiguration in networked environments such as Flickr, Facebook and Pinterest, unlike in the photo album or shoebox (Lister, 2013; van Dijck, 2007). Indeed, the materials and social practices of photography have always been associated with making and sharing memories or at least with remembrance in a general sense (Barthes, 1982; Sontag, 1977), but these appear outmoded and outpaced in the context of ubiquitous imaging machines and visual data.

This redistribution of agency between user, object, database, and algorithm has been a key theme within STS and Information Science (e.g. Bowker, 2005; Van House & Churchill, 2008). From the perspective of 'relational materiality' developed in STS, networks, databases and algorithms do not determine but actively shape their content as elements within heterogeneous networks of people and things (see van Dijck, 2013). New possibilities of storage, circulation, retrieval and multifaceted classification are proliferating, with significant consequences for how the production and circulation of digital traces is being organized. The invisible structuring capacities of algorithmic classifications are 'ambiently' shaping remembrance (Hoskins, 2011a, 2011b), in tandem with the recursive negotiations between users and platforms (van Dijck, 2013). Furthermore, as contemporary media are 'increasingly integrated into the fabric of everyday life' (Silverstone, 2007, p. 5) it becomes essential to understand how the digital technologies routinely being used by individuals are articulated and domesticated within the rhythms of everyday life (cf. Shove, Pantzar, & Watson, 2012; Silverstone, 1994). Moreover, digital traces and to some extent memory objects (e.g. photos), are often the unintended outcome of intersecting practices. Understanding this requires an analytic focus upon the materiality and mediating capacity of digital devices, both in terms of the quotidian contexts in which they are used, and the ways in which combinations of devices and platforms form a broader 'arrangement' for the accomplishment of diverse social practices (Couldry, 2012; Shove et al., 2012).

In both projects I have adopted a broadly relational approach to technology and practice, and orientated the empirical research towards exploring the dynamics of devices (cameras, smartphones, etc.) and their uses as material and mediating objects in daily life. By daily life, I mean the context of established routines and habits – the dynamics of what people regularly do – explorations of which can assist in grounding some of the grander claims about the ephemerality of digital images and the constant connectivity afforded by networked media.

METHOD

The two research programs discussed below employed a range of methods, including archival work, content and discourses analyses of popular magazines, plus policy, commercial, and trade documents related to national and regional archives and consumer electronics industries, institutional observation, and in-depth interviewing. It is the processes of in-depth interviewing that I wish to concentrate on here.

In the first project on personal photography in the digital age[1] (2006–2009), I conducted in-depth interviews ($n = 75$) with four specific groups in order to explore constellations of belief, technologies, and practice influencing patterns of use. Each group was designed to focus (in principle) around different trajectories of digital imaging and personal photography: archivists and curators; members of a well-established amateur photographic society; undergraduate students; and residents from different areas of a local city. As well as investigating different forms of convergence between technologies at that time (cameras, PCs, printers, email, social media), interviews were designed to reveal current *variations* in the ways in which people assemble, use and make meaning through these technologies. How are the materials, meanings and purposes of digital photography being assembled and reproduced in practice?

In the ongoing project on digitization and memory practices[2] (2010–2014), I am conducting semi-structured in-depth interviews ($n = 80$) with individuals and families with children in three cities in Ontario. The interview-based research asks how digital devices, especially smartphones and other mobile media, are situated within domestic contexts of memory making also involving cameras, diaries, scrapbooks and so forth. Again, these interviews are designed to reveal variations in how these technologies are framed, and precisely what role they play in shaping what is remembered, how, and whether this is changing. For this chapter I want to reflect upon the data from 30 in-depth interviews with 18 current undergraduates and 12 employed recent graduates. These specifically examined the detail of both routine and self-reflexive modes of forgetting and remembering related to the prevalence of devices and visual digital traces produced in ordinary conduct. In this sample (not all reported on here), 20 participants were women and 10 were men, aged between 20 and 30 years. All were living independently of parents, possessed at least one smartphone and had regular access to networked media. Smartphone and related device ownership among 20-year olds to 30-year olds with high educational attainment is high, and it is this group which survey data suggests are early adopters of such technologies, and are 'always on' and 'connected' to web-based platforms of distribution and exchange throughout the day (Rainie & Wellman, 2012). In both projects, all names are pseudonyms.

DIGITAL PHOTOGRAPHY AND MEMORY MAKING

In the interview-based element of the research on personal photographic practices, I wanted to explore people's engagements with the potential of digital cameras and connected systems to vastly increase the quantity of images made, stored, viewed and shared. Alongside issues of saturation and 'deluge', this raised questions of how people go about organizing and managing ubiquity, and what the contexts are for doing so. In what follows I report on previous findings and also reflect upon them in terms of the process of interviewing and what this allowed me to 'see' in terms of the continuities and discontinuities of digitization in practice.

Continuities: Reconfiguring the Family Album

A first example highlights the potential for digitization to enable continuity as well as disruption in cultural practice. The photo album in all its forms has arguably defined photographic order and memory during the 20th century. There is a rich literature on the relationships between photography and domestic sphere (e.g. Chalfen, 1987; Csikszentmihalyi & Rochberg-Halton, 1981; Hirsch, 1981; King, 1986; Slater, 1995; Spence & Holland, 1991). The production of family albums (rather than photographs per se) can be seen as relatively self-conscious efforts to *produce* memory, constructing and ordering ideal and partial narratives of the past (Spence & Holland, 1991). In digital culture, it has been almost universally argued that the collectively produced family album is disappearing as photographic memory-making reorients from fixing images to *exchanging* them (e.g. Murray, 2008; van Dijck, 2011; Van House & Churchill, 2008).

Digital cameras appear to problematize album-orientated practices immediately as they enable the unprecedented production of images-as-data. For example, is there any reason to make prints of digital images when they can be stored in software generated or web-based 'albums'? Should I keep *all* the images I have produced? Should I store my images on multiple formats such as external hard drives, CDs, memory sticks and so on? The ways in which people answer these questions through practical engagements are of great significance for what kind of material lives digital images may have. By interviewing participants in their homes, and with them knowing in advance that the interviews were about photography and photographs, there was of course an element of 'staging' whereby participants tried to remember in advance where they have stored their old photos such that they can be retrieved. But this also served to encourage reflection on the fact that they haven't necessarily thought about their photos for some time, and would be hard pressed to find a specific image should it be called for. Moreover, the physical handling and description of images, cameras and other technologies during the interview allowed for conversations about the material infrastructure of image making to be pulled into view – constitutive processes of assembling and appropriation that would otherwise remain hidden, much like albums themselves. In addition, by being asked to find and handle their technologies and images, and demonstrate what they do with them, participants articulated their material and mediating capacities in the surroundings where they are used.

Although one of the main features of digitization is this *over-production* of photos made possible by the storage capacities of the camera-computer-cloud, many people used film in similar ways, producing vast collections of negatives and prints that never see the light of day. At the level of practice people are more likely to view photos on the screen rather than those stored in printed albums. This is partly a matter of classifications ('Why did I store those prints in that order'?). Talking to Anna while surrounded by envelopes, albums, cameras and a laptop enabled her to think about the different ways her images have been classified:

> But I don't look at those [pictures in envelopes] I only go through those if I'm looking for something specific. If I have to get pictures from a past event or if I'm doing a photo contest and I think 'oh I took a picture of …'. One time … I couldn't remember exactly what year it was so I went back through those boxes to find it. And then took that in and got it reprinted. It's a lot easier to find things now on the computer. (Anna, Legal Secretary)

For some, the sheer quantity of their digital images completely destabilizes previous storage and retrieval practices. For Caroline, the already burdensome task of collating and classifying has become more intense as she continues to print all the (now thousands) of digital images she makes:

> Before I had children [laughs]… then they got really far behind. And then I spent an entire winter and that's where I got to 2004. I spent an entire winter with these because I couldn't stand that I couldn't find pictures. Now I've sort of fallen into that trap with the digitals that are printed, they're not as organized as this yet. No, they're kind of half and half. I'm just waiting for that lottery ticket, you know, the one that lets me have a holiday and sort through those things. It hasn't come yet. (Caroline, Nurse)

Classification practices associated with album making (such as chronology) are sometimes automatically *reproduced* through software or are intentional. The key dynamic here is between the software *defaults* (automatically classifying and ordering downloaded photos in date order, but also as events, places and faces) and the reflexive engagements of users. In contrast to the myth of seamless interoperability and digital standardization there are often different practices of classification and different *senses of being organized* operating in alternative systems:

> I don't get into this automated software stuff that people put out for this I just find it way too complicated for me to. So I think I am definitely organized on the computer, I'm not so organized with the disks that I've made as a backup. I don't have a filing system for them. I have to go through all those disks to find where are those zoo shots?

> Cause I can't even tell you how I've labeled them. I'm hoping I've labeled them properly, but I have no idea so. So I have to put those in the computer look at them, see what they are and then label them. (Sarah, Administrator)

The ambivalent and often idiosyncratic practices of classification apply to both print and digital images, including the multiplication and continual renaming of 'folders', the recognition of the inexhaustible ways of sorting images, and differences in thinking about images individually or collectively. In other words different combinations of devices, systems and classificatory conventions and schemes are employed for locally specific reasons, from the making of scrapbooks, printed and digitized albums, to the use of shared online folders. In focusing upon such specificities, we are able to see that digitization allows for a *reinvigoration* or 'remediation' (Bolter & Grusin, 2000) of album making, which can co-exist with other forms of digital memory making. In some ways, conventional linear narratives of the family have remained intact. In other ways, domestically anchored memory making is simultaneously individualized and multiplied.

Discontinuities: Sharing and the Management of Circulation

A second example highlights the discontinuous potential of digitization in practice. Much has been made of the notion that the private lives of others are becoming increasingly public, as they are often voluntarily made visible and retrievable through the uploading of personal photographic and moving images to social networking/media sites such as Flickr, Facebook, Vine, Snapchat, Pinterest and so on. This is producing novel aspects to how photos are contextualized, re-contextualized, classified and re-classified through metadata and 'social browsing' (Lerman & Jones, 2006; Rubenstein & Sluis, 2008). In Flickr, user-generated content is tagged by users and generates 'clouds of tags' described as *Folksonomies*. Flickr tracks the popularity of specific tags in order to create new suggestive categories for photo searching: tags are *read by other software* to create new classifications in 'performative infrastructures' (Thrift, 2005) that shape flows of data. In Facebook, tagging is used primarily to name individuals within images. On Facebook, tagging *individuals* in an image opens the albums of others (to whom one may have no relationship or tie) for social browsing. I want to concentrate here on the *practices* of 'tagging' and 'commenting' specifically, as they signal both an expansion of who is deemed *responsible* for memory making and also the intimation of anxieties about the nature of digital photographic traces in wider flows of data. There is little ethnographic or sustained qualitative research specifically on photo tagging and commenting that draws upon the accounts of users themselves. I will reflect here upon extensive interview data, in this case with undergraduate students, to explore the increasing distribution of digital images in social media.

When asked about their photographic practices students talked about how they assemble the components of photo making, storage and sharing, how they use or do not use elements of the software and social media, how they see their relationships with images, and how social relations are mediated through their images. In complete contrast to what I had expected, all presented detailed ways of organizing and making sense of their photos. Care was taken to explain how not all photos have the same value. Some photographs were stored without much thought in a variety of systems (again, they often found it difficult to find specific images they wanted to refer to in the interview), others were instantly shared on social media blogs or through email and messaging but could barely be remembered or recalled. 'Special' moments were often kept in additional folders and/or printed and displayed in frames, albums or scrapbooks, and some photographs were only seen by a very select number of people, namely relationship partners (and social researchers). Even at the individual level we find a multiplicity of photo-memory practices incorporating durability *and* ephemerality.

The majority of students expressed degrees of anxiety, concern and fascination with the visual landscapes encountered through Facebook. But a number of consistent themes emerge here, about ownership as a mode of classification, about viewing the photo-streams of others, and about the sheer numbers being uploaded in social media:

> It's just like this alternate universe that I don't want to be a part of … It's like this fake surreal way of making relationships, but they're always backed up by the fact like, oh, I just want to see people's photos, like I just need to see what they're doing. (Harry, student)

Many of these general comments were about the sheer numbers of images uploaded and the uncertainty of how to interpret this in terms of how meaning could be attributed to them. As an artefact of the interview process (as a device), there was often a feeling that normative stances about 'what others are doing, uploading too many images' were being deliberately taken, perhaps assuming that this is 'what the interviewer wants to hear'. However, other more specific concerns related to the movement and potential circulation of these images beyond the control of the maker. As Jack explained:

> Facebook I think is too networked for me. There's too much possibility for information to come across ... I see Facebook as a really great way to connect and make sure that I've got everyone's email address correct and telephone numbers correct and I think it's a good way to send people notes back and forth. But I don't buy into the piles of photos and the piles of videos. (Jack, student)

Practices of photo sharing on Facebook were discussed in terms of three key processes: tagging, de-tagging and commenting; image selection; and image making. Each of these processes involved modes of classification and implications for potential photo-orientated memories. But what was intriguing here was how participants related their anxieties about tagging back to their sense of the appropriate ways to make images in the first instance. In this way, although these processes are inextricably related, it made sense to examine them in what appears to be a reverse chronological order (working back to the image making process) because this is what was so clearly articulated by participants: issues arising from tagging processes make them reflect reflexively organize their image making processes in several ways.

On example of this is how the near ubiquitous presence of image-capture devices at social events has a direct bearing upon practices of tagging and commenting. Participants explained that after social events, or even during them, tagging and de-tagging operates as a mode of owning and disowning images. With the proliferation of digital cameras someone is always there to capture the event in ways that are far less manageable than in the past. The 'right' to place a tag on a particular photograph in the first instance belonged to the photographer, but most students reported that, in the end, they have little control over what images of them end up on Facebook. The most that they could do was to either ask for the picture to be removed or they could 'un-tag' themselves, a process which has the effect of both removing the name on the photo and the photo itself from the profile of the tagged individual and the newsfeeds of their 'friends'. This has to be done almost immediately if the unwanted circulation of the photo is to be effectively managed. Jack, for instance, said he was not tagged in any photographs. He explained that he removed *any* tagged images and refuses to tag anyone in his photos.

> I'm sure there are lots of pictures of me out there. But my thing is that I don't want people to be able to see a picture, click on it and go to my profile. That kind of creeps me out. (Jack, student)

The use of tagging as a mode of inserting and removing oneself within images and of managing the mobility of images speaks to one of the most novel aspects of photo sharing in Facebook. If one of your 'friends' is tagged in a photo, the photo appears in your news feed. By clicking on the photo you are able to access the entire photo stream of which it is part, even if the 'owner' of that stream is not known to you. If there was a print album equivalent of this, it would be asking a complete stranger if you might leaf through their photo albums simply because you have a mutual acquaintance. In this instance, tagging produces a scenario in which one can have unprecedented access to the visual lives of unknown others. This exemplifies how ordinary life has *become* visual content, and in some cases public to an unprecedented degree. In terms of tagging and de-tagging, it demonstrates the ethical terrain within which these processes of image management and memory work have become so significant.

Although I was aware of these processes as a Facebook user at the time, tagging emerged here as a novel mode of multifaceted management, memory work and surveillance for participants. Photos that they had not even known had been taken suddenly appeared in their list of tagged images. Students' profile images were clearly not entirely under their control. By posting an image of someone and tagging them in it, the 'tagger' asserts ownership over that image and the others in it. This seems especially significant in a visual environment in which, for these students, self-images have strong connections with concerns over self-perception and their social identity. As Andrew explained:

> I guess we are very vain and self-obsessed sometimes and we put a lot of meaning in photographs … such that they really kind of have this kind of fundamental impact on our consciousness and our sense of identity. I guess when people see photos of themselves that aren't too flattering we tend to react poorly to them, negatively, rather than just brush them off. (Andrew, student)

Some of these issues are resolved or exacerbated by the ability to make comments in a thread attached to images. These are most commonly a central aspect of the dialogic nature of photo sharing (van Dijck, 2007); how photos become vehicles for often elaborate conversations about their meaning, significance, and most interestingly their contested nature as a reflection or representation of a person or event ('that's how I remember this'). The ever more elaborate personal archive is an unexpected turn enabled primarily because of digital photography. Students had a range of opinions on 'what to do' with the multiple versions and accounts of events circulating around them, all of which are contributing to the collective construction of individual memory. While it added to their own archive of images, it also presented a new (and often daunting) task of *constantly monitoring their own public image*, or in other words, of reflexively engaging with potential memories in the present.

Students were not only more cautious about what images were tagged and therefore linked to their public profiles, but had become also more *selective* in the images that they posted of themselves and of others in the first instance. Van House (2009, 2011) has documented how young people are intensely focused upon calibrating online photos to suit specific audiences. For the students here, this concern has been intensified by the possibilities of future mobility beyond their control. In other words, it was possible to identify a heightened reflexivity about what to post in the first instance due to a sense of unintended consequences.

In this sense, the students in many ways had become their own public relations manager. In some ways the proliferation of cameras and the possibilities of online distribution have taught respondents to be more *critical* of images and their ability to 'accurately' represent their subjects. This turned out to be a strange mixture of 'vanity', as Andrew called it, with a considerable awareness of the subjective or arbitrary nature of the camera. Students made numerous mentions of having friends who would refuse to have a bad picture of them taken, anticipating the 'hard work' that would then be required to manage their own Facebook profiles and the types of images circulating of them.

> Well like there are some people that I have on Facebook that are from camp, so they're younger, like I have 'Emma' on Facebook who's like 10, I have her siblings on Facebook, and like there are some pictures there that I don't really want her to see. Not because I'm like drinking or anything like that, cause I don't put those kinds of pictures up, I don't think that's a good way to represent myself and like who I am .... (Diana, student)

Again, what I found most intriguing during these interviews was this sense that concerns about potential tagging practices were collapsing in on issues of which images to upload, and then, in turn, into considerations of what image to make in the first instance. In this way Facebook and other social media have the dual roles of enabling digital photography to become and remain so pervasive and in reconfiguring many elements of it that extend well beyond these interfaces. The enfolding of digital photography into the dynamic interfaces of social networking sites is making the connections between personal and collective memory and the routine activities of daily life visible and explicit in the sense that it then *requires* intervention and management. This seems entirely consistent with the notion of the 'connective turn' (Hoskins, 2011a, 2011b) highlighted at the outset. But the attention to some of the specificities of practice here has contributed to a critique of the 'from-to' story of digitization. Instead, we see the *multiplication* of the materials of memory making, both print and digital, combined and recombined in novel ways and with surprising affects.

SMARTPHONES, TIME AND MEMORY

The second piece of research on memory practices in the digital age is focused primarily upon smartphones, in terms of their specific roles in mediating social life but also how they become part of interconnected suites of technologies, applications and associated practices. I wanted to avoid simply documenting 'smartphone use' and treating smartphones as novel 'gadgets', but rather seek to situate them within the lived experiences of people and aim to understand them as 'active relays' at the intersection of data and practice. The focus on smartphones emerged primarily because of their ubiquity in people's lives, and partly as an extension of the previous work on photography. In contrast to much of the scholarship on social media and data, I wanted to explore the *materialities* of social media practices and think about whether the *material means through which* most people encounter, produce and consume social media data shapes those processes.

In terms of their sheer prevalence, in North America smartphones are an increasingly significant device within suites of mobile technologies that mediate social life (Rainie & Wellman, 2012). According to the Pew Research Center, 56% of American adults have a smartphone, and 43% have a tablet computer or e-reader. In the September 2013 survey, taking photos, sending texts and accessing the Internet were the dominant uses of smartphones and cellphones. Smartphone ownership in the United States shows little difference in gender and ethnicity, but increased ownership according to higher educational attainment, household income, and levels of urbanity. In Canada, the focus of my research, adult smartphone usage increased from 33% in 2011 to 48% in 2012. Smartphone use is higher among 18–34 years old with 72% ownership among 18–24 year olds. Smartphones are used far more regularly than cellphones in accessing social media and social networking, web content and for uploading and distributing photos (Canadian Wireless Telecommunications Association (CWTA), 2012 Cell Phone Consumer Attitudes Study).

Useful those these data are, especially in documenting particularly rapid rates of adoption, they tell us little about how and why people do the things that they do with these technologies, and on what basis continuous and discontinuous practices frame and are framed by the adoption of smartphones. In using in-depth interviews to focus on *processes of negotiation*, I want to simply suggest what I think are three prominent configurations of smartphones and practices worth exploring further, involving a range of efforts to manage the relationships between timekeeping, temporalities and visuality on the screen.

Coordinating and Managing Multiple Mediated Practices

As observed throughout this volume, people increasing engage in practices that generate digital data. The use of apps is a key example of this. Much of the data produced is a byproduct rather than an intention of use. But what are the contexts for engaging in such practices? If we look at how smartphones are being used, specifically to schedule events and processes, and 'scaffold' our memories of what we are supposed to be doing, we can see that the sum total of arranging and coordinating social life is increasing. This is a familiar process if we think of the promises of labour saving technologies that simultaneously reduce one kind of labour while producing new expectations that then have to be met (see Hand & Shove, 2007; Shove, 2003). In this case, smartphones offer the promise of detailed temporal coordination and control, while at the same time producing new expectations about the capacity to coordinate events and co-presence in social media platforms and physical locations. It is possible to detect several prevailing assumptions about contemporary temporality by examining smartphone apps. For example, the notion that our daily lives would benefit for being 'more organized' is writ large: the potential to 'control everything', while multiplying the number and range of things to control, all in the name of increasing productivity. There are several thousand iPhone apps and iPad apps that promise to 'improve your productivity'. There are apps for managing your 'to-do' list (e.g. *Ta-Da List, Toodledo, Wunderlist, Producteev*), remembering what you wanted to purchase (e.g. *Remember the Milk*), organizing daily routines (e.g. *HomeRoutines, ChoreHero*), and the broader services associated with enabling what is known as 'universal capture' in the cloud: text files, web pages, audio and photos are all instantly available, on all devices, everywhere.

Apps that promise to specifically organize temporal sequences are suggestive of the 'end of forgetting' – there is no excuse to forget anything. But they also involve a redistribution of memory, from remembering via the post-it note on the fridge to remembering to look at your smartphone lists. Participants spoke of how the continual presence of the smartphone meant that it does indeed gradually become the default for 'syncing' a range of reminders, fulfilling in part the notion of being 'more organized'. As an element within the emergent practices of 'personal analytics', participants also talked about how they are using smartphones to produce new information about the temporality of a practice, event or process. For example, there are a range of apps that integrate temporal and other information – time + calorific burning + running distance – and so on. These have become routine accessories for gym work and related exercise, in turn visualizing aspects of the self that can become resources for self-governance (see Ruckenstein, 2014).

In contrast to an overplaying of novelty here, in interviewing early adopters and enthusiastic 'updaters' of smartphones, I found that they are almost always relays in broader systems of scheduling and temporal coordination that are simultaneously multiplying or being reconfigured. In a similar way to how the photo album is both reproduced and transformed, the analogue and digital techniques of scheduling are all being utilized to record, schedule, produce dairies, and various other modes of temporal self-analysis and reflection. For example, the sense of proliferating schedules was particularly apparent in talking to Melissa (graduate, 30), living and working in a major city with her graduate student partner, who spoke in detail about how they coordinate their scheduling technologies:

> So we have a wall, sort of wipe off calendar in the kitchen where we'll write things that aren't just personal schedules, so we'll write on there when we both, say, have dinner plans with friends or somebody's coming over we'll schedule that in, and then he uses his phone for his calendar, and then in the office we have a place where both of our school calendars are, so when I'm at home I can see where he is ... so kind of like 5 calendars I guess. (Melissa)

Here we see the smartphone operating in tandem with other technologies and practices, perhaps behaving something like a 'ratchet' (see Shove, 2003), both enfolded into and further enabling an increase in *practices of coordination*. In other words, the smartphone is enfolded into an existing regime of memory making that is itself on the move, with an increasing number of events recorded and multiplying media for recording them, both digital and non-digital.

Managing the Real-Time

Aside from the increase in ownership of smartphones there is also something novel about how they are both constantly present as a material object and enable a constant presence across platforms. The attachment of the material device to bodies is the topic of much debate in popular discourse, from the dangers of texting while driving, to the sense of a constant 'pull' of the smartphone in every aspect of people's personal lives ('let me just check to see …'). Such anecdotal accounts abound, as we have all seen people thumbing and scrolling while walking, talking, watching, eating and so on. But again, this tells us nothing about what activities are taking place, in what ways, for what reasons, and how people are making sense of and negotiating their engagement in such practices.

As the smartphone tends to be carried at all times, it became an integral part of the interview process. As with photography, this was partly a matter of 'show and tell', enabling the participant to both demonstrate their uses and to remember and reflect upon some of their own data during the interview. A second aspect of this was the ways in which participants negotiated the physical presence of the smartphone *during the interview*. Where should it be placed? Should I check it when not asked to do so? What should I do when it vibrates or beeps? Such questions were present in every interview, and most importantly thus became a key topic of interviews as participants were prompted to think about this physicality in other contexts of daily life. For example, Jade continually monitored her device through the interview, recognized this at one point, prompting her to talk about the appearance of the smartphone as altering the dynamics of physical co-presence in all sorts of other situations:

> …[L]ike how I have it right now, on the table, in the middle of our conversation, it's very visible it's right there … when people do that it makes me think that they are SO anticipating, they're just waiting for some call or email and I can tell they're going to take it as soon as it happens you know, whereas I tend to keep it in my bag zipped away, because I value personal contact more than I do anybody who's messaging me. (Jade)

The smartphone, as a physical device, is thus very different from the camera and the screen-less cellphone in its constant presence. This presence both enables the continual production of byproduct and other data, but it also has the capacity to 'puncture' temporal regimes – to intervene and interrupt a conversation, regardless of whether it is answered or looked at. What was interesting about this was how it often led the interviews in the direction of normative concerns among participants. It is useful here to think of the interview as a continuous method, using a device that continually records, producing a different temporal frame to that of the devices under discussion. One might be tempted to think that the clearly intimate relations between person and phone are unproblematic. But this is far from the case. These relations are often 'uneasy'. Participants reflected upon two key aspects of this uneasiness. Firstly, awareness that specific pockets of time need to be allotted to the practices of friendship. Some aspects of close friendship, especially 'deep conversation', need to be 'saved' for moments of physical co-presence. The smartphone 'threatens' this, enabling continual conversation that 'flattens' distinctions between friendships. This requires management. Secondly, this also leads to what participants called 'meaningless conversation' in the form of continual scrolling messages that subsequently feel like 'wasted time'. Participants stressed the need to construct and manage different temporalities – real-time flows are appropriate for some practices and not for others. The capacity of the smartphone to afford continual connected presence and flow problematizes demarcations people want to make.

The management of the real-time, then, involves complex issues of materiality and mediation as people try to negotiate and to some extent control the intervention of the device *into* temporal flows and the affordances of the device in *enabling* alternate and often multiple temporal flows.

Managing Visual Time

In the digital photography research described above, a key theme among the younger participants was the management of image circulation partly achieved through strategic 'tagging' and 'commenting' to control flows of visual data. In many ways, the smartphone has exacerbated these existing concerns through its continual presence and the possibilities of something approaching the real-time documentation of social life. In the research alluded to here, the management of visual material is also becoming a matter of managing the *visualization of temporalities*. Part of this involves the speeding up of data circulation, as the outcome of continual device use, shaping the production of social media data in the first instance. Similarly, because smartphones are routinely configured with other screens and social media, an unprecedented range of traces are made visible and available for reflection, requiring continual management in a negotiation of *instantaneousness*. There are three temporal aspects to this new visuality. First, as noted in the introduction, past traces are reactivatible (or 'undead') and have to be visually managed – this both visualizes time (the temporal distance between event, seizure, and circulation has to be monitored) and *takes time* (and work). Secondly, the visibility of social media activity often provides unintentionally temporal data, from simply the time of posting to the anxiety that one's Twitter feed betrays a 'lack of attention' at work. Some participants spoke about the 'need' for multiple social media accounts (e.g. a 'professional' and 'friendship' Twitter feed), prompting complex forms of synchronization between devices and systems in trying to produce different 'speeds' – that is twitter feeds that are 'off the top of my head', and those that require more considered reflection, and that also demonstrate *appropriate uses* of time.

Thirdly, participants articulated increasing awareness of and efforts to intervene in the intentional and unintentional visualization of spatiotemporal location. As an example of how changes in the architecture of a platform can shape social media practices (see van Dijck, 2013), the advent of 'timeline' in Facebook is something that all participants talked about, and in many ways captures some of the most important issues in digitally mediated social life for younger users. It also provided a mechanism in the interview to talk about issues of time and memory and the practices of adaptation being explored. Facebook timeline visualized temporal sequences of people's social media lives that they had thought 'forgotten'. An aspect of this that was important to participants was how it 'publicly' *located them* in time and space. For some, it was the 'undead' presence of this information, producing a visual memory of location and co-presence that requires retroactive management:

> On Facebook I'll go back and, even though ill say yes I'm attending an event every couple of months I go back and remove myself from all of the events, because Facebook will keep a list of all the events you've been to and they sit there forever so if somebody stumbles across an old event page on Facebook they can see that you went .... (Lucy)

Of course, such locative practices are increasingly common and intentional. The fine grain of daily life and the deliberate construction of visual timelines of personal activity are increasingly locative (see de Souza e Silva & Frith, 2012). From 'checking in' on Facebook to the reward driven Foursquare, geolocational applications have the effect of signalling presence in location, thus either by design or default inviting others to meet physically. How is this locativity situated and negotiated? For three participants in particular (Emily, Lucy, Miles), this practice raised problems not just in terms of privacy but also in producing a 'continuous co-prescencing' of others in their newsfeeds:

> I think I had an initial distaste for it [Foursquare] because when I was on Facebook I was constantly seeing 'such a person has checked in here' and I'm like 'I don't care, I have no interest about where you are, if I'm meeting you then just send me a text, my mom doesn't need to know that you're at the A&P or whatever'... and then I realized when I was able to use it myself that you can block all of that ... people are either just not aware of the fact that they're pushing that information out to those platforms or they want to be. (Emily)

The intersection of visual and textual data with multiple temporalities paints a complex picture of emerging practices and their negotiation on the ground. Software does indeed increasingly 'intervene' in the constitution of social life – it is both invited and uninvited, embraced and resisted, negotiated and put to work. That people, such as those above, are to some extent required to 'enter' digital social life 24/7 means that they have to engage with data in multiple ways, often simultaneously, without necessarily knowing what the implications are.

DATA, DEVICES AND PRACTICES OF ADAPTATION

This has not been a chapter about qualitative methods as such. By drawing upon two pieces of qualitative research focused upon digitization and memory making, I have simply tried to show – at least imply – that there are real benefits to the in-depth interview process if we are trying to understand the enfolding of digital technologies *into* everyday life in order to account for the shaping of personal data production and interpretation. There are of course clear limitations to a complete reliance on interview data such as this. Researchers are prone to rely on people's accounts of image content, there are often self-presentation issues that skew access to the detail of practices, and the fine grain of individual engagements perhaps neglects the formation of more networked publics that remained hidden. Furthermore, while the argument might be made that 'digital data' often tells us about that data rather than the practices that have produced it (see Smith, 2014), it might also be said that interview data tells us primarily about individual practices of self-reflection and confession, rather than the practices that they are actually referring to. That acknowledged, the capacity of the interview process to reveal some of the how and why of uses, and some considered reflection on the contexts of those uses, certainly provides avenues for demystifying and perhaps deflating the digital in terms of its novelty and its mythical seamlessness.

The empirical material drawn upon in this chapter shows how people actively (sometimes very self-consciously) negotiate the digital, both in terms of its shifting material forms, the range of data that it makes visual, and the continuous and discontinuous practices it enables. This takes many forms that taken together suggest rich territory for future, qualitatively enhanced, digital social research. In terms of the claims made about digitization and memory making, the concepts of the 'connective turn' and the 'continuously networked present' developed by Hoskins (2011a, 2011b, 2013) appear particularly useful in making sense of many of the anxieties and ambivalences of living in digital (visual) culture. The emphasis on personal engagements in the context of social practices provides some empirical substance to these ideas, and also highlights the *ongoing* negotiations involved, which of course require certain forms of know-how on the part of participants.

In exploring reflexive engagements with digital devices and varieties of data it seems clear that the analytic separation of that data from the devices through which it is produced and circulated would be an error. People have intimate yet uneasy relationships with their devices, their devices are part of co-evolving systems both within and beyond the participants' control, all of which is shaping their relation to data and therefore the data 'we' see in social media. There is a need for qualitative empirical data of this kind at present that pulls together both devices and data in these ways, as a means to explore, for example, the management of connected presence and personal analytics. It is not being proposed that this is the only or best way to capture digitally mediated social life, but rather that it is a particularly useful way of grounding many of the claims being made in the present that are developed from interpreting social media data. It is equally important to explore the material culture of data production and circulation in practice. Qualitative attention to the specificities of practice might enable the grounded analysis of how new data visibilities and temporalities are being imposed, enacted, negotiated and appropriated.

NOTES

1. This research is published in my book *Ubiquitous Photography* (Hand, 2012), with elements of chapter 5 reworked here.

2. Some of this research is published as 'Persistent traces, potential memories: smartphones and the negotiation of visual, locative and textual data in personal life', *Convergence*, forthcoming.

REFERENCES

Barthes, R. (1982). *Camera Lucida: Reflections on photography*. New York, NY: Hill and Wang.

Bauman, Z. (2007). *Consuming life*. Cambridge: Polity.

Bolter, J., & Grusin, R. (2000). *Remediation*. Cambridge, MA: MIT Press.

Bowker, G. (2005). *Memory practices in the sciences*. Cambridge, MA: MIT Press.

Bowker, G. (2013). Data flakes: An afterword to raw data as an oxymoron. In L. Gitelman (Ed.), *Raw data as an oxymoron* (pp. 167–171). Cambridge, MA: MIT Press.

Canadian Wireless Telecommunications Association. (2012, April 23). *Cell phone consumer attitudes study*. Quorus Consulting Group Ltd. Retrieved from cwta.ca. Accessed on June 21, 2014.

Chalfen, R. (1987). *Snapshot versions of life*. Bowling Green, OH: Bowling Green State University Popular Press.

Couldry, N. (2012). *Media, society, world*. Cambridge: Polity.

Csikszentmihalyi, M., & Rochberg-Halton, E. (1981). *The meaning of things: Domestic symbols and the self*. Cambridge: Cambridge University Press.

De Souza e Silva, A., & Frith, J. (2012). *Mobile interfaces in public spaces*. London, UK: Routledge.

Featherstone, M. (2000). Archiving cultures. *British Journal of Sociology*, *51*(1), 161–184.

Gane, N. (2006). Speed up or slow down? Social theory in the information age. *Information, Communication & Society*, *9*(1), 20–38.

Garde-Hansen, J. (2009). My memories? Personal digital archive fever and Facebook. In J. Garde-Hansen, A. Hoskins, & A. Reading (Eds.), *Save as ... digital memories* (pp. 135–150). Basingstoke, UK: Palgrave.

Garde-Hansen, J. (2011). *Media and memory*. Edinburgh, UK: Edinburgh University Press.

Gillespie, T. (2010). The politics of 'platforms'. *New Media & Society*, *12*(3), 347–364.

Grusin, R. (2010). *Premediation: Affect and mediality after 9/11*. Basingstoke, UK: Palgrave.

Hand, M. (2012). *Ubiquitous photography*. Cambridge: Polity.

Hand, M., & Shove, E. (2007). Condensing practices: Ways of living with the freezer. *Journal of Consumer Culture*, *7*(1), 79–104.

Hirsch, J. (1981). *Family photography: Context, meaning and effect*. New York, NY: Oxford University Press.

Hoskins, A. (2011a). Media, memory, metaphor: Remembering and the connective turn. *Parallax*, *17*(4), 19–31.

Hoskins, A. (2011b). 7/7 and connective memory: Interactional trajectories of remembering in post-scarcity culture. *Memory Studies*, *4*(3), 269–280.

Hoskins, A. (2012). Digital network memory. In A. Erll & A. Rigney (Eds.), *Mediation, remediation and the dynamics of cultural memory* (pp. 91–106). Berlin, Germany: DeGruyter.

Hoskins, A. (2013). The end of decay time. *Memory Studies*, *6*(4), 387–389.

King, G. (1986). *Say cheese! Looking at snapshots in a new way*. New York, NY: Dodds Mead.
Lash, S. (2002). *Critique of information*. London, UK: Sage.
Lerman, K., & Jones, L. (2006). Social browsing on Flickr. *Proceedings of the international conference on weblogs and social media*. ICWSM, Boulder, CO, USA.
Lister, M. (Ed.). (2013). *The photographic image in digital culture* (2nd ed.). London, UK: Routledge.
Mayer-Schonberger, V. (2009). *Delete: The virtue of forgetting in the digital age*. Princeton, NJ: Princeton University Press.
Murray, S. (2008). Digital images, photo-sharing, and our shifting notions of everyday aesthetics. *Journal of Visual Culture*, *7*, 147.
Rainie, L., & Wellman, B. (2012). *Networked*. Cambridge, MA: MIT Press.
Rubenstein, D., & Sluis, K. (2008). A life more photographic. *Photographies*, *1*, 1.
Ruckenstein, M. (2014). Visualized and interacted life: Personal analytics and engagements with data doubles. *Societies*, *4*, 68–84.
Schwarz, O. (2014). The past next door: Neighbourly relations with digital memory-artefacts. *Memory Studies*, *7*(1), 7–21.
Shove, E. (2003). *Comfort, cleanliness and convenience*. Berg: Oxford.
Shove, E., Pantzar, M., & Watson, M. (2012). *The dynamics of social practice*. London, UK: Sage.
Silverstone, R. (1994). *Television in everyday life*. London, UK: Routledge.
Silverstone, R. (2007). *Media and morality*. Cambridge: Polity.
Slater, D. (1995). Domestic photography and digital culture. In M. Lister (Ed.), *The photographic image in digital culture*. London, UK: Routledge.
Smith, R. J. (2014). Missed miracles and mystical connections: Qualitative research, digital social science and big data. In M. Hand & S. Hillyard (Eds.), *Big data? Qualitative approaches to digital research* (Vol. 13, pp. 181–204). Studies in Qualitative Methodology. Bingley, UK: Emerald Group Publishing Limited.
Sontag, S. (1977). *On photography*. Hammondsworth, UK: Penguin.
Spence, J., & Holland, P. (1991). *Family snaps: The meaning of domestic photography*. London, UK: Virago Books.
Sturken, M. (1997). *Tangled memories*. Berkeley, CA: California University Press.
Sturken, M. (2007). *Tourists of history: Memory, kitsch, and consumerism from Oklahoma city to ground zero*. Durham, UK: Duke University Press.
Thrift, N. (2005). *Knowing capitalism*. London, UK: Sage.
Tomlinson, J. (2005). *The culture of speed: The coming of immediacy*. London, UK: Sage.
van Dijck, J. (2007). *Mediated memories in the digital age*. Stanford, CA: Stanford University Press.
van Dijck, J. (2011). Flickr and the culture of connectivity: Sharing views, experiences, memories. *Memory Studies*, *4*(4), 401–415.
van Dijck, J. (2013). Facebook and the engineering of connectivity: A multi-layered approach to social media platforms. *Convergence*, *19*(2), 141–155.
Van House, N. A. (2009). Collocated photo sharing, story-telling, and the performance of self. *International Journal of Human-Computer Interaction*, *67*, 1073–1086.
Van House, N. A. (2011). Personal photography, digital technologies, and the uses of the visual. *Visual Studies*, *25*(1), 125–134.
Van House, N., & Churchill, E. (2008). Technologies of memory. *Memory Studies*, *1*(3), 295–310.

PART V
INVISIBILITIES, GAPS, AND WAYS OF KNOWING

'WHERE NO-ONE CAN HEAR YOU SCREAM': AN ANALYSIS OF THE POTENTIAL OF 'BIG DATA' FOR RURAL RESEARCH IN THE BRITISH CONTEXT

Sam Hillyard

ABSTRACT

Purpose – *This chapter describes how the technologies of big data might apply to rural contexts. It considers the relative advantages and disadvantages of such 'new' innovations.*

Design/methodology/approach – *It uses two case studies, one of online community specialist groups linked to rural activities and a second from a policy shift relating to firearm legislation in the English context.*

Findings – *The chapter suggests that digital data in the forms discussed here can be both benign and underutilised in its potential. In relation to the management of datasets holding information on firearm owners, these need careful reflection regarding their establishment, access and general use.*

Big Data? Qualitative Approaches to Digital Research
Studies in Qualitative Methodology, Volume 13, 231–249

ISSN: 1042-3192/doi:10.1108/S1042-319220140000013014

Originality/value – *The chapter provides insight into the rural context and makes a case that such locales are not immune from the influence of the dataverse. The appearance of 'big data' here is not without political implications. The case of UK firearm legislation reform demonstrates the implications of policy falling short of its potential and how a social science analysis can unpack the operation of power as well as position the debate more broadly.*

Keywords: Rural; sociality; firearms; twitcher; digital data

OVERVIEW

The chapter discusses the role and potential of digital data of many kinds for rural research. The discussion operates on two levels. First, that the current climate of theoretical ideas in rural studies is appreciative of the complexity of rural spaces. Second, and flowing from the first, that the advent of new empirical resources (such as digital data) is therefore timely and well-placed to speak to such complexity. The chapter then considers by example what is the best way in a rural context to 'get at' the impact of the use of digital technologies, datasets and, generally, the dataverse? Two situations are discussed, where online forums and the management of databases have had social consequences – one enhancing sociality and failing to realise the benefits of linkages. These are two very different uses of digital data and therefore show that what we mean by digital rural research speaks to the very ambivalence of digitisation. What digital social research is should be questioned, but at its most basic level, it can be argued to include the 'bottom up' and 'top down' manifestations of digital data discussed here – simply because they become socially enacted and have consequences. The chapter's overall stance is positive: digital data offers possibilities for 'opening up' the countryside by broadcasting its assets to interested parties. However, a predictable caveat is made, namely that digitalisation's potential is curtailed in the rural settings because of lack of both density and a proliferation of virtual mediums and media – as reflected in the title. Hence, empirically it is best positioned alongside existing research techniques, rather than delivering some of the transformative promise heralded in urban environs. Therefore the chapter concludes that the rural penalty[1] includes a digital imbalance, too, that limits what digital rural research is feasible. Nevertheless, the very complexity of what the rural has become in the twenty-first century context means that rural is neither separate nor immune from the impact of digitised forms of datasets and these, in the case of National Police Databases relating to firearms, are not benign.

INTRODUCTION – A SOCIOLOGY OF THE RURAL

Theoretical representations of the rural have undergone a sea change in recent decades. What was once a 'retarded' over-reliance upon political-economic or agricultural economic explanatory models has been replaced with a more plural array of theoretical and empirical approaches to studying rural spaces (Halfacree, 2009; Marsden, 2006; Woods, 2011). Key metaphors for representing the countryside have shifted, from differentiated, contested, constructed and appreciating 'otherness' to a situation now where the rural is complex and global. Rural studies no longer sees the countryside as a separate entity, along a continuum with 'the urban' as its opposite, but rather a networked, interconnected and mobile society which is both influencing and influenced. The rise in the number of scholars engaged in rural research reflects the vibrancy of the sub-discipline and informs a growth in the number of theoretical models applied to rural contexts. These have ranged from themes of consumptive gentrification (Phillips, 2009), Bourdieuvian capitals (Heley, 2010), Lefebvre on space (Halfacree, 2007), actor-network theory on relational agency (Lowe, Phillipson, Proctor, & Emery, 2014), Habermas' communicative action (McKee, 2014) and non-representational theory (Wylie, 2005). There is, it seems, a theory to account for all rural eventualities. In summary, rural studies has benefited from the proliferation of different theoretical paradigms present in associated disciplines and, importantly, been receptive towards new ideas. So whereas the sociology of health and medicine has become an important site – but not quite synonymous – with the application of actor-network theory, there is no such theoretical dominance within rural studies.

Significantly, however, a concern with the analysis of inequalities has been retained. For example, Shucksmith's (2012) Presidential Address to the European Society for Rural Sociology (ESRS) Congress in 2011 was a call-to-arms for research offering an understanding of the impact of the global recession upon rural spaces. Interestingly, his argument also called for more research at the micro-level. So the theoretical richness of contemporary British rural studies has an *applied* character: an empirical steer and a concern that theory be able to unlock how inequalities are maintained and reproduced. These characteristics are sufficiently broad that they avoid becoming prescriptive.

Theoretical pluralism, for all of its advantages, is not without caveats and this stems from rural studies having long been a site of inter-disciplinary collaboration and overlap. For example, at the recent Trans-Atlantic Rural Research Network (TARRN) meeting hosted by Newcastle University, UK, delegates from both sides of the Atlantic represented at least eight disciplines – from fine art to criminal justice. This was the foundation for fruitful and constructive discussions, yet closer readings reveal a lack a common stock of knowledge or epistemological antecedents (Atkinson, 2014; Hillyard, forthcoming). For example, Atkinson (2014) is tenacious in his view that the research tradition of ethnography is informed by sociological and anthropological interests, and, too, symbolic interactionism. If combined with Shucksmith's call to pursue micro-worlds as sites of investigation, there is a risk that such new ethnographic works become sheered away from the intellectual tradition motivating their use. The ethnography applied in this way would become a kind of atheoretical research tool akin to a musical instrument played by anyone; at that moment and; without continuity or cumulation of knowledge across performances.

It is this theoretical and inter-disciplinary environment that the advent of 'big data' and digital social research must be positioned. So within rural studies, there is a receptive theoretically plural environment engaged with empirical work, but too a need for caution with respect to Atkinson's (2014) argument. As with any new method or dataset – promising or otherwise – there is a need to consider compatibility vis-à-vis existing theoretical trajectories and whether it meets Shucksmith's interest in rendering visible sources of inequalities. This exploratory spirit informs this chapter: in favour of the potential of digital data for rural studies, but with a commitment towards a sophisticated application and reflexive engagement that avoids over-claiming or, worse, the discovery of an emperor's new set of clothes.

ON THE POSSIBILITY OF A 'DIGITAL RURAL STUDIES'

In the past, when new empirical research 'moments' have been proclaimed, a number of stances have been adopted in response. Hammersley (1992), for example, in a discussion of the emergence of qualitative research from out of the shadow of quantitative techniques, described a number of reactions. One perceived that there were many commonalities and hence that no epistemological breach had occurred. Another claimed that qualitative research constituted a new paradigm in its own right. What Hammersley (2012) subsequently showed was that those claiming such stances were not always accurate in describing their own position. So, for example, those claiming to use a grounded theorising approach were more accurately operationalising a more conventional form of analytic induction. There are clear parallels with the emergence of 'big data'. One parallel are claims that it can offer something truly distinctive – the 'promise' of 'big data' to be a game-changer. A second has been 'by doing', namely what 'big data' can deliver in empirical practice. Relating to the former, it is not perhaps the radical newcomer as may first appear to be the case, given the recognition that a 'knowing capitalism' surrounding and influencing us is well-established (Thrift, 2005) and datasets generated through the networks and objects engaged with by research participants have a long history (Bancroft, Karels, Murray, & Zimpfer, 2014). Nevertheless, if the rural is truly global, then the permeation of the dataverse into our everyday lives will include rural spaces, agents and objects. How might rural digital data offer insight?

What is much messier is the second parallel of how to 'get at' and practically apply this evidential base and sociology is not alone in facing this challenge. Hargreaves Heap (2014) and *Times Higher* (2014) noted the calls for curricula reform economics has faced in the wake of the financial crisis – and the associated phenomenal rise of behavioural economics. Are rural studies, too, capable of a relational turn steered by the new possibilities of handling hitherto unimaginably large datasets? Established ethnographic research communities have, too, explored whether co-location replaces co-presence (Beaulieu, 2010; Hallett & Barber, 2014). Can you conduct a study of rurality without being in a rural space? Plus, diversionary activities that fetishise the technology above what it can actually tell us, a modern narrow technical solipsism, after Merton's (1972, p. 14) 'methodological solipsism'. Is the *availability* of new masses of data stopping us from thinking about good questions to then ask of that dataset? In thinking about how digitalisation applies in the rural context soberly reminds us that whilst we might *think* we are using 'big data' for our purposes, there is the danger that it may actually be using us.

Collectively, this context – that we are in such interesting times – makes the rural sphere a very different test case study. This is because the methodological principles of best practice are in-progress (Hand, 2014) and the very incongruity of the rural vis-à-vis the digital. Rural sociology is an outlier or neglected sub-text of sociology, since the impetus of industrialisation brought about societal change and the demographic shift from country to city. The very territories that sociology has made its own look to the city, after all, what kind of study of social practices can be done where there are no people? The question posed here is challenging – what sociology can be done where the dataset all around us and about us, but how to make use of it effectively, consistently and reflexively in more remote, rural contexts too? The interest in the urban within sociology needs re-focusing onto the rural stage. For if 'big data' can deliver in such circumstances, then arguably it can deliver anywhere. Hammersley's two-tier way of seeing status claims is used here: (i) the modest view that it sits well within existing canons and (ii) alternatively 'big data' as a game-changer. There might, too, be scope to ask whether in either case 'big data' offers some means to understand and alleviate the inequalities identified by Shucksmith (2012).

Big Data as a New Addition to the Research Toolkit

The rural community researchers of 1950s described arriving in their village fieldwork sites like landing in a foreign country (Williams, 2008). In fictional works, even a hardened industrialist confesses to finding the prospect of a field of cows frightening (Lodge, 1988). In the twenty-first century, the 'chattering classes' (Pawson, Owen, & Wong, 2010, p. 211) descending on rural spaces for edutainment purposes (Edensor, 2006) encounter the rural penalty and its associated privations, as campaigns for equal amenities provision (i.e. broadband) by the Countryside Alliance demonstrate. The rural is simultaneously a leisure zone and yet unequal in terms of the networks city spaces take for granted. Furthermore, the consumption of the countryside has been increasingly acknowledged by rural scholars to shape what those spaces become, so Hand's (2012) recognition of the ubiquity of imagery is intensified here: imagery around the rural informs the understanding and interpretation of that experience. Collectively, any use of digital data encounters a rurality that is both physical (absent or limited facilities) and cultural (a 'fear factor' of the unknown/ discomforting) and these fold together to constitute the rural. Has the rural mediated the usage of new modes of technical usage, or merely accommodated it?

In their awarding-winning overview, Halford et al. (2012) discuss practical scenarios of the use of linked data as grassroot initiatives. These are the kind of websites that allow runners to up-load a preferred route, to then share with other runners. The working of this 'operational infrastructure' is mediated when applied to rural sites (Halford et al., 2012, p. 177). The question of signal reveals the different spatial-material distributions as well as a cultural disconnect within rural spaces that impact upon our everyday practices. In addition, the datafication of everyday life is inconsistent in rural spaces. For example, fewer amenities, reduced population density and greater inconvenience are all to be found in rural areas, but this varies in the British context. Banbury, in Oxfordshire, to provide a famous example from community studies, is actually now heralded as a 'Cotswold commute' ideal for the city worker due to improved rail access (*Financial Times*, 2014; Stacey, 1960). Therefore Banbury is now extraordinarily different to the remote Scottish communities discussed by McKee (2014) and does not share the significance of the landowner in the latter, but instead has much greater population density and comprehensive mobile coverage (Ofcom, 2014 http://maps.ofcom.org.uk/mobile-services).

Access to telephone networks (landline and mobile) has become habitualised and routinised. The impact of the invention of the telephone, Berkeley sociologist Claude Fischer reminds us, worked out in unforeseen ways (Fischer, 1994). After initial perceptions of intrusiveness (what was the cold-calling of its time) and social-policing of acceptable usage (it should not be used for gossip), the telephone became of more importance for women and for those in rural spaces (Fischer, 1994). So what was once seen as intrusive is today's unsettling loss of network. It shows how diverse rural spaces are and also how social actors have shifted in their capacity to accommodate initially intrusive digital apparatus. The technologies are not dissimilar, merely we have become accustomed to its cloak of availability.

The modern-day smartphone, as a small, sleek multi-faceted technical device (Bancroft et al., 2014), has a capacity for tracking via their global positioning systems (GPS), an innovation derived from military research funding. When it works well in present-day rural contexts, its GPS capacity can, via a satellite navigation system (satnav), help navigate through the winding back lanes of the British countryside that are very different to the grid pattern of the US or Canadian road networks. When it fails, there can be a delivery gap between the rural and how mediums such as GPS technology interface with a given locale. GPS directions via postcode (zip code) are notorious for their inaccuracy, for example directing traffic down one-way country back lanes. Far more seriously, emergency services' reliance upon inaccurate satnav systems highlights these imperfections (West Briton, 2011). Hence, handheld GPS guidelines stress that they should not be relied upon due to the vagaries of signal reception in remote rural spaces. 'Big Brother' here is unable to deliver a constant monitoring of place in the rural environment, both for those who actively seek to use it and for those who might be in need of it. Therefore, the rural curtails some of the capabilities of data-objects when the spatial-material distribution deselects them before they can become enabled through social practices.

Whilst no-one might be able to hear you scream down your mobile device without a signal in a rural locale, it does not mean that all listening is impossible. Another example, drawing inspiration from urban research, shows a more collaborative relationship between data-object and end-user. Gabrys (2014) discusses smart-city projects and whilst that scale of data capture is not feasible in the rural environment for the reasons discussed above, her argument regarding the social lives of data-objects (such as smartphones) and the importance of their enactment remains important. It is also in synergy with recent rural theorising that stresses how rural spaces are now *collectively* shaped by the environment, technology and ways of life. So a benign practical example of how the web can enable very specialist social practices in the countryside, and indeed open the countryside up by broadcasting its attributes, is that of birdwatching. Furthermore, it is circular: enacted co-presence leading to co-location.

Birdwatchers, or 'twitchers' as they are more colloquially known, are a specialist group that use rural spaces in their pursuit of this leisure activity, as the rarer bird species are to be found there. Twitchers are rural cultural consumers, without necessarily being rural residents. Enhanced participation involves specialist knowledge and sightings accrued. A rare warbler, like the eastern crowned[2] for example, may attract more visitors to an area, as specialists think nothing of travelling a hundred miles to view a special bird. The online forums and newsgroups of this community provide the means to spread news of rare sightings, but there is also an etiquette within this community that is wary of revealing too much of very special species for fear of nest disturbance, etc. So like Mazanderani (2012) discusses how HIV positive online community group users very carefully use and screen their interactions with potential romantic partners, what she terms 'viral sociality', birdwatcher forums also have their own protocols. This is an example of where the instantaneous nature of the web and its capacity to form its own communities (with self-policing rules) can enhance interactional processes, rather than replace them. Co-presence online facilitates co-location (both between the birders, the birds that they watch and the rural environment). The environment (and the bird), becomes a presence online via technology – digitised as it were – and then becomes enacted through the watchers' consumptive lifestyles. This is, then, a digitally linked rural data and 'twitcher sociality' (after Mazanderani, 2012).

Examples, such as GPS and birdwatching, do not push the boundaries of the promise of 'big data' or a digital rural studies. There are echoes of the mobilities literature's observation about the freedom to travel is actually curtailed by the direction of the roads available. The real task is recognising that 'developing algorithms is not simply an opportunity for invention but also a route through which power to define and know is mobilised (however unreflexively)' (Halford et al., 2012, p. 177). So much of the direction of travel has been predetermined by capitalism's interest (such as the military underpinnings of the development of GPS) and, of course, capitalism continues to collate mass data with different obligations in mind (to the extent that clubcard datasets are capable of predicting pregnancies before a mother-to-be's family). Arguably Halford et al.'s (2012) argument that it is key for sociologists to participate in the debate before it is too late is itself a little too late.[3] Yet simply because the flow of data was stunted in these two rural instances does not undermine the more generic capacity of digitisation to retain some transformational capacity. As Halford et al. (2012) argue, it becomes a question of thinking more *sociologically* about the point of interface. A final case discussion is possible and links with their discussion of the issue of privacy. This policy issue holds scope to be a game-changer in that domain at least.

Digitisation as a Game-Changer – An Evaluation of UK Firearm Licence Policy Innovation

The assessment of suitability to hold a firearms licence is one policy field where digitisation can be evaluated and where it too could speak to the rhetoric of social responsibly and openness surrounding digital data. A significant part of Halford et al.'s (2012) argument paid attention to the principles of computational thinking underpinning the construction of the semantic web. This appears technicist, but how these tools are built have implications, as when the assessment of suitability to legally hold firearms in the United Kingdom failed in the past with tragic consequences. Therefore, a 'critical politics of data' is needed for the semantic web, where linkages *across* datasets replace the existing system within which the storage of fairly autonomous documents prevails (Halford et al., 2012, p. 173). This is a metaphorical equivalent of replacing an old-fashioned filing cabinet with a computer's sub-folder containing all manner of material – and new possibilities for accessible linkages (see Tummons, 2014). So linkages are all about politics, power and ultimately the unknown fall-out of 'open data' (or data that is yet to be linked), as 'technical developments are neither inevitable nor neutral' (Halford et al., 2012, p. 174). Applied to a rural context, the implications of who does the linking, what is linked, indeed the definition of the very units *to* link are all significant and in the case of a specialist area of policing – the administration of firearm licences – show the complexity of rurality. Therefore, seeing how firearms policy is enacted with reference to a digital dataset opens up a role for the social scientist, to evaluate this convergence of method, politics and power. As it is operationalised in County Durham, United Kingdom, the granting and monitoring of firearm holders has yet to realise its potential of synergising environment, technology and ways of life (after Gabrys, 2014). But, prior to the discussing the nuances of licence issue and review, firearms legislation is like game shooting participation and etiquette (cf. Hillyard, forthcoming), somewhat complex and merits explanation and overview.

Firearm legislation was introduced in the UK post WWI as a means to assess the extent of private weapon ownership (many weapons coming back into the United Kingdom as 'trophies' or were overlooked during the demobilisation of troops). The context is therefore one of a right to own, where the legislation captures the extent of ownership via a process that will exclude those deemed unsuitable under the remit of protecting the public safety. The process is one of application and assessment, whereby the Police bring together a variety of datasets to assess each applicant and, once issued, monitor the licence holders' continuing suitability. The Police (via regional forces) have always had oversight of this process, delivered currently via their database checks, references and a home visit. This is the current framework surrounding the legislation and its historical antecedence.

The fatal shootings in Britain of family members by a legal owner of both shotgun and firearm certificates was reviewed by the Independent Police Complaints Commission [IPCC] (2012). This reviewed the granting of certificates to this individual (Michael Atherton) and concluded that these shootings using legally owned firearms were avoidable. They found that question marks about his character and suitability that could have been flagged were not (reports of domestic violence alongside intemperate behaviour) and this regional force did not consistently deliver existing policy. As one shooting specialist argued, in another county his licence would have been revoked (Harriman, 2013).

The Atherton case is problematic and should not be over-stated as an example, given that the faultline lay with the inadequacy of Durham Constabulary's delivery of the policy process via its Firearms Licensing Unit (FLU) (and particularly one Firearms Officer) rather than the policy per se. What has occurred subsequently, using the IPCC's findings and the Association of Chief Police Officers' (ACPO) acknowledgement of shortcomings, is an attempt to use the information that is available to greater effect. Much like we all now possess a data shadow (Wall, 2013, p. 6), 'big data' has the potential to bring together databases relating to firearm users' profiles across their lifecourse in order to filter and revoke those unsuitable to legally possess firearms in the same way that it failed to make those linkages in the case of Michael Atherton. Therefore the specific potential of a connected national police database for the assessment and monitoring of suitability the potential is clear – it can but only enhance public safety, its primary policy task. The discussion now considers what Durham Constabulary have done to make such linkages and whether it delivers the promise of enhanced public safety, without compromising privacy, security and offers a balanced use of surveillance.

The changes that have been implemented since the IPCC (2012) report include the ACPO issuing clearer Home Office guidelines and the consolidation of the application process into one form (previously they were separate for shotguns and firearms). Any ambiguity as to Home Office directives Durham's FLU could claim in the past has been nullified. However, there is a new initiative specially introduced by Co. Durham's Constabulary that merits evaluation. Can the information a 'knowing capitalism' (Thrift, 2005) already collates about us be used in a legitimate way by the police force or is it an invasion of privacy, defended by the promise of policy enhancement?

The key 'big data' resource here is the national police database and associated debates surrounding the right to privacy and the administration of such datasets. Wall (2013) argues that databases are open to abuse by deviant or rogue users and the exposure of such resources to a human element in generating, maintaining and accessing them threatens the quality of data captured (Lawless, 2013). In relation to firearms, this risk is demonstrated by recent admissions by a number of constabularies that they permitted unrestricted access to their police databases to external agencies, such as the RSPCA (Hemming, 2013) and DVLA. Given the historic the right to own,[4] as recognised by the ACPO chair CC Andy Marsh, this becomes not only a question of how to better make linkages across datasets to enhance the assessment and review of suitability, but of the very security of private individuals' information contained there. For example, the RSPCA is currently undergoing an internal review following criticisms that it is politically motivated and hence has exceeded its animal welfare remit and charitable status. The legal ownership of firearms is not neutral, for example the government minister has clearly stated his personal view is against the right to own (Green, 2013), without consultation or political mandate. In such a politically charged and sensitive context in the wake of the tragedy in Peterlee, information submitted on a voluntary basis to the police force by applicants if accessed by those opposed to shooting is open to abuse.

C. I. Steven Ball of Durham Constabulary has responded proactively to the criticism of his constabulary's past shortcomings. He has claimed Co. Durham is now the lead in the field and sought to enhance the dataset available to FEOs and issuing Firearms Officers (who do so on behalf of the Chief Constable). To this end, Durham Constabulary introduced a new pilot for trial. This involves the applicant's GP providing a letter of support in addition to the standard application form (and reference system) stating that they know of no reason why the application should not hold a licence according to their records. This has not been required before, although a GP could act as a referee. It is a pilot and therefore voluntary, although this is not made clear from the website where the application form and guidance are available for download. Following the logic of the earlier discussion about the political ramification of datasets – and their linkages – these are social, political and economic infrastructures. Therefore, the most mundane of seemingly 'practical' difficulties – of filling in forms – has generated contradictions in policy and regulation. The sheer 'messiness' of seemingly straight-forward tasks such as inputting data from forms, etc., is prone to human-error and abuse. Nevertheless, the very mundane everyday exchanges 'produce knowledge' that is acted upon and has performative effects on actual individuals and abstracted populations.

The pilot scheme of Durham Constabulary, with its rhetoric of enhanced accountability and the use of enhanced datasets, on close analysis risks offering only a mirage. The GP's evidence cannot consistently deliver quality data because, as sociologists recognise, even rural populations live in highly mobile times and it is highly unlikely that a GP will be familiar with all of their registered patients nor in possession of their complete medical history. They are therefore unable to offer a consistency of insight that will deliver enhanced public safety. Durham's Constabulary's decision to make this pilot appear compulsory (with the incurred additional costs to be met by the applicant) and to then pursue its completion, should the applicant omit it, exceeds its remit to administer the policy. Rather here the allowances of digitisation have led one organisation to attempt to reconstitute policy. The shooting community, including the organisation representing those who use shotguns as a professional tool, not a lifestyle object (i.e. gamekeepers), has expressed concern (Waddell, 2013; Wallace, 2014).

The shooting community has also responded to the further possible reforms mooted by the Police. Proposals have called for the establishment of an anonymous 'tip-off' database, whereby members of the public can anonymously raise concerns about individuals holding certificates. The quality or accuracy of these reports is in effect unverifiable, as the burden of proof would be much lower than that of a criminal court. The right to respond to such instances by the accused is therefore lost in such cases and appeals by those whose licences were revoked have been upheld on that very basis. Given, too, the specialist activities that game shooting can involve (Hillyard, forthcoming), combined with the rural fear factor of the unknown combined with the presence of firearms, such an initiative risks being entirely, ineffective and disproportionate. Here, raw data (i.e. that is already in the public domain) differs to that which would actively gathered – and that there may be potentially contradictions between them. Neither form of dataset would be entirely neutral, despite rhetorics of openness and accountability.

Where the licence holder's behaviour comes to the attention of the police, for example by drink-driving or reports of domestic violence, when linked in the database the issue of unsuitability is more clear-cut. If such a link had taken place in the Atherton case, his licences would have been permanently revoked. The calls for better handling of domestic violence reports by the police supports the potential of what 'big data' management can deliver for both the public and individuals' safety (Westmarland & Kelly, 2012). Again, there will be a risk of inconsistencies and how the promise of digital data for improved efficiency and policy does not see through the ways in which data production, storage and circulation is always grounded in both mundane practicalities and abstractions. As such, it cannot be the game-changer of foil-proof, gold-standard evidence.

The rural, of course, is subject to processes of monitoring and technologies of control. For example, it would be naïve to assume that, just because there is not the extensive CCTV network in the British countryside, that no watching takes place. Privacy – like coverage – is relative in rural space. The anonymity the stranger (cf. Simmel, 1971) is different to the 'forced' co-operation of the occupational communities (Newby, 1977). Being a good neighbour is sociability balanced with privacy (Crow, Allen, & Summers, 2002). Here, being watched, but not being seen is the key nuance. For those who wield power on the local level possess the ability to do as they please (Neal & Walters, 2008). So, in the absence of external watching there remains an element of self-policing (Hillyard, forthcoming) that can be welcome (Neal & Walters, 2008). Yet the role digital data linkages could fulfil in less ambiguous instances, where serious illegal and harmful activity does occur, is unclear. Whilst precision farming can calculate the highest yield, and quite literally plough the field itself using a tractor's GPS, what can it offer to solve the theft of that same tractor in a context of rising rural crime? A new brokering between what digitalisation can feasibly deliver and how it could be enacted in the rural sphere is yet to be realised, but not impossible.

Halford et al. (2012) make an important point that the motivations underpinning the use of 'big data' may differ, between disciplines and also transnational corporations (TNCs). The case of firearms licencing suggests that capitalism is far ahead of policy, in how it manipulates the web in the control or operation of markets. Yet some disciplines are well-placed to make an impact. It is unlikely, for example, that computer scientists, for all their technical competence, will have a better grasp than sociologists as to the unintended fallout of what the semantic web will become simply because the discipline of sociology takes as its subject-matter the broader view of societal implications. Pragmatics will feature, but as Halford et al. (2012) suggest, being able to fix the web should also be underpinned by an understanding of its operation. Alternatively, perhaps a new strand of computational science ethics will emerge. Given that the founding of even hallowed institutions such as MIT have been underpinned by vast tranches of defence research spending, the ethics of what the semantic web will produce merits prominence. Otherwise, as Halford et al. (2012) argue more strongly, 'risk ceding the field to a tsunami of positivism tied to the ascendency of computer science and/or other technical forms of cultural capital in the digital age' (Halford et al., 2012, p. 185). The case of UK firearm legislation reform demonstrates the implications of policy falling short of its potential and how a social science analysis can unpack the operation of power as well as position the debate more broadly.

EVALUATION AND CONCLUSION

It is in the handling or understanding of new knowledge linkages that is rendered possible by the semantic web that the real scope for sociologists' role is most clear. Strangely, Halford et al.'s (2012) ultimate position, for all their positive rhetoric, favours triangulation despite the capacity of the semantic web to be a game-changer. The few rural case studies presented here demonstrate that the sociologists' task can be more than merely acting as a referee, by noting instances where applications of 'big data' hold unintended consequences. For firearm licencing when contrasted with 'twitcher sociality' showed the relevance of digital data for the rural. Two superficially similar areas of 'data', when analysed, is that not all examples of potential enactments of big datasets are benign. They show how they can come to mean very different things. They, too, have very different implications for (a) what the rural is (i.e. a site for leisure) and (b) what can be accurately known and stored about it. Therefore, digitisation is having effects on the rural and, with greater impact, digitisation might also provide new 'ways of knowing' about the rural. Hence, sociology may be better place to contribute a sociology of knowledge that can speak to the implications of a data phenomenon that is not only just about us but now, too, capable of making linkages – particularly given that we are for the most part technologically unconscious (after Beer, 2009).

The argument has been that even in the outlier case of the rural, there is no avoidance of some kind of data shadow (Wall, 2013). The advent of the semantic web is insidious, holding the potential to not just *link* data already there, but *create* linked data that then associates with other relevant datasets (i.e. shared URIs[5]). The sociology of knowledge also allows us to understand that those able to access these datasets are in a privileged position. Hence the irony, as Halford et al. (2012) point out may be that the very openness of data in its 'raw' format requires greater technical competency in its use: 'as increased technical mediation reduces the transparency of these data. The rhetoric of 'openness' may, paradoxically, mean *less* openness for some' (Halford et al., 2012, p. 182, original emphasis). We do, therefore, need to engage in these debates despite capitalism already being better placed to capture its synergies.

There is a history within sociology of over-promising and under-delivering in research innovations. Visual methods, the potential of which was clearly articulated (Strangleman, 2004), has not delivered the anticipated impact upon the sociology of work. Claims made about innovation in research have been exaggerated (Travers, 2009; Wiles et al., 2011) and, as stated earlier, inaccurate (Hammersley, 2012). Theoretically, rural studies have too been accused in the past of wearing emperor's clothes in relation to its theoretical explanatory power (Pahl, 1989). At the moment, the sociological approach risks being on the backfoot and reacting rather than proactively imagining the possibilities. Yet this chapter's rural focus and examples from the past show that early forms of technological innovation came to actually hold more import for rural communities than for their urban counterparts (Fischer, 1994). The rural is not excluded from experiencing the impact of this new infrastructure – expressive or operational – and nor should it be from the associated ethical and sociology of knowledge implications. Therefore, a more ambitious portfolio of techniques than simply triangulation is merited. This would be informed by theoretical ideas appreciating the complexity of interrelationships between space, people and objects – a sensing multi-strategy research that reflexively explores but also challenges how they operate in synergy.

NOTES

1. The additional costs rural households incur.
2. The birdwatching equivalent of winning the World Cup (Daily Express, 2009).
3. Given capitalism's ability to move to forge new markets and unwitting consumers for those markets. Business is therefore unlikely to place all of their data into the public realm (cf. p. 176).
4. Shotguns only.
5. URIs (uniform resource identifier) replacing URL.

REFERENCES

Atkinson, P. (2014). *For ethnography*. London: Sage.

Bancroft, A., Karels, M., Murray, O. M., & Zimpfer, J. (2014). Not being there: Research at a distance with video, text and speech. In M. Hand & S. Hillyard (Eds.), *Big data? Qualitative approaches to digital research* (Vol. 13, pp. 137–153). Studies in Qualitative Methodology. Bingley, UK: Emerald Group Publishing Limited.

Beaulieu, A. (2010). Research note: From co-location to co-presence: Shifts in the use of ethnography for the study of knowledge. *Social Studies of Science*, *40*(3), 453–470.

Beer, D. (2009). Power through the algorithm? Participatory web cultures and the technological unconscious. *New Media & Society*, *11*(6), 985–1002.

Crow, G., Allen, G., & Summers, M. (2002). Neither busybodies nor nobodies: Managing proximity and distance in neighbourly relations. *Sociology*, *36*(1), 127–145.

Daily Express. (2009). Rare warbler has twitchers in a real flap. *Daily Express*. Retrieved from http://www.express.co.uk/news/uk/135870/Rare-warbler-has-twitchers-in-a-real-flap. Accessed on September 20, 2014.

Edensor, T. (2006). Performing rurality. In P. Cloke, T. Marsden, & P. Mooney (Eds.), *Handbook of rural studies*. London: Sage.

Financial Times. (2014). New fast train link opens up Banbury area to London commuters. *Financial Times – House & Home*, April 25, p. 4. Retrieved from http://www.ft.com/

cms/s/2/51306608-c4bb-11e3-9aeb-00144feabdc0.html#axzz3E3T3RUXQ. Accessed on September 22, 2014.

Fischer, C. A. (1994). *America calling: A social history of the telephone*. Berkeley, CA: California University Press.

Gabrys, J. (2014). Programming environments: Environmentality and citizen sensing in the smart city. *Environment and Planning D: Society and Space*, *32*(1), 30–48.

Green, D. (2013). Foreword. *Firearm and shotgun certificates in England and Wales 2012/13*. London: HMSO.

Halfacree, K. (2007). Trial by space for a 'radical rural': Introducing alternative localities, representations and lives. *Journal of Rural Studies*, *23*(2), 125–141.

Halfacree, K. (2009). Rurality and post-rurality. In N. Thrift & R. Kitchen (Eds.), *International encyclopedia of human geography*. Oxford: Elsevier.

Halford, S., Pope, C., & Weal, M. (2012). Digital futures? Sociological challenges and opportunities in the emergent semantic web. *Sociology*, *47*(1), 173–189.

Hallett, R., & Barber, K. (2014). Ethnographic research in a cyber era. *Journal of Contemporary Ethnography*, *43*(3), 306–330.

Hammersley, M. (1992). *What's wrong with ethnography?* London: Routledge.

Hammersley, M. (2012). Qualitative causal analysis: Grounded theorizing and the qualitative survey. In B. Cooper, J. Glaesser, R. Gomm, & M. Hammersley (Eds.), *Challenging the qualitative-quantitative divide: Explorations in case-focused causal analysis*. London: Continuum.

Hand, M. (2012). *Ubiquitous photography*. Cambridge: Polity.

Hand, M. (2014). Digitization and memory: Researching practices of adaption to visual and textual data in everyday life. In M. Hand & S. Hillyard (Eds.), *Big data? Qualitative approaches to digital research* (Vol. 13, pp. 205–229). Studies in Qualitative Methodology. Bingley, UK: Emerald Group Publishing Limited.

Hargreaves Heap, S. (2014, May 15). *The state of economics*. Centre for humanities engaging science and society lecture. Durham, UK.

Harriman, W. (2013). Peterlee was entirely avoidable. *Shooting Times*, March 7, pp. 32–33.

Heley, J. (2010). The new squirearchy and emergent cultures of the new middle classes in rural areas. *Journal of Rural Studies*, *26*, 321–331.

Hemming, D. (2013). Anger at RSPCA's access to Cumbria police records. *News and Star*. Retrieved from http://www.newsandstar.co.uk/news/anger-at-rspca-s-access-to-cumbria-police-records-1.1077809#. Accessed on June 23, 2014.

Hillyard, S. H. (forthcoming). Bullshot: Sporting shooting, alcohol and the two cultures. *International Review for the Sociology of Sport*.

Independent Police Complaints Commission (IPCC). (2012). Mr. Michael Atherton IPCC investigation into the granting, management and review of his shotgun certificate and firearm licence by Durham Constabulary. *Independent Investigation Final Report*. IPCC Reference No. 2012/000063.

Lawless, C. (2013). The low template DNA profiling controversy: Biolegality and boundary work among forensic scientists. *Social Studies of Science*, *43*(2), 191–214.

Lodge, D. (1988). *Nice work: A novel*. London: Secker and Warburg.

Lowe, P., Phillipson, J., Proctor, A., & Emery, S. (2014, April 3–4). Inter-professional expertise. *Trans-Atlantic Rural Research Network (TARRN) Conference*, Newcastle.

Marsden, T. (2006). Pathways in the sociology of rural knowledge. In P. Cloke, T. Marsden, & P. Mooney (Eds.), *Handbook of rural studies*. London: Sage.

Mazanderani, F. (2012). An ethics of intimacy: Online dating, viral-sociality and living with HIV. *BioSocieties*, *7*(4), 393–409.

McKee, A. (2014, April 3–4). Legitimising the laird? Communicative action and the role of private landowner and community engagement in rural sustainability. Trans-Atlantic Rural Research Network (TARRN) Conference, Newcastle.

Merton, R. K. (1972). Insiders and outsiders: A chapter in the sociology of knowledge. *American Journal of Sociology*, *78*(1), 9–47.

Neal, S., & Walters, S. (2008). Rural be/longing and rural social organizations: Conviviality and community-making in the English countryside. *Sociology*, *42*(2), 279–297.

Newby, H. (1977). *The deferential worker*. Harmondsworth: Penguin.

Ofcom. (2014). *UK mobile services map 2013: Level of outdoor mobile coverage by administrative authority*. Retrieved from http://maps.ofcom.org.uk/mobile-services. Accessed on September 22, 2014.

Pahl, R. (1989). Is the emperor naked? Some questions on the adequacy of sociological theory in urban and regional research. *International Journal of Urban and Regional Research*, *13*, 709–720.

Pawson, R., Owen, L., & Wong, G. (2010). The today programme's contribution to evidence-based policy. *Evaluation*, *16*, 211–213.

Phillips, M. (2009). Rural gentrification. In R. Kitchin & N. Thrift (Eds.), *International encyclopedia of human geography* (Vol. 4, pp. 368–375). London: Elsevier.

Shucksmith, M. (2012). Class, power and inequality in rural areas: Beyond social exclusion? *Sociologia ruralis*, *52*(4), 377–397.

Simmel, G. (1971). The stranger. In D. Levine (Ed.). *Georg Simmel: On individuality and social forms*. Chicago, IL: University of Chicago Press.

Stacey, M. (1960). *Tradition and change: A study of Banbury*. Oxford: Oxford University Press.

Strangleman, T. (2004). Ways of (not) seeing work: The visual as a blind spot in WES? *Work, Employment and Society*, *18*(1), 179–192.

Thrift, N. (2005). *Knowing capitalism*. London: Sage.

Times Higher. (2014). Bubble bursts on economist's 'alternative' course. *Times Higher Education*, May 15. Retrieved from http://www.timeshighereducation.co.uk/news/bubble-bursts-on-economists-alternative-course/2013313.article. Accessed on September 23, 2014.

Travers, M. (2009). New methods, old problems: A sceptical view of innovation in qualitative research. *Qualitative Research*, *9*(2), 161–179.

Tummons, J. (2014). Using software for qualitative data analysis: Research outside paradigmatic boundaries. In M. Hand & S. Hillyard (Eds.), *Big data? Qualitative approaches to digital research* (Vol. 13, pp. 155–177). Studies in Qualitative Methodology. Bingley, UK: Emerald Group Publishing Limited.

Waddell, L. (2013). Upland keeper. *Shooting Times*, October 30, p. 23.

Wall, D. S. (2013). Policing identity crimes. *Policing and Society*, *23*(4), 437–460.

Wallace, G. (2014). The answer is "No! Now what did you want?" *Keeping the Balance*, (Summer), 40.

West Briton. (2011). Emergency services warned of rural satnav risk to lives. Retrieved from http://www.westbriton.co.uk/Emergency-services-warned-rural-sat-nav-risk/story-13069331-detail/story.html. Accessed on May 27, 2014.

Westmarland, N., & Kelly, E. (2012). Why extending measurements of 'success' in domestic violence perpetrator programmes matters for social work. *British Journal of Social Work*, *43*(6), 1092–1110.

Wiles, R., Crow, G., & Pain, R. (2011). Innovation in qualitative research methods: A narrative review. Qualitative Research *2011*, *11*(5), 587–604.

Williams, W. M. (2008). From continuing tradition to continuous change, W. M. Williams interviewed by Paul Thompson. *International Journal of Social Research Methodology*, 11(2), 97–102.

Woods, M. (2011). *Rural*. London: Routledge.

Wylie, J. (2005). A single day's walking: Narrating self and landscape on the South West Coast path. *Transactions*, *30*, 234–247.

INVESTIGATING THE OTHER: CONSIDERATIONS ON MULTI-SPECIES RESEARCH

Nik Taylor and Lindsay Hamilton

ABSTRACT

Purpose – *The last few decades have seen the rise of a new field of inquiry – human–animal studies (HAS). As a rich, theoretically and disciplinarily diverse field, HAS shines a light on the various relations that humans have with other animals across time, space and culture. While still a small, but rapidly growing field, HAS has supported the development of multiple theoretical and conceptual initiatives which have aimed to capture the rich diversity of human–animal interactions. Yet the methodologies for doing this have not kept pace with the ambitions of such projects. In this chapter, we seek to shed light on this particular issue.*

Design/methodology/approach – *We consider the difficulties of researching other-than-human beings by asking what might happen if methods incorporated true inter-disciplinarity, for instance if social scientists were able to work with natural scientists on multi-species ethnographies. The lack of established methodology (and the lack of cross disciplinary research between the natural and social sciences) is one of*

Big Data? Qualitative Approaches to Digital Research
Studies in Qualitative Methodology, Volume 13, 251–271

ISSN: 1042-3192/doi:10.1108/S1042-319220140000013016

the main problems that we consider here. It is an issue complicated immensely by the 'otherness' of animals – the vast differences in the ways that we (humans) and they (animals) see the world, communicate and behave. This chapter provides the opportunity for us to consider how we can take account of (if not resolve) these differences to arrive at meaningful research data, to better understand the contemporary world by embarking upon more precise investigations of our relationships with animals.

Findings – *Drawing upon a selection of examples from contemporary research of human–animal interactions, both ethnographic and scientific, we shed light on some new possibilities for multi-species research. We suggest that this can be done best by considering and applying a diversity of theoretical frameworks which deal explicitly with the constitution of the social environment.*

Originality/value – *Our methodological exploration offers the reader insight into new ways of working within the template of human animal studies by drawing upon a range of useful theories such as post-structuralism and actor network theory (ANT) (for example, Callon, 1986; Hamilton & Taylor, 2013; Latour, 2005; Law, Ruppert, & Savage, 2011) and post-humanist perspectives (for example, Anderson, 2014; Haraway, 2003; Wolfe, 2010). Our contribution to this literature is distinctive because rather than remaining at the philosophical level, we suggest how the human politics of method might be navigated practically to the benefit of multiple species.*

Keywords: Ethnography; human-animal studies; interdisciplinary; ontology; epistemology; politics

INTRODUCTION

The authors of this chapter have been working together for around three years investigating human relations with other species. While we both work within a sociological template, we write from very different perspectives. One of us has been involved with animal rights/liberation for over three decades and approaches the study of human–animal relations politically, critiquing those embedded structures that (in her analysis) lead to myriad institutionalised animal abuses. The other has focussed on management and organisational studies, and is more concerned with the lived experiences of identity, relations and structures in social – and particularly working – life with animals (Hamilton, 2013). We have devoted our joint attention to the processes, experiences and social worlds of work where humans and animals come together (Hamilton & Taylor, 2012). We have used ethnographic techniques to investigate communities of front-line animal workers such as veterinary surgeons and employees in animal shelters. We have also extended our research into less well-known areas such as slaughterhouses (Hamilton & Taylor, 2013; Taylor & Hamilton, 2014). In doing this, we have developed a heterogenous theoretical outlook, informed by a range of useful theories such as ANT (Callon, 1986; Hamilton & Taylor, 2013; Latour, 2005; Law, 2004; Law, Ruppert, & Savage, 2011) and post-humanist perspectives (Haraway, 2003).

Despite our ideological differences we have found our working relationship to be a productive, useful and above all *interesting* one. Perhaps this is because however we come at our research conceptually, we are both interested in the '*hows*' of the inclusion of other animals in social life: *how* do people interact with other species; *how* are species differences and similarities made known; *how* do other animals fit into daily life; *how* does power operate in and through species difference, and perhaps most importantly, *how* on earth do we begin to investigate these issues? In other words we are preoccupied by methodological questions and these form the basis for the current chapter.

This chapter investigates the troubling, often vexatious but always interesting methodological issues that we have come across in the context of our interest in human–animal research. We begin with a brief overview of the literature in the field of post-humanism (as it pertains to methodological insights in human–animal studies) before turning more closely to research methodology. We summarise and explore some of the differences between qualitative and quantitative methods and investigate the potential hindrances to multi-disciplinary research in the field of human–animal relationships. We then make some (tentative) suggestions as to how this might be thought through and approached. We offer a brief example to illustrate this and then turn to a more in-depth analysis of the emerging method of Multi Species Ethnography (MSE). We draw upon that debate to conclude with a number of suggestions for further analysis and speculation.

THE PROMISE OF POST-HUMANISM: DOCUMENTING HUMAN–ANIMAL RELATIONSHIPS

Studies of inanimate, technological artefacts have flourished within recent literature, particularly within the emerging discipline of post-humanism.

Yet despite this growing interest in 'others', the realities of our lived entanglements with different species have yet to be adequately documented in academic accounts even within the growing sub-field of human–animal studies. This is largely because until very recently, animals have been excluded from sociological ways of seeing culture; an 'affected ignorance' towards animals as 'others' (Haraway, 2003). And where this has been challenged, very few of the studies involve consideration of the methodological difficulties involved in trying to make sense of our lives with other species (for a notable exception see Birke & Hockenhull, 2012).

Indeed, when animals do crop up in the literature, they are often portrayed as passive *commodities*, a narrow view that neglects the ways in which animals play active roles in social processes, as workers (Hamilton & Taylor, 2013; Porcher & Schmitt, 2010) or – at worst – as resources (Cudworth, 2011). Yet we have noted that humans and animals often deconstruct and 'mess up' species distinctions in situ (Alger & Alger, 2003; Taylor, 2010), a fascinating blurring of supposedly clear boundaries between species which is deserving of far more attention. The fact that such a concept has received so little academic attention is linked to and predicated on the moral humanism that is sociology's intellectual legacy and often, still, its default setting. Troubling these anthropocentric underpinnings at a theoretical level has been occurring (with differing degrees of success) for the last couple of decades but this hasn't yet been tracked by methodological innovation.

There is a degree of dissatisfaction with the limits of contemporary human–animal research, however. Consider, for example, Cary Wolfe's admonishment that, 'we must take yet another step, another post, and realise that the nature of thought itself must change if it is to be post-humanist ... when we talk about post-humanism we are not just talking about a thematic of the decentring of the human in relation to either evolutionary, ecological, or technological coordinates ... we are also talking about *how* thinking confronts that thematic, what thought has to become to face those thematic' (2010, p. Xvi, in Anderson, 2014). Just as Wolfe calls for the nature of thought itself to be scrutinised, Anderson (2014) reminds us that our human 'tool-kit'; that is, the very language that we use, leaves us relegated, 'within the bounds of humanist discourse' and thus underpins and reinforces the humanism that we seek to trouble. There are no clear solutions here but there are, at least, a number of thinkers now addressing these profound epistemological and linguistic complications (e.g. Haraway, 2003).

While the rise of post-humanist thinking has done much to provoke and challenge received wisdom on our implicit status as (human) thinkers and writers, what is often missing is a practical consideration of what this might mean for the methods we use to produce knowledge and, by extension, the ways in which we present research findings. With few exceptions, the inroads being made into multi-species research remain theoretical and abstract, even within what might arguably be considered the most practical disciplines of animal and veterinary science. At the same time, the veterinary sciences have access to vast amounts of data which has yet to be capitalised upon by those working within the humanities. What is needed, then, is a way to lay out new templates for the research, documentation and understanding of human–animal relationships; templates that seek out analytic and representational 'meeting points' between academic disciplines and between the datasets that they produce. In short, we are advocating closer contact between the social and natural sciences at both a paradigmatic and methodological level. This has the potential to prompt greater attention to be paid to the strategic methods by which we gain and present 'knowledge'.

This sounds simple on paper. It has often been claimed that multidisciplinary teams might profitably bring their own knowledge, experiences and methods to bear on particular issues. But, as we shall go on to discuss, there is a fundamental (and some would say intractable) problematic to navigate before such a strategy might take shape in real world form. Here we refer to the fact that the production of knowledge is inextricably bound up with the interplay of power in and through societies and, in turn, that this is manifest through the choices we make about the study of multispecies relations. We have choices about writing and representing those relations just as we have the choice to overlook or 'edit out' particular actors, events, mistakes, or even entire species from our studies (Latour & Woolgar, 1988). But the unwillingness to recognise and confront the overt ideological and political aspects of all research presents perhaps the single biggest blockage to inter-disciplinary collaboration. The next section of the chapter excavates this particular issue by turning to methodological concerns in more detail.

POWERFUL METHODS: POLITICAL METHODS

Our own research of inter-species relations draws upon a constructivist standpoint summed up by the idea that research methods not only describe but 'enact' the world they purport to study. It is a cornerstone of our shared philosophy that methods help to both create and *re*-create the social world, that they are produced by and productive of that world. The various barriers one has to negotiate throughout the entire research process (including the writing up or selection of results) are indicative of the power games that suffuse the research process. Our research methods and our research questions have effects: they make differences and boundaries, they enact realities, and they help to bring into being what they also discover. They shape the direction of the findings and, often, determine how those findings will be edited and presented to the broader world. The power of methodological choices to create, enact and embody reality applies just as much to those working in human–animal studies fields as it does without. As Law et al. (2011) remind us when discussing the double social life of methods:

> ... social realities are being constituted by social research methods way below the radar, and quite independently of what we think we are doing when we undertake social research. 'Definitions of the situation' prevail – and are enacted – even when we don't make them explicit. But if this is right then it becomes important to excavate the versions of the social embedded in our methods, to bring them into the light, and to debate them. Do we actually want the kind of collectivities implied by ethnographies, by surveys, by focus groups, or by collations of transactional data? Do we even know what they are? And what kind of subjectivities and collectivities are they propagating? As you'll see, we are no longer dealing only with methodological questions. We're also trading in politics, in questions about the kinds of social worlds and subjectivities we want to help to make more real – to realise – in and through our methods. (Law et al., 2011, p. 12)

In considering how our 'definitions of the situation' might play out in practical, methodological terms, for example, it is often supposed by researchers that carrying out large-scale quantitative data collection mitigates the effect of a variety of potential biases. Such methods often seek to generate big data to shed light on 'real life' problems, for example, investigating the health and welfare of whole populations of animals[1] (Whay & Main, 2009). Within the veterinary industry, for example, there has been a turn towards 'evidence-based' medicine which seeks to draw a firm link between day-to-day work with animals and the underlying scientific research 'knowledge' base produced by university faculty (Cockroft & Holmes, 2003). The evidence-based approach has become increasingly accepted as the veterinary industry norm because, it is argued, with the 'right knowledge' even non-experts like farm workers might feasibly make decisions for individual animals based upon 'good science'. This is precisely what Law et al. (2011) refer to as making 'real' in and through methods, but how are such realities crafted and made powerful? We can begin to answer to this question by looking again at research methods.

Many quantitative methodologists draw upon mathematical estimates of the risks and benefits of particular actions, derived from research conducted on large-scale population samples (rather than individual cases). Such research is often 'validated' by a range of mathematical evaluation criteria such as computer-assisted sensitivity testing, statistics and frequency counts. The positivist science traditions that inform such approaches rest upon a core assumption that the real world can be discovered tested and measured, that reality can be presented via mathematically informed methods that decode that reality from sizeable and 'valid' samples of data. This is where the politics of research and, indeed, the politics of 'making real' become acute (Law et al., 2011). Following Law, however, our thesis is that apparently value-free and rigorous methods are never as simple and objective as we are led to believe.

All methods, including statistics, are subject to professional and methodological decisions regarding what to collect and how; how to manage data problems and how to analyse, redact, edit and present the findings in ways that will make them usable, interesting and – above all – powerful. The selection of which methods and/or results to prioritise and how to determine them, is always a political as well as a technical issue. The uses and/or generation of big data is also an exercise in the performance of multiple realities. In the quest for generalisable findings, quantitative methods often rely upon an editing process which seeks to disregard outlying results, exceptional cases or other 'hard to measure' factors such as human motivation and unpredictability (Latour & Woolgar, 1988; Law, 2004). Thus, it is a mistake to adopt an uncritical acceptance to any findings – no matter how 'scientific' they might appear. For example, even the biggest of datasets may tell us little more about human–animal relations than what one species (humans) thinks about another.

Qualitative research methods, by contrast, prioritise investigation of the 'quality' rather than the 'quantity' of data. Proponents of the qualitative tradition privilege a rather different array of methodological tools including semiotics, discourse analysis, survey research, focus groups and interviews, ethnomethodology and ethnography (to name but a few). All these practises draw upon long histories with their own distinctive literatures and – of course – they are tied to a wide range of theoretical approaches from the positivist and humanistic to post-human, post-modern and constructivist sensibilities. As Nelson, Treichler, and Grossberg (1992) argue, qualitative research embraces a range of forms and methods and can crosscut a number of disciplines, including the natural and medical sciences. With its interest in 'processes and meanings', however, qualitative research does not rely upon experimental examination in terms of 'quantity, amount, intensity, or frequency' and instead turns its attention to questions that 'stress *how* social experience is created and given meaning' (Denzin & Lincoln, 2003, p. 13). There is usually a core appreciation from the outset – albeit superficial in some cases – of the tangled and interwoven politics of method, epistemology and ontology.

Even though our own research to date has relied heavily upon the qualitative approach, we are aware of a number of shortcomings which limit its usefulness for exploring human–animal interaction. The tendency towards small-scale datasets in qualitative research carries its own set of problems, for instance. There are questions of access and sample size, persuasiveness, and – as we have already acknowledged – small datasets become even smaller when we exclude certain species on the basis of their biological differences. Savage and Burrows (2007) have gone as far as to argue that there is a 'crisis of empirical sociology' stemming from the realisation that other sectors (particularly private enterprises like veterinary practices) have access to more information, often in the form of 'big data', which can be used to generate greater impacts upon everyday working practises. The argument goes that qualitative researchers should respond to this 'crisis' by re-imagining their methods and, indeed, their 'worlds' of research which is a position echoed by a number of scholars (for example, Law & Urry, 2004, p. 390).

Yet, as we have already suggested, the virtual boundary between quantitative and qualitative approaches, often tracked by disciplinary differences between social and natural sciences, goes far beyond questions of scale, validity or impact. While large datasets might exist, for example, on animal behaviour and health within the veterinary sciences there are, very often, major differences in epistemological and ontological sensibility between those who might find value in them. The profound philosophical tensions between factions of scholars interested in human–animal interactions undermines the benefits of sharing data as part of truly inter-disciplinary research. In drawing attention to some of the potential blockages to interdisciplinarity, we are not seeking to point out that one methodological approach is superior to another nor are we aiming to reignite old debates regarding qualitative versus quantitative methods. Instead we are seeking to highlight that we have to attend much more rigorously to the 'ontological politics' of methods, be they socially or naturally scientific, qualitative or quantitative, because these politics (or at least a lack of acknowledgement of them) are perhaps the biggest hindrance to cross-fertilisation between disciplines and paradigms (Law et al., 2011).

As Law (2004) explains in his discussion of the results of the Eurobarometer investigation into animal welfare, 'we need an archaeological reading if we are to start to articulate the realities they [methods] imply. Such an archaeology is relational, always incomplete, always capable of articulating new versions of performativity' (p. 12). The incompleteness, the politics and the frustrated possibilities of research are deserving of far more 'archaeological' scrutiny than they have been afforded to date. And, when we include other species into this mix of already knotty issues, we find that matters become even more problematic – precisely how are we to include nonhumans in such a way that *their* reality is represented, never mind performed, by method?

CAN MULTI-DISCIPLINARY RESEARCH WORK IN PRACTICE?

Lowe, Phillipson, and Wilkinson (2013) argue that effective inter-disciplinarity depends upon 'overcoming basic assumptions that have structured past interactions: particularly, the casting of social science in an end-of-pipe role in relation to scientific and technological developments'. This is best summed up in the words of the UK Commission on the Social Sciences (2003, p. 29):

> [The role of] social sciences as a back-end fix to the problems arising from new scientific developments ... can be parodied by 'we have invented this, now find a market for it' or 'we have invented this but it has a few unfortunate side effects. How do we get people to accept it?'

There are certainly examples of such an approach in recent animal science. Several projects have attempted to draw upon the literatures and techniques of management, marketing and communication to make evidence-based research more powerful 'on the ground' (see, e.g. Atkinson, 2010; Horseman, Whay, Huxley, Bell, & Mason, 2013; Kristensen & Enevoldsen, 2008). Such studies often seek to 'tag on' the apparent benefits of 'soft science', for example, to encourage vets and animal owners to adopt the recommendations suggested by research findings, a style of working that echoes contemporary policy discourses which stress the 'mantra' that the analysis and resolution of current problems (like animal disease or welfare) calls for the 'active engagement of a wide range of sciences' (for a fuller discussion and critique, see Lowe et al., 2013). As to how this might be achieved, or even discussed, however, there is little guidance or practical help for academics of any discipline. We reject the notion that qualitative methods and data should be utilised simply as the 'back end fix' or as the 'whip hand' of the scientist, which prompts us to consider different approaches and methods; ways of working that would bring researchers closer together. In the next section, we offer a brief 'real world' example to sketch out how this might work in practice.

An Example: The Case of Bovine Lameness

Cattle lameness is one of the most significant welfare problems in contemporary dairy farming. Veterinary surgeons usually define lameness as 'any abnormality which causes a cow to change the way that she walks' (DairyCo, 2014). It can be caused by a range of foot and leg conditions (e.g. bruising, sores and cuts), themselves caused by disease, management or environmental factors. A number of studies in the veterinary sciences have pointed to a significant relationship between lameness in dairy cattle and human management practises on the farm. To simplify and summarise just one aspect of this research work, it has been argued that cattle herds, if allowed to walk freely (that is, without being herded, rushed or driven) will suffer fewer cases of lameness (Whay & Main, 2013). A number of action plans have been produced in recent years that suggest practical ways for farmers and their staff to make use of findings like these (e.g. Bell et al., 2009). The question that has yet to be answered by research teams in this area, however, is how to encourage front-line workers to take action plans and research findings seriously in carrying out their own everyday practises (Whay & Main, 2013) and how to effect meaningful change in the lives of the animals afflicted by lameness.

In such studies, the burning issue can be summed up in the following terms; if the facts show that certain practises lead to lameness, why do farmers and their operatives persist with 'old ways' of managing their animals? The puzzle is not easily answered but it is a starting point of our argument that it cannot be tackled with positivist, quantitative methods alone. Imagine, for example, that research into bovine lameness took a more complex view from the start; avoiding the question of 'how to make the scientific facts stick' and instead treating knowledge itself as a co-created process – never resolved or fixed – but rather impacted and embedded within a whole range of unpredictable and vague social, cultural, economic, and above all political factors. In short, the question becomes deeply epistemological, '*how* and *why* does knowledge become powerful?' Rather than '*what* do farmers know and how can we change this?'

Excavating this epistemological debate would help bring about a radical shift in focus, one that would require consideration of knowledge not as a 'product' requiring discovery, communication and 'uptake' but rather an artefact of a highly political nature (from the very start of the research process) (Lam, Jansen, van Veersen, & Steuten, 2008; Lowe, 2009; Penny, Paine, & Brightling, 2009). This is a far more tricky matter altogether, straying outside the purview of traditional science methods into interactional spaces, voids and grey areas between scientific practice, knowledge and belief – the domain more usually associated with the critical social sciences. Yet the benefits of taking this step would offer a much more rounded view of the social life of the farmyard (or any other area of investigation). If such research involved qualitative techniques such as ethnography from the outset, we think that it would be possible to understand more about the ways that farmers feel about 'knowledge', about advice and the interactions between animals and humans on the farm.

A similar approach has already been used successfully by Emery (2014) in his longitudinal ethnographic fieldwork with farmers in the North York Moors (UK). In his investigation of the relationship between environmental policy and on-farm practice, Emery's research pointed out that there are cultural rather than purely utilitarian economic values associated with work on the farm. Emery showed how the over-riding ethic of 'hard work' in the farming community had the potential to bring individuals into conflict with government policy or the (evidence-based) advice given to them by experts. Emery's work echoes a number of other qualitative studies of farming work within labour and migration studies, cultural geography and anthropology (e.g. Gray, 1998; Penrose, 1993; Ravetz, 2001; Wallman, 1979) which have pointed overwhelmingly to the finding that 'the task of meeting obligations, securing identity, status and structure, are as fundamental to livelihood as bread and shelter' (Wallman, 1979, p. 7). The bulk of this literature suggests that work is far more than a simple exchange between wage and effort (Baldamus, 1967), or in the case of bovine lameness, between 'finding the facts' and putting them into practice. Work is also a human identity investment resting upon processes through which complex cultural and ideological values are developed, enacted and made powerful. A farm should be considered not simply as a place where animals are managed, then, but as a site of value and meaning-making or perhaps as 'an evolving testimony to the life's work of those who have left their mark on [it]' (Ingold, 1984, p. 116). Considering and applying just a fraction of this wealth of critical, qualitative research, to the initial research design has the potential to offer far more insight into the reasons why farmers often appear to resist action plans and the benefits of applying 'scientific facts'.

COMMUNICATING ACROSS RESEARCH DISCIPLINES

So far we have argued that research methods are political as well as analytical and that multi-disciplinary approaches to human–animal entanglements might be of benefit. In making this suggestion, and while drawing attention to the limited recognition of the human politics of knowledge, we think that inter-disciplinary research drawing upon a range of work – resting upon strong communication between differing disciplines – could bring together a range of paradigms and perspectives that would turn 'findings' into far more subtle and multi-faceted accounts. The benefits of drawing on different datasets and differently qualified researchers as part of team-based project work could be significant (Lowe et al., 2013).

Importantly, we also think that developing relations and communication strategies between disciplines might help us to adopt new ways of thinking about our relationships with nonhumans, and specifically, ways that do not perpetuate perceptions of power as uni-directional (Hamilton & Taylor, 2013). We are aware that most research into human–animal relations privileges the point of view of the human and that constructionist accounts fall victim to this when considering how it is that *humans* construct *animals* in particular ways and settings. We are also aware that while the discussion above outlines some of the benefits of multi-disciplinary work when considering human–animal relations, it does not necessarily circumvent this. For us, then, the purpose of thinking and re-thinking methods is twofold: one as outlined above, to consider how it is we might better understand animal lives through multi-disciplinary teamwork, and two, how we might literally include animals in this research. While we are cognisant of the huge barriers to this rather noble, and possibly idealistic sentiment, given that we believe methods enact the social world as much as they investigate it, then the exclusion of animals from the research process hinges upon important social issues of power, agency and representation.

In seeking to tackle this, we are supported by a number of qualitative scholars – particularly those working in the post-humanist or ANT templates – who have already argued that social and physical changes in the world are and need to be, paralleled by changes in the methods of social inquiry (e.g. Law & Urry, 2004). For us to speak more confidently about human–animal relationships, organisations and societies and to effect lasting impact in 'real world' situations, such as on the farm, we feel that we now require adapted methods or – at the very least – new ways of considering our existing techniques and strategies of 'doing research' to make further inroads into this worthwhile project. We also need to consider how large datasets might (or might not) be helpful in generating ideas for tackling small-scale problems or issues. In the next section, we consider what might happen if such methodological work (which incorporated interdisciplinary research) also considered the agency and perspective of the animal, as much as is practicable, for instance if social scientists were able to work with natural scientists on *multi-species ethnographies.*

MULTI-SPECIES ETHNOGRAPHY

Multi-species ethnography (MSE) is a qualitative research method with a small but concerted following, primarily in anthropology. Proponents of the multi-species approach not only question what researchers mean by society and culture (Abu-Lughod, 1991; Gupta & Ferguson, 1992), but they also interrogate assumed species variances as an assumed base-line for research; that is, 'for articulating biological difference and similarity' (Kirksey & Helmreich, 2010). In doing so, MSE seeks to foreground a number of philosophical dilemmas and questions. But the very notion of MSE is a troublesome one for 'multi species ethnographers are studying contact zones where lines separating nature from culture have broken down, where encounters between Homo sapiens and other beings generate mutual ecologies and coproduced niches' (Kirksey & Helmreich, 2010, p. 546).

Drawing on various post-humanist debates, MSE practitioners refuse simplistic binaries such as nature and culture, human and animal, social and natural and instead point out that entanglements, 'hybrids' to use Haraway's terminology (1991), are the basis of our reality, not pure distinctions. One idea following from this is that agency can be attributed to nonhuman actors (which includes but is not limited to other species) that have normally formed part of the 'background' of traditional social science research, for example, technological artefacts. The agency and importance of such 'others' be they insects, fungi, plants or animals has a powerful bearing upon the data collected and the manner in which it is reported. It is also acknowledged that such forms of agency may or may not extend into forms of communication (like speech) which have been the traditional mainstay of social scientific research data. Taking this as a cornerstone of the research process, then, those interested in MSE use photography, visual and audio data recordings and even art to convey the complexity of the human–animal engagement.

Avoiding over-reliance upon traditionally humanist modes of enquiry such as interview, a richer portrayal of daily life is achieved, one which does not rely solely upon human discourse. If MSE were to utilise existing big data, such as those generated by the veterinary sciences, for example, researchers would be able to take this a-lingual approach even further. Perhaps the continuing problem of bovine lameness could be better attacked with large scientific datasets that could generate research questions for MSE. What, then, might attempts to look at lameness from the perspective of the cow (through using video data gathered from the cow's perspective in the barn, the field or the yard for example) tell us beyond the theory of 'management techniques'? We think that blending qualitative and quantitative resources would help to sharpen the focus upon the interactions and exchanges between farmers and cattle to provide a more rounded picture of daily life on the farm. This would add depth to existing quantitative information concerning husbandry, housing and other physical factors, just as it would add weight to qualitative observations done with small samples. We think this is a way for researchers of all disciplines to find out more about the impact of 'scientific facts' upon daily life.

For those working within MSE frameworks, ethnographic methods are key. As Lestel points out 'the profound renewal of ethology itself' (2006, p. 148) spearheaded by the pioneering work of Jane Goodall is based on a transformation of ethology into ethnology; 'it became accepted and understood that the societies of animals studied were far more complex than expected and that an ethnographic approach was crucial to their understanding' (p. 149). Kirksey and Helmreich (2010) also point to the importance of ethnography in opening up new ways of seeing the world: 'Creatures previously appearing on the margins of anthropology – as part of the landscape, as food for humans, as symbols – have been pressed into the foreground in recent ethnographies. Animals, plants, fungi, and microbes once confined in anthropological accounts to the realm of zoe or "bare life" – that which is killable – have started to appear alongside humans in the realm of bios, with legibly biographical and political lives' (p. 545).

With its emphasis upon the animal part of the interaction, the veterinary sciences are particularly well placed to add value to such research. Taking MSE out of its anthropological context – and mixing its disciplinary footings – will help us to ask some very difficult questions about our intellectual heritage as well as about the methods we use to study the social world. There is also the potential to expand the horizons of those working within other paradigms. For example, there is a wealth of big data available online for the everyday social scientist interested in human–animal relations (e.g. chat rooms devoted to dog 'owners'; Facebook groups full of pictures of humans with their animals and accompanying stories). While not unproblematic (as much of the current volume demonstrates) for those conversant with online ethnographic techniques this data is incredibly rich. Uncluttered by the usual considerations of, for instance, the asymmetrical power relations between interviewer and interviewee in an artificial setting, this data offers an unparalleled glimpse into everyday life. Finding ways to utilise it in multi-disciplinary research projects, which may well necessitate convincing those from other disciplines of its authenticity, offers much promise.

FINAL DISCUSSION

There's an excitement in contemporary human–animal studies, you can't help but be swept along by it; how interesting it is to read about how bees are co-constitutive of urbanised city life (Moore & Kosut, 2013), or of how chimpanzees have a culture that has similarities (and differences) to our own (Read, 2012), or that animals might somehow participate in and object to the ways we study them (Alger & Alger, 2003). But this excitement often covers an important point. As attractive as '"Becomings"– new kinds of relations emerging from non-hierarchical alliances, symbiotic attachments, and the mingling of creative agents' are in the development of multi species ethnography (Kirksey & Helmreich, 2010, p. 546) one is struck by a certain amount of hubris in these philosophical imaginings. We may live lives entangled with other species but in most of these entanglements there is a clear power disparity seen, not least, in the very fact that it is *we* who study *them*.

It is our choice of research agenda, and our methods, which make them intelligible to us in certain ways, which make them matter (or not). It is here that critical, qualitative disciplines can lead the way – drawing upon a long history of attention paid to the workings of power, including that which is manifest throughout the research process. As part of that, we need to find new methods that challenge our beliefs about the neat binaries between culture, nature and technology. We need these precisely because we are investigating phenomena that itself troubles existing neat schema between what constitutes nature and what constitutes culture. Moreover, to do this within multi-disciplinary teams further disrupts entrenched divides. Using methods that are in keeping with these disruptions then makes sense. While MSE is in its infancy we believe it has boundless potential and possibilities and we 'watch this space' avidly.

We would like to conclude this chapter by opening out a few further considerations as food for thought. We have argued that we need a degree of theoretical and methodological heterodoxy if we are to be pragmatic in our investigations of human–animal relations, and we have pointed out that this may mean softening some epistemological/paradigmatic allegiances in the name of pragmatism. We think it would be feasible, for example, that work within multi-disciplinary groups could be planned through a central overlapping phase of the research, followed by a phase of more specialist considerations such as MSE. Of course, navigating the ethical, political, epistemological and methodological terrain will prove difficult but – as we have already argued – this is likely to benefit all precisely *because* it is difficult.

The difficulty comes, we think, from having one's own allegiances and boundaries challenged and we are not suggesting that one 'side' is better at this than the other; rather, we are acknowledging that we all come to research as creatures with belief systems that we hold dear. Of course, we realise that we are advocating that people from different sides of the fence 'get together' and work through the issues openly and we acknowledge that this is difficult both as an intellectual exercise and in its 'real world consequences' (e.g. in getting grants, publishing papers and so on). But we consider that the passion that often goes with intellectual curiosity will go a long way to offset all but the most intractable here.

There are a number of considerations that arise from such seemingly practical suggestions, however; knotty issues and dilemmas which require significantly more analysis that we have been able to offer here. For example, if we follow the argument that methods are performative, that they enact the social world as much as they tell us about it, then it isn't the case that qualitative methods are simply better because they tell us more about the world and less about the politics of the research (or the research funder), or that quantitative methods are better because they are value free. Instead, we have to confront the problematic that all methods are political, all methods bring the world into being and make it known. To use the terminology of Law et al. (2011), all methods are linked to advocacy – they come into being because they have advocates behind them:

> We will need to understand that methods inhabit and help to reproduce a complex ecology of representations, realities and advocacies, arrangements and circuits. … The implication is that there's a kind of triple lock at work here. And this, if it's right, makes it very, very, difficult to know differently, to shape new realities, or to imagine different 'methods assemblages' or modes of knowing. For all of these have to be shifted together. … But, here's the bottom line, until we can find ways of rethinking knowledges, realities and methods together in the same breath, we won't have the tools that we need to understand the work being done by our methods. Neither will we be able to imagine a social that is radically different. (pp. 13–14)

Acknowledging this takes us in interesting directions. If we choose, then, to advocate on behalf of animals through human–animal studies, or advocate that we include species in our studies of organisations and work practises then we also have to advocate on behalf of certain methods, or at least advocate that we give time to understanding the role methods play in bringing these 'realities' to light. We have suggested that MSE might be one such method, a means of incorporating human and animal 'actors' in our field research. If methods come into being because they have a purpose and because they have advocates, then we human–animal scholars might do well to think not only about what our method choices omit (animal agency for instance) but also what they might include. In other words, we can use our power to advocate methods that include other beings, that give them 'voices', allow them to be heard and above all politicise their life (and death) experiences. Perhaps in the sharing of such values, the natural and social sciences might complement each other more readily than might be supposed, not least because – as we have suggested in the foregoing analysis – there is often an underlying interest in promoting the welfare and health of animals.

While it has become de rigueur in social science to acknowledge one's own intellectual/ideological biases (particularly in those aspects of social science that address the disempowered or otherwise ostracised) we think that there is more work to do in acknowledging and working through our methodological biases. We end this chapter, then, by advocating that researchers of all stripes become attuned to the idea that methods create reality as much as they study it and that this is acknowledged – along with its consequences – in our research. We are also advocating that scholars from different disciplines pay closer attention to the datasets that already exist but have yet to be fully explored. While this may make multi-disciplinary research in some ways more difficult, it also has the potential to make other – previously deeply entrenched – points of divergence more easily reconciled. If we move away from discussions of whose methodological approach is better, and why, to one where we accept *all* approaches are implicated in performing reality, we might actually find we stand closer than we thought.

NOTE

1. The 'Bristol Cats' study (2013) was run by vets, behaviourists and epidemiologists at the University of Bristol, United Kingdom. It was designed to improve knowledge of common diseases and behaviour problems of cats, for example unwanted elimination (i.e. urinating), obesity and hyperthyroidism. It was hoped that findings from the study would be used by veterinary practitioners, cat breeders and owners to improve the health and welfare of cats. Approximately 2,200 kittens were registered with the study between May 2010 and December 2013 and the research was questionnaire based. Cat owners were asked to provide information on the living standards of their pets and that dataset was subsequently analysed to shed light on the causes of common behaviour patterns and diseases of cats; the extent to which their characteristics (e.g. aggression towards humans) or conditions (e.g. obesity) were connected with the cat's management (e.g. diet, life-style) and other factors (e.g. breed).

REFERENCES

Abu-Lughod, L. (1991). Writing against culture. In R. G. Fox (Ed.), *Recapturing anthropology: Working in the present*. Santa Fe, NM: School of American Research Press.

Alger, J., & Alger, S. (2003). *Cat culture: The social world of a cat shelter*. Philadelphia, PA: Temple University Press.

Anderson, N. (2014). We have never/have always been posthuman. In J. Weinstein & C. Colebrook (Eds.), *Inhuman rites and posthumous life*. Durham, NC: Duke University Press (forthcoming).

Atkinson, O. (2010). *The role of the vet in knowledge transfer in the dairy industry* report of the Nuffield Farming Scholarships Trust. Retrieved from http://www.nuffieldinternational.org/rep_pdf/1295259764Owen_Atkinsonreport_edtedl.pdf. Accessed on April 26, 2014.

Baldamus, W. (1967). *Efficiency and effort: An analysis of industrial administration*. London: Tavistock.

Bell, N. J., Bell, M. J., Knowles, T. G., Whay, H. R., Main, D. C. J., & Webster, A. J. F. (2009). The development, implementation and testing of a lameness control programme based on HACCP principles and designed for heifers on dairy farms. *Veterinary Journal*, *180*, 178–188.

Birke, L., & Hockenhull, J. (2012). *Crossing boundaries: Investigating human-animal relationships*. Boston, MA: Brill Academic Press.

Bristol University 'Bristol Cats Study'. (2013). Summary of research. Retrieved from http://www.bristol.ac.uk/news/2013/9406.html. Accessed on April 26, 2014.

Callon, M. (1986). Some elements of a sociology of translation: Domestication of the Scallops and the fishermen of Saint Brieuc Bay. In J. Law (Ed.), *Power, action and belief: A new sociology of knowledge?* Sociological Review Monograph. London: Routledge and Kegan Paul.

Cockroft, P. D., & Holmes, M. A. (Eds.). (2003). *Handbook of veterinary evidence-based medicine*. London: Blackwell.

Cudworth, E. (2011). *Social lives with other animals: Tales of sex, death and love*. London: Palgrave Macmillan.

DairyCo. (2014). '*Lameness*' *online report*. Retrieved from http://www.dairyco.org.uk/technical-information/animal-health-welfare/lameness/#.U1eZGfldX6Q. Accessed on April 26, 2014.

Denzin, N. K., & Lincoln, Y. S. (Eds.). (2003). *Collecting and interpreting qualitative materials*. London: Sage.

Emery, S. (2014). Hard work, productivity and the management of the farmed environment in anthropological perspective. In L. Hamilton, L. Mitchell, & A. Mangan (Eds.), *Contemporary issues in management*. Cheltenham: Edward Elgar.

Gray, J. (1998). Family farms in the Scottish borders: A practical definition by hill farmers. *Journal of Rural Studies*, *14*(3), 241–356.

Gupta, A., & Ferguson, J. (1992). Beyond "Culture": Space, identity, and the politics of difference. *Cultural Anthropology*, *7*(1), 6–23.

Hamilton, L. (2013). The magic of mundane objects: Culture, identity and power in a country vets' practice. *The Sociological Review*, *61*, 265–284.

Hamilton, L., & Taylor, N. (2012). Ethnography in evolution: Adapting to the animal 'Other' in organizations. *Journal of Organizational Ethnography*, *1*(1), 43–51.

Hamilton, L., & Taylor, N. (2013). *Animals at work: Identity, politics and culture in work with animals*. Boston, MA: Brill Academic Press.

Haraway, D. (1991). A Cyborg manifesto: Science, technology, and socialist-feminism in the late twentieth century. In *Simians, Cyborgs, and women: The reinvention of nature*. New York, NY: Routledge.

Haraway, D. (2003). *The companion species manifesto: Dogs, people and significant otherness*. Chicago, IL: Prickly Paradigm Press.

Horseman, S. V., Whay, H. R., Huxley, J. N., Bell, N. J., & Mason, C. S. (2013). A survey of the on-farm treatment of sole ulcer and white line disease in dairy cattle. *The Veterinary Journal*, *197*(2), 461–467.

Ingold, T. (1984). The estimation of work in a Northern Finnish farming community. In N. Long (Ed.), *Family and work in rural societies: Perspectives on non-wage labour*. London: Tavistock.

Kirksey, S., & Helmreich, S. (2010). The emergence of multi-species ethnography. *Cultural Anthropology*, *25*(4), 545–576.

Kristensen, E., & Enevoldsen, C. (2008). A mixed methods inquiry: How dairy farmers perceive the value(s) of the involvement in an intensive dairy herd health management program. *Acta Veterinaria Scandinavia*, 50, 50.

Lam, T. J. G. M., Jansen, J., van Veersen, J. C. L., & Steuten, C. D. M. (2008). Improving cattle health: Knowledge transfer and motivation. Alltech Symposium, Dunboyne, Ireland, November.

Latour, B. (2005). *Reassembling the social: An introduction to actor-network-theory*. Oxford: Oxford University Press.

Latour, B., & Woolgar, S. (1988). *Laboratory life: The construction of scientific facts*. Chichester: Princeton University Press.

Law, J. (2004). *After method: Mess in social science research*. London: Routledge.

Law, J. (2009). Seeing like a survey. *Cultural Sociology*, *3*(2), 239–256.

Law, J., Ruppert, E., & Savage, M. (2011). *The double social life of methods*. CRESC Working Paper No. 95. Open University, Milton Keynes.

Law, J., & Urry, J. (2004). Enacting the social. *Economy and Society*, *33*(3), 390–410.

Lestel, D. (2006). Ethology and ethnology: The coming synthesis, a general introduction. *Social Science Information*, *45*(2), 147–153.

Lowe, P. (2009). *Unlocking potential: A report on veterinary expertise in food animal production*. London: Department for Environment and Food Rural Affairs.

Lowe, P., Phillipson, J., & Wilkinson, K. (2013). Why social scientists should engage with natural scientists. *Contemporary Social Science*, *8*(3), 207–222.

Moore, L. J., & Kosut, M. (2013). Among the colony: Ethnographic fieldwork, urban bees and intraspecies mindfulness. *Ethnography* (published online before print, 27 September 2013).

Nelson, C., Treichler, P. A., & Grossberg, L. (1992). *Cultural studies*. New York, NY: Routledge.

Penny, J., Paine, M., & Brightling, P. (2009, February). A*chieving sustainable improvement: Enhancing services to dairy farmers through effective partnerships between public and private sectors*. Research report to Dairy Australia.

Penrose, J. (1993). Reification in the name of change: The impact of nationalism on social constructions of nation, people and place in Scotland and United Kingdom. In P. Jackson & J. Penrose (Eds.), *Constructions of race, place and nation*. London: UCL.

Porcher, J., & Schmitt, T. (2010). Les vaches collaborent-elles au travail? Une question de sociologie. *Revue du Mauss*, (35), 235–261.

Ravetz, A. (2001). *Vision, knowledge and the invention of place in an English town*. Unpublished PhD Thesis, Faculty of Economic and Social Studies, University of Manchester.

Read, D. W. (2012). *How culture makes us human: Primate social evolution and the formation of human societies*. Walnut Creek, CA: Left Coast Press.

Savage, M., & Burrows, R. (2007). The coming crisis of empirical sociology. *Sociology*, *41*, 885–899.

Taylor, N. (2010). Animal shelter emotion management: A case of in situ hegemonic resistance? *Sociology*, *44*(1), 85–102.

Taylor, N. (2012). Animals, method, mess: Post-humanism, sociology and animal studies. In L. Birke & J. Hockenhull (Eds.), *Crossing boundaries: Investigating human-animal relationships*. Boston, MA: Brill Academic Publishers.

Taylor, N., & Hamilton, L. (2014). Care of the underdog: Animals, culture and the creation of moral certainty in the rescue shelter. In L. Hamilton, L. Mitchell, & A. Mangan (Eds.), *Contemporary issues in management*. Cheltenham: Edward Elgar.

UK Commission on the Social Sciences. (2003). *Great expectations: The social sciences in Britain*. London: Commission on the Social Sciences.

Wallman, S. (Ed.). (1979). *The social anthropology of work*. London: Academic Press.

Whay, H. R., & Main, D. C. J. (2009). Improving animal welfare: Practical approaches for achieving change. In T. Grandin (Ed.), *Improving animal welfare: A practical approach*. Wallingford: CABI Books.

Whay, H. R., & Main, D. C. J. (2013). Reducing cattle lameness: Making it happen on farm. *Cattle Practice*, *21*, 240–242.

Wolfe, C. (2010). in Anderson, N. (2014). We have never/have always been posthuman. In J. Weinstein & C. Colebrook (Eds.), *Inhuman rites and posthumous life*. Duke University Press (forthcoming (awaiting further publication details)).

ABOUT THE AUTHORS

Angus Bancroft is a lecturer in Sociology at the University of Edinburgh. He has written on intoxication culture and policy, pre-drinking and femininity, drinking and drug use rituals, drug control, social theory, and Gypsy-Traveller ethnicity and discrimination. He is currently researching trafficking, cannabis production, intensive care survivorship and the sociology of pleasure.

Andrew Goffey is an associate professor of critical theory and cultural studies and director of the Centre for Critical Theory at the University of Nottingham. He is the author (with Matthew Fuller) of Evil Media (MIT), the editor (with Eric Alliez) of The Guattari Effect (Continuum), with Roland Faber, of The Allure of Things (Bloomsbury) and is co-editor of the journal Computational Culture. His research explores the intersections of science, technology, and culture within computing and software, and he has a particular interest in exploring the philosophy and politics of knowledge and technical practices. He also works as a translator and has translated work by Felix Guattari, Isabelle Stengers and Philippe Pignarre, Barbara Cassin and others.

Lindsay Hamilton received her Ph.D. in Management from Keele University in 2009 with a thesis that addressed the issues of dirty work and professional identity in the veterinary industry. Since then, Lindsay has worked on a number of research projects which have explored the human–animal interaction further, particularly in organisational contexts. Recent book publications include the monograph, Animals at Work: Identity, Politics and Culture in Work with Animals (with Nik Taylor; Brill, 2013) and the edited collection Contemporary Issues in Management (with Laura Mitchell and Anita Mangan; Edward Elgar, 2014).

Martin Hand (BA, MA, PhD) is an Associate Professor in Sociology at Queen's University, Canada. He is the author of Ubiquitous Photography (2012; Polity), Making Digital Cultures (2008; Ashgate) and co-author of The Design of Everyday Life (2007; Berg), plus articles and essays about visual culture, technology, and consumption. His current SSHRC-funded research program is designed to bring together recent theorizing of digital memory with qualitative empirical studies of how emerging technologies of memory-making are being incorporated, interpreted, and used within a range of institutional, household, and individual contexts in Canada.

Mariann Hardey (BA hons, MA, PhD) is Co-Director for the Institute of Advanced Research in Computing (iARC) at University of Durham, she is also a Lecturer in Digital Communications and Programme Director at Durham University Business School. Mariann's presence is 'old' in technology terms with her research interests in subjectivities, sociality and digital content. Her academic work is often featured on the BBC and she is also the BBC North East commentator on social media and correspondent for BBC Radio York. Many of her debates become popular commentary on her website mariannhardey.com. Since 2004 she has authored the award winning blog properfacebooketiquette.com (Tweet @thatdrmaz).

Sam Hillyard (BA, PhD) is a Reader in Sociology at Durham University, UK. She is the author of The sociology of rural life (2007; Berg) and series editor of Studies in Qualitative Methodology (Emerald). She has written articles and essays about game shooting (with Burridge), rural elites, rural communities (with Bagley) and theorising through qualitative research. Past ESRC-funded research compared and contrasted two rural locales in order to understand the role of the school in the performance of community.

Emma Hutchinson has recently completed her PhD entitled "Performative Identity and Embodiment: An Online Ethnography of Final Fantasy XIV" in the Sociology Department at the University of Warwick. Her work concerns the performative relationship between identity and embodiment online in the context of online gaming. This research maps how performative identity and embodiment via an avatar can be enacted within an environment that is structured by social norms including heteronormativity and racism. The thesis also charted different ways of researching online gaming using qualitative methods including participant observation, asynchronous interviewing and forum observation. Her research interests include Digital Sociology, Digital Social Research Methods, and Visual Sociology.

Martina Karels is a doctoral researcher at the University of Edinburgh where she is looking at the performance of public remembrance in relation to September 11 memorial sites. Influenced by her background in theatre she is interested in collaborative projects involving visual and sensory methods of inquiry.

Christine Lohmeier works as an assistant professor at the University of Munich, Germany. Her research interests encompass issues around memory, media, migration, digital culture and qualitative methods. Christine is the author of Cuban Americans and the Miami media (2014). Her work has been published in Media, Culture & Society, M/C Journal and the International Journal of Media and Cultural Politics among others. She has co-edited a special issue of Media, Culture & Society on 'Social Media – Social Memory'. Before joining the University of Munich, Christine taught and researched at the University of Stirling, Scotland, and the University of Rotterdam, Netherlands. She holds a PhD from the University of Glasgow. Christine has been awarded a Fast-Track fellowship with the Robert Bosch Foundation. She serves as the Managing Editor of Communication Theory.

Órla Meadhbh Murray is a Sociology PhD candidate at the University of Edinburgh researching higher education in the UK alongside mapping out applications of institutional ethnography, an approach to research developed by Dorothy Smith. Her interests range from knowledge production practices, power, and identity, to activism, research methodologies, and feminist theory and praxis. She is also the founder and convener of the Institutional Ethnography Network.

Lynne Pettinger is Assistant Professor in Sociology at the University of Warwick. She researches the intersections of work, consumption and markets, and is interested in understanding the transformations of work brought about by technological change. She has recently written about commercial sex and is currently researching on 'green collar' work.

Robin James Smith is Lecturer in Sociology at the Cardiff School of Social Sciences, Cardiff University. His research is informed by the work of Erving Goffman and ethnomethodology and has been concerned with the ways interaction and mobilities in public space get done in the course of everyday life and in interactions between outreach workers and the homeless. He has also studied sense-making and membership categorisation in research team meetings. He has published a number of articles reporting on these matters, as well as other articles contributing to debates in qualitative methodology, and was co-editor of Urban Rhythms, (The Sociological Review monograph series). The Sociological Review monograph.

Ewen Speed is Senior Lecturer in Medical Sociology in the School of Health and Human Sciences at the University of Essex. His research is concerned with sociological understandings of the changing relations between states and citizens in public service provision, with particular reference to ongoing policy reforms in neoliberal welfare contexts. He has written extensively about health and health policy in the UK (most recently the reform of the NHS in England).

Nik Taylor received her Ph.D. in Sociology from Manchester Metropolitan University in 1999 where she addressed the sociology of human–animal interaction. Since then Nik has been active in human–animal studies researching issues such as links between human and animal directed violence, and humane education and animal assisted therapy. As well as working on academic issues pertaining to human–animal relations Nik is also involved in grass roots work, for example, in consulting over the establishment of a pet foster service for women and children entering refuges. Now an Associate Professor in Sociology at Flinders University, Dr Taylor maintains this focus on various aspects of human–animal interaction. Recent publications include Animals at Work: Identity, Politics and Culture in Work with Animals (with Lindsay Hamilton; Brill, 2013), Humans, Animals and Society: An Introduction to Human-Animal Studies (Lantern Books, 2013) and The Rise of Critical Animal Studies: From the Margins to the Centre (ed. With Richard Twine, Routledge, 2014).

Daniel Trottier is an Assistant Professor in Media and Communications at Erasmus University Rotterdam. Prior to this appointment, he held Postdoctoral Fellowships in the Social and Digital Media at the University of Westminster, in the Department of Informatics and Media at Uppsala University, and the Department of Sociology at the University of Alberta. His current research considers the use of social media by police and intelligence agencies, as well as other forms of policing that occur on these platforms. As part of this research, he has participated in two European Commission projects on security, privacy and digital media. He has authored numerous articles in peer-reviewed journals on this and other topics, as well as Social Media as Surveillance with Ashgate in 2012, Identity Problems in the Facebook Era with Routledge in 2013, and Social Media, Politics and the State: Protests, Revolutions, Riots, Crime and Policing in the Age of Facebook, Twitter and YouTube with Routledge in 2014 (co-edited with Christian Fuchs).

Jonathan Tummons (BA, MA MEd, PhD) is lecturer in education and pathway leader for the MSc in Educational Assessment at Durham University. In addition to ongoing research into learning, teaching and assessment in further and higher education, he is currently acting as co-investigator for

'Higher Education in a Digital Economy: An Institutional Ethnography', a three-year research project based at Dalhousie University, Nova Scotia, and funded by the Canadian Social Sciences and Humanities Research Council. He is the author of a number of books and book chapters relating to further, higher and adult education, and has published in a number of leading journals, including Studies in Higher Education, Assessment and Evaluation in Higher Education, Higher Education Research and Development and International Journal of Educational Research.

Jade Zimpfer is a doctoral candidate in the Department of Sociology at the University of Edinburgh. Her dissertation concentrates on the acquisition and distribution of cultural and social capital in contemporary Appalachian culture through the employment of an artifact-based ethnography. Her research interests are: ethnicity and culture, Appalachia, the American South, and Community Development.